This book belongs to:

Mrs. Ruby Cassanese

A YEAR
OF
CHANGE
AND
CONSEQUENCES

MARK SINGEL

SUNBURY
P R E S S

Mechanicsburg, PA USA

Published by Sunbury Press, Inc.
105 South Market Street
Mechanicsburg, Pennsylvania 17055

www.sunburypress.com

For information about special discounts for bulk purchases, please contact
Sunbury Press Orders Dept. at (855) 338-8359 or orders@sunburypress.com.

To request one of our authors for speaking engagements or book signings,
please contact Sunbury Press Publicity Dept. at publicity@sunburypress.com.

ISBN: 978-1-62006-695-9 (Hard cover)
ISBN: 978-1-62006-696-6 (Mobipocket)

Library of Congress Number: 2016943334

FIRST SUNBURY PRESS EDITION: June 2016

Product of the United States of America
0 1 1 2 3 5 8 13 21 34 55

Set in Bookman Old Style
Designed by Crystal Devine
Cover by Lawrence Knorr
Edited by Jennifer Cappello

Continue the Enlightenment!

CONTENTS

PREFACE

Some things that fly there be—
Birds—Hours—the Bumblebee—
Of these no Elegy.

> —Emily Dickinson

My involvement in public service began with a life-changing experience.

I was in the fifth grade in a ramshackle building that housed St. Mary's Elementary School in Johnstown, Pennsylvania. Sister Athanasius, in the black habit with unbearably starched head- and neckwear, was responsible for teaching an entire range of subjects to ten year olds. She also insisted on a healthy dose of religion and tradition that infused us with an awe of Jesus and an awareness of the founders of the Byzantine sect of Catholicism. By the fifth grade, we were well aware of the lessons of the New Testament, but we also knew about Constantine, the Great Schism of 1054, and St. John Chrysostom.

While our orientation was a little different than the Irish Catholics at St. Columba's or the Polish Catholics at St. Casimir's, the entire ethnic community was committed to the pope. This was not without some bitter confrontations between Orthodoxy and Catholicism that occurred a generation earlier. By 1963 though, we Byzantines, like all Catholics, also had a reverence for President John Kennedy that was exceeded only by our love of Pope John XXIII.

It was, therefore, catastrophic when the good Sisters of St. Basil the Great interrupted class that November afternoon to give us the news: John Kennedy had been shot.

The standard response was to get on our knees and begin to recite the rosary. Sister led and we responded in a subdued chant that filled the room with an air of sadness and confusion. In the middle of this somberness, a valve on a clunky old radiator broke, spewing steam into the classroom, breaking our reverence like a heckler in a movie theater.

"It's the devil," I thought. "And he is gloating."

I carried the sound of the devil's hiss in my head for years. I became determined that it was up to me to do something about it. That something turned out to be following John Kennedy into public service.

While I am grateful for the experiences I've had in the public realm, they do not compare with the stories of more prominent historical figures. My journey through the political landscape took me to Washington as a congressional aide, the Pennsylvania State Senate, lieutenant governor of Pennsylvania, acting governor of Pennsylvania, and the president of my own government relations business. Along the way, the interactions with leaders in the public and private sectors, my involvement with issues at the federal and state levels, and my constant amazement at the huge potential and, especially, the connections I made with people going about their daily lives, have enriched me beyond any of my expectations.

I am painfully aware of my own failures. In the glow of youthful exuberance, I intended and expected to reach some political pinnacle. After all, how could I battle with the devil if I wasn't in the arena? Governor or US senator seemed to be the appropriate "calling," but, as I would learn, the terrain along the way could be rough and, ultimately, impassible.

This book is not about the entire journey.

I did, in fact, run for governor in 1994. Before that I was a candidate for the US Senate in 1992. I was also mentioned as the replacement for US Senator John Heinz, who died in a tragic airplane crash in 1991. Those events hold memories for me that would each fill their own book. The reality though is that those stories would be a lot more compelling had I won. Like "some things that fly," I did exist. Like birds-hours-bumblebees, however, I expect no elegy.

I do, however, have a tale to tell about circumstances that converged into a spiral of past and present realities with implications for the future. I found myself in this kind of vortex in 1993.

The idea of how life quickens when roles change from peripheral to central, when power changes from illusory to dangerously real, may be of some interest to current and future political leaders. I am convinced that the events of 1993—what led to them, what occurred in that year, and how they made a difference—is worth exploring.

***

My brother, David, is an associate provost at Montana State University. He is an accomplished scientist and academician. Not long after our father passed away, we were reminiscing about the many life lessons he taught us both. One unsettling sentiment that he conveyed to us often was: "I haven't accomplished much."

My brother and I could not have more different personalities, but we are identical in the restlessness that we got from a father who thought of himself as an underachiever. It is that restlessness that can make a great scientist or a great political leader. Great scientists and great leaders look for fertile opportunities, and sometimes those opportunities are thrust upon them by chance. Grasping those opportunities and performing at a "quickened" level can make all the difference in the world.

And now, if I may, a word about lieutenant governors.

In a brief biography by the Pennsylvania Capitol Preservation Committee, John Latta, Pennsylvania's first lieutenant governor, is memorialized this way:

Latta was elected as a Pennsylvania state senator in 1863, and was again elected to the legislature in 1871 and 1872, serving for two terms. Two years later he was nominated and elected lieutenant governor of Pennsylvania, serving in that office for four years. When his term expired, Latta returned to Greensburg, resuming the practice of law. Latta was regarded as one of the most gifted speakers in the General Assembly. He passed away on February 15, 1913. Burial location is unknown.

The other 31 lieutenant governors are treated with similar brevity.

Two of them, Arthur James and Ray Shafer, were elected governor. Two others, John Bell and Mark Schweiker, assumed the office when their governors took roles at the federal level (Governor Edward Martin took a seat in the US Senate; Governor Tom Ridge was appointed Secretary of Homeland Security).

The others all had interesting careers in business, the legal profession, agriculture, and academia. Most were active leaders in their communities before and after their service as lieutenant governor.

By and large, however, they are denied any effusive elegies because their flight is ancillary to those who have risen higher.

Yet, every one of them met challenges and served honorably—not just in a supportive role to their respective governors, but in contributing substantively to their communities and to their Commonwealth.

Thomas Kennedy, for example, was the president of the United Mine Workers of America and served on the National War Labor Board under Franklin Delano Roosevelt.

John Gobin was brevetted a brigadier general in the Civil War and was a founder of the Grand Army of the Republic.

Ernie Kline was Governor Milton Shapp's point person in a dangerous labor dispute. His skill in defusing that situation and ushering in a new era of labor management relations is rarely noted.

At my first national conference of lieutenant governors I met a host of politicos brimming with ambition and potential. Some seemed to be destined for higher office, and others were quietly enjoying the pinnacle of their political careers. All of them, however, deserved recognition for getting to that level in the first place and for performing their functions—with or without adequate recognition.

John Milton wrote: "They also serve who only stand and wait," and I think this sentiment captures the essence of lieutenant governors quite well. While they may labor in relative obscurity, history is full of those who are second-in-command, rising to challenges that present themselves. The ordinariness of waiting in the wings becomes crucial training when extraordinary circumstances quicken the pace of those who have been standing by.

My story may provide one such example.

ACKNOWLEDGMENTS

The people mentioned in this book and many others continue to help and inspire me.

My wife, Jackie, has been with me through every adventure. My children and grandchildren are a source of pride and comfort to me.

My parents, Steve and Jean Singel, set me on my path and all of my siblings—Carol, David, Joyce, Myra, and Amy—know how important they are to me.

Family (including the "outlaws"), colleagues, and friends from every phase of my life have, as Frost said, "made all the difference."

I thank the good folks who worked with me in public service and private business.

The Winter Group team assisted whenever I needed them and was patient with me when I was locked away in writing mode.

I have tried to be as accurate as possible but it is likely that there are some errors and omissions. These mistakes are mine alone.

Finally, my thanks to the intrepid folks at Sunbury Press for their editing skills. This book is much more readable because of their professionalism.

1993

PART ONE — THE GATHERING

Watch long enough, and you will see the leaf
Fall from the bough. Without a sound it falls:
And soundless meets the grass. . . . And so you have
A bare bough, and a dead leaf in dead grass.
Something has come and gone. And that is all.

But what were all the tumults in this action?
What wars of atoms in the twig, what ruins,
Fiery and disastrous, in the leaf?
Timeless the tumult was, but gave no sign.
Only, the leaf fell, and the bough is bare.

This is the world: there is no more than this.
The unseen and disastrous prelude, shaking
The trivial act from the terrific action.
Speak: and the ghosts of change, past and to come,
Throng the brief word. The maelstrom has us all.

—Conrad Aiken

JANUARY

I found myself with some downtime in the lieutenant governor's office. There were still calls to return, mail to sift through, and schedules to review, but it was late on a weekday afternoon and I allowed myself some personal time.

Here's what I was thinking: It's time to move on.

Don't misunderstand, public service was, and is, my calling. The opportunity to serve as a state senator and lieutenant governor was a privilege and full of unexpected highs and lows.

For example, I was fortunate to serve with a governor whose personal morality was beyond question. Bob Casey was solid, and his example set the tone for an administration that saw no trace of scandal. Early on in the administration, I had approached him at the request of several Democratic chairman who thought we were not replacing holdovers from the previous Republican administration fast enough. In fact, Casey was more concerned with the quality of job seekers than their party. What he said to me was: "Mark, if we start hiring all Democrats, we'll all be in jail in six months!"

Instead, together, we got elected and reelected, weathered the storms of an economic recession, fought partisan battles on issues like taxes, education funding, child health care, recycling and landmark environmental reforms, and faced many other challenges.

But there was definitely some tension between the front office and mine.

At that moment in January of 1993, I was thinking about some of the events that had occurred during the Casey/Singel tenure so far.

Just four days into the administration, we were rocked by the suicide of R. Budd Dwyer, the state treasurer. He had been convicted in a scandal that involved Computer Technology Associates (CTA), a California-based company that purportedly offered bribes to Dwyer to help secure a lucrative contract for computer services for the state. Budd was an easygoing politician from northwest PA. I liked him and found it hard to believe that he would be mixed up in anything like bribery or extortion. In a dramatic live press conference that was called for him to announce his resignation prior to sentencing, Budd shocked the entire press corps by pulling out a .357 magnum handgun and placing it in his mouth. When he pulled the trigger I still had on my desk a handwritten letter that said: "Best of luck to you as you begin your service as Lieutenant Governor. I am sorry I will not be around to work with you."

I realized only then that he wasn't talking about going to jail—it was a suicide note.

I represented the governor at Budd's funeral. My first press conference as lieutenant governor was an impromptu exchange with several television reporters outside of a church in Hershey just after the service. One reporter asked: "How do you like the job so far?" I said, "Let's hope it gets better than this."

There were other wrenching moments and some victories during the first term; a few of them are worth noting.

Governor Casey and I worked closely together on lowering auto insurance rates, cleaning up toxic waste sites, battling drugs, and creating jobs. There were harrowing moments like the Ashland Oil spill that threatened Pittsburgh's water supply. We faced severe droughts and record-setting floods and endured energy shortages that affected home heating supplies and business operations.

During these hard times, I was assigned tasks in three key areas:

1. Working with some talented folks at the Pennsylvania Energy Office, we developed a new state energy policy that stressed conservation and support for safer, cleaner alternative fuels. My state car was the first in the state to be equipped to operate on gasoline and compressed natural gas. I was proud that Pennsylvania led the nation in developing alternative natural gas supplies—twenty years before anybody ever heard of the Marcellus Shale formation.

2. Emergency management responsibilities fell to the lieutenant governor. Building on lessons learned from the Three Mile Island incident of 1979, we developed the national model for effective response capabilities for natural and man-made disasters.

3. Recycling was a new concept when Governor Casey won the battle for the strongest law in the country to mandate the recovery and reuse of plastics, newspapers, and other items. My role was to find new uses for the mountains of recyclable materials that began to grow as a result of that law. Through

grants, loans, and technical support, we were able to launch several hundred businesses and create nearly 15,000 jobs— all using recyclables as their raw material.

While my constitutional duties were limited to presiding over the Senate and chairing the Board of Pardons, the governor added an unusual amount of other items to my plate: chairman of the Emergency Management Council, chairman of the Heritage Affairs Council, member of the Economic Development Partnership, and governor's representative on the Penn State Board of Trustees to name a few.

While I was relatively young when I assumed these responsibilities, I had been involved in government for years.

I had worked as a legislative assistant and then as chief of staff to two different members of Congress. I had also spent six years in the PA Senate. One biographical sketch about that earlier period said:

As a state senator, Singel distinguished himself by his aggressive efforts to promote economic development and educational opportunities. He played a leading role in the enactment of the nation's first Emergency Mortgage Foreclosure Assistance program, a prescription drug program for the elderly, and a nine-point economic development program which included the Ben Franklin Partnership—still one of the state's most successful programs for business and job creation.

Casey and I took a strong record of accomplishments to the voters in our 1990 reelection campaign. The wily James Carville, who had guided us through the bare-knuckled battleground of the first campaign, had a much easier time presenting the governor and Pennsylvania's economic condition as "rising stars." Casey cruised to reelection with a million vote plurality.

The governor and I connected at his home in Scranton to celebrate the day after the November election. There was a press conference outside of the Casey residence, and looking back on it, some cleavage began to occur the moment a reporter raised a question or two about the future:

"Governor, will you be seeking the Democratic nomination for US Senate in 1992?"

"No," Casey responded with a Coolidge-like brevity that ended speculation then and there.

The next question was tossed casually but landed heavily. Like a seed planted into the ground that was likely to poke through at some point, the reporter turned to me and said:

"How about you?"

Privately, I was thinking, "Heck, yes!" but it was neither the time nor place to blurt that out.

"We'll see," was all I said.

Having been the recipient of the famous "Casey freeze" on occasion, I could feel the iciness coming from the man. My innocuous "We'll see" was, in his mind, inappropriate and unacceptable. I found out soon enough that he opposed any thought I might have of running on my own for US Senate, just as he had closed off any possibility of appointing me to the position a year before.

In lighthearted moments I would tell people that Casey and I had a father/son relationship and that all I wanted to do was to have the keys to the car once in a while. The reality was that the governor began being downright elusive with me, and I suspected that there was something more going on here. It was not until June of 1993 that I learned, along with all of the citizens of Pennsylvania, that he was battling a rare blood disorder that would threaten his life and incapacitate him for more than six months.

In retrospect, Bob Casey was right: my place was by his side, standing by ready to serve as acting governor should the need arise.

Had I known more about the governor's health issues over the years, I am certain that it would have altered my own political trajectory. Had I known, there is no way I would have actively sought his support for the US Senate seat that was vacated by the tragic death of John Heinz in 1991. I would not have sought the nomination for US Senate for the seat held by Arlen Specter in 1992, either.

The problem was that he never confided in me about his health challenges. I was left with what I considered to be a governor who simply didn't want me to pursue my own dreams. It felt condescending and unfair to me.

It felt especially unfair given the gauntlet of political and legislative jousting that I had already endured for the cause.

The unusual events of 1991 included the tragic plane crash that took the life of US Senator John Heinz and the sudden death of the formidable Frank Rizzo, who was seeking reelection as mayor of Philadelphia. The deaths occurred within weeks of each other and changed the landscape of Pennsylvania politics.

I was brash enough to think of myself as a good candidate for the US Senate seat. Because of Casey's reticence on his health concerns, I could not have known the real reasons behind his disagreeing. The statewide media drew all kinds of inferences about Casey's three week delay—many of which were at my expense—suggesting a possible lack of confidence by the governor regarding his second in command. The eventual appointee, Harris Wofford, was a scholar and a compassionate leader with whom I already had a deep personal friendship. Still, it was hard not to feel chastened by my own teammate. What I didn't know was that it was just the beginning of several such slights. Whether deliberate or not, they had a direct impact on my own political career.

With the deaths of Heinz and Rizzo, my chief of staff, Joe Powers, spent some time developing a confidential memo on succession. Joe was a strong Irish Catholic Democrat whose credentials included a St. Joseph's University degree and a lifetime of service to his family, his party, his community, and his state. He first learned about politics from his ward-leader father in the cigar-chomping backrooms of Harrisburg. Joe was a walking history book on Pennsylvania politics and had participated in campaigns going back to the 1960s. His succession memo was neither ghoulish nor opportunistic. It was just Joe looking out for my interests and making sure all bases were covered.

He carefully pointed out constitutional and statutory requirements in the case of the demise of the governor. Part of the document said:

We should reasonably expect to have chaos outside our office. You yourself will be swamped with phone calls. You will be amazed at the number of close friends that you have suddenly gained. Perhaps all of this can be handled if some forethought is given now to all the possibilities.

He went on to suggest a "to-do" list that included first calls, staffing needs, security concerns, and interaction with the governor's staff. On that last issue, and in retrospect, his words were both prescient and amusing:

The changeover of the Governor's staff, it seems to me, should be approached from both a long-term and short-term direction. On the short-term, it is not considered seemly to start firing people immediately under these circumstances. However, many of the inner circle will most likely want to move on in a short time. There are others that you might encourage to move on.

9

Before any rash decisions are made, it seems to me that there is a need for complete evaluation of the 300 or so employees in the Governor's Office to determine what precisely they all do and how well they are doing it. To illustrate this point, in the last month three senior staff employees left their positions. None was replaced. They do not seem to be missed.

Even today, I am struck by the candor and gutsiness of his guidance. Joe was famous for his calm, steady demeanor, and I am sure that some of his peers in the governor's office would have had a stroke if his comments had surfaced. This is especially true given the potentially fatal illness with which the governor was afflicted.

I, on the other hand, deeply appreciated his counsel, just as I appreciated his friendship. I put the memo into safekeeping believing that no such scenario would develop.

Republicans will not forget the budget battle of 1991. A dramatic economic downturn in the final quarter of the previous year had put us in a billion dollar budget hole. This, just as the Casey/Singel reelection campaign was crowing about Pennsylvania's "rising star."

To this day, Republicans rail about the historic tax increase package that was necessary to right the ship. Casey and I had an unrecorded moment on this issue when I stopped by his office one Saturday morning. It was just after we had settled in to the new term. I noticed that the governor's car was in his spot and thought it would be a good time for a purely social call.

Casey and a speechwriter were putting the final touches on his budget presentation. I was just observing, but the governor was in an upbeat mood and was pleased to take a break from the wordsmithing.

The conversation was cordial and friendly until he turned back abruptly to the issue at hand.

"We have a bit of a problem with the budget, Mark," he said.

I may have spoken a little too quickly and casually when I said, "I'll say!"

Those closest to Casey have all been on the receiving end of the "Casey stare." This was when his dark, bushy eyebrows furrowed into an arrow between his eyes and seemed to point directly at you.

"What do you mean, Mark?"

"Just what you said, Governor." I was nearly stammering by now. "The economy's a mess."

"What are they saying out there?"

Casey knew that I was "on the circuit" regularly and that I could give him an assessment of what the average person was saying. I thought he wanted a straightforward answer.

"They're kicking the shit out of us out there," I said, regretting the words as they were leaving my mouth.

I am not exactly sure, but there may have been smoke coming out of Bob Casey's ears. He gored into me like he was preaching to hostile voters in the state. His tirade included a defense of the positive message of the campaign, the reality that he couldn't control international trends, and a challenge about his most recent opponent (who had raised the issue of the state's fiscal condition in her campaign material).

Almost shouting, he said rhetorically, "Do you think Hafer could do any better?"

"No, Governor," I said looking desperately for the door.

After a few minutes, Casey calmed down enough to understand that I was on his side and genuinely trying to help.

"What would you do about it?" he asked.

Discretion has never been my strong suit. Deference would have been in order. Silence would have been smart. Again, I mistook his question as a genuine request for an answer.

"Call in the press corps and come clean," I said. "Tell them that we didn't intend to mislead anyone with our rosy campaign rhetoric and that the economic downturn was completely beyond our control. Then ask for everyone's cooperation—especially the Republicans—to roll up our sleeves and get to work."

I thought it was the correct advice under the circumstances. Casey exploded.

"I am not going to apologize to ANYONE!"

Things had just taken a turn for the worse, and I did my best to regroup and get the heck out of there.

While our journey together to this point had been eventful, it was going to get a whole lot more intense. While I look back on the relationship and recall some unfortunate snubs and deliberate shots from Bob Casey, I readily admit that some of these pains were self-inflicted. Recalling the 1991 botched budget strategy session, I am reminded of the famous Jimmy Buffett line from "Margaritaville": "Hell, it could be my fault!"

There were endless hours of negotiations and flat-out legislative deals to get the general fund budget and the revenue packages passed. While it can't be denied that taxes went up, the effect of that adjustment in Pennsylvania's income stream meant that we had secured our economic vitality for the next ten years.

The next year was about political repositioning toward the presidential race, to a hotly contested US Senate seat, and to other battles at the federal and state levels. For me, 1992 was a grueling mixture of campaigning and official functions that culminated in a loss in the primary for the US Senate seat. That race sent me back, somewhat chastened, to the daily grind. Somewhere in that year of dashed hopes, I recall being summoned to the governor's office for one of my several trips "to the woodshed."

I don't remember the issue, but something I had said appeared in the newspapers and was not exactly in sync with the "spin" that the governor wanted on the subject. Fair enough, but I remember protesting to the governor and to his closest confidant, Jim Haggerty, who was then serving as general counsel:

"Governor, I must have given a thousand speeches on your behalf. I am more than respectful every time. I toe the company line every time. The first words out of my mouth are 'Greetings from Governor Bob Casey.' I couldn't possibly be more loyal to you. Why is it that you focus on the one time I screw up?"

It was Jim Haggerty who put it all in perspective for me:

"Mark, he has Irish Alzheimer's—he only remembers his grudges."

Ah, I thought to myself. I get it. I also got that I would probably never expect complete support coming from that quadrant.

Still, I understood my place and was determined to fulfill all of my duties, even if I thought I would never get the keys to the family car.

The 1991-92 legislative session ended with an upheaval that required tact, patience, and strength on the part of all of the Democratic leaders. After years of subjugation in the minority, an election to Congress (Senator James Greenwood of Bucks County), and a defection from R to D (Senator Frank Pecora of Montgomery County) gave the Democrats a whopping three days to exert their newfound 25-24 majority in late November 1992.

The Republicans were having none of it, however. They focused their wrath on Senator Pecora and labeled the erstwhile Republican as a traitor and a carpetbagger. The 44th District had been redrawn as a new district in Montgomery County—300 miles from its original location. Frank Pecora simply moved with it and became a new senator from his new territory. It is true that Pecora was now residing in an area far from his boyhood home of Allegheny County. But it is equally true that it was the Republican leadership that gerrymandered him into that position. In other words, they were hoist with their own petard.

Pecora delighted in telling reporters, "I didn't leave the Republicans; they left me."

On November 23, 1992, the Democrats were unusually prepared. Senator Bob Mellow had alerted his troops that there was mutiny in the air, and he even had a judge standing by to swear him in once the coup had occurred. By a vote of 25-23 (one R was absent), the Democrats elected Bob as the new president pro tempore and installed all of their folks as majority committee chairs and leaders. This gave control of the legislative process back to the Democrats for the first time in ten years. It also allowed them to strut their stuff.

Within hours of the takeover, they had dusted off a long-delayed child health care initiative that the governor favored. The so-called CHIP program provided for low cost health care coverage for uninsured children in Pennsylvania. It was landmark legislation that served as the model for health insurance initiatives across the country.

The Democrats also pushed through legislation to shore up the PA Lottery, with an eye on securing the prescription drug benefits for senior citizens.

By being prepared to move these two popular initiatives, the Democrats showed their leadership aptitude. This led to a rapid-fire session in which 80 bills were dislodged from committee, passed by the Senate, and sent to the governor.

The three-day season of governing was not without intense growling from the other side, though.

Senator Loeper, now the minority whip, led the offensive against Pecora (as recorded in the transcript of the Senate Journal):

Senator Loeper: *"Mr. President, once again, I would raise the issue that Senator Pecora . . . comes from Allegheny County, and because of his failure to meet the constitutional qualification to serve as senator from the 44th District, I question the validity of his vote."*
The President (Lt. Governor Singel): *"The gentleman's point has been raised before and answered. The chair does not intend to expend any more time refuting the gentleman's point. The chair considers his point out of order."*

13

It didn't happen often, but I was capable of slamming the gavel down when necessary. It would happen with much more regularity when the new session began in January.

In January 1993, it was clear to me that I needed to set my own course with an eye on the governor's seat in 1994.

That effort would begin over the next few days with newspaper editorial board meetings in central and eastern Pennsylvania. There were also a few radio talk shows and television interviews that were ostensibly to discuss the new legislative session and highlight Casey/Singel administration priorities. The exposure, my team thought, couldn't hurt.

One interview specifically requested by WPVI in Philadelphia was about a rumor that I was about to be named to a position in the new Clinton administration. It was true that I had played an active role in the Pennsylvania organization for Bill Clinton's presidential campaign. It was also true that the Pennsylvania Energy Office, which I led, had received national recognition for some groundbreaking work in the area of natural gas development, alternative fuels, and energy conservation. The rumor was that a deputy secretary spot in the US Department of Energy was on tap.

The reality is that there was no formal offer. This was partly because I had already declined any such appointment because of my own interest in pursuing higher office in Pennsylvania. It was flattering to be asked about the appointment, however, and the week or two of speculation enhanced my reputation as having some expertise in the energy policy field.

I had a standing meeting with Jim Brown, the governor's chief of staff, every Tuesday morning. The first item on the agenda was to discuss the rumor of the position in the Clinton administration. I reassured Jim that I would remain in Harrisburg for the foreseeable future. The next subject was the newly-elected president. More specifically, we had a frank conversation about the governor's continued reticence toward Bill Clinton.

That conversation was the first indication that the political realities of Mark Singel and Bob Casey were about to collide. I was headed toward a possible campaign that would require Democratic support and a working relationship with the president of the United States. Governor Casey, literally, "had his Irish up" and was prepared to distance himself to give conservative, pro-life Democrats an alternative.

The governor would not be attending the inauguration. I had my tickets and plans already in place.

The governor was still smarting from the Democratic Convention. He was denied an opportunity to speak because his position on abortion was at odds with the Democratic platform. The Clinton folks were concerned that Governor Casey would generate an unnecessary kerfuffle on the issue, while the Casey folks were stunned that the governor of a major state like Pennsylvania would be denied his moment at the platform—regardless of his topic.

While we didn't dwell on the subject, the rift and the cause of the rift had deep implications. Casey went on to harden his pro-life stance and began to position himself as an ideological alternative to President Clinton on the issue. Most political leaders—Republican and Democrat—struggled with the issue and did not see it in the black and white terms that Casey espoused. Yes, we were all influenced by our religious orientations. Yes, we all wanted to limit abortions to protect innocent life. But the Supreme Court had handed down a decision that carefully protected a woman's right to choose, with clear restrictions on abortion relating to length of pregnancy and outlining states' prerogatives. The Blackmun opinion also acknowledged the history and difficulty of deciding when life itself begins.

While the Democratic platform accepted the 1973 *Roe v. Wade* decision as dispositive on the subject, activists in the pro-life and pro-choice worlds did not.

But it wasn't just the abortion issue that caused Casey serious concerns about the new president. Governor Casey was a stickler for ethics and morality. His personal and professional codes of behavior could not accept someone with a history of indiscretions of the magnitude of the president-elect. His qualms about Clinton proved to be somewhat justified when the country endured the circus of Monica-gate.

Before the inauguration, though, there were a number of commitments on the calendar. For the most part, those commitments reflected the normal workload of the lieutenant governor with an added emphasis on key issues that my staff and I had focused on. This is what the early part of 1993 looked like from the lieutenant governor's perch:

Monday, January 4, 1993, was fairly routine with office time, correspondence, calls, and staff. I met with the Governor's Legislative

Secretary Helen Wise to discuss some strategy for key issues that were in front of the House and Senate at that time. Senator Bill Lincoln, the Democratic leader, dropped by to share his caucus' perspective on several of these items.

Later that evening I hosted the Governor's Cabinet at the lieutenant governor's residence. After a lifetime in and around politics, Governor Casey had assembled one of the finest groups of leaders for his cabinet in the history of Pennsylvania. They were sharp, capable individuals with a high standard of ethics. I made it my business to learn from each of them and to be aware of the key issues that related to their departments. This would hold me in good stead when I had to step in as acting governor.

For now, we were relaxing at a completely social post-Christmas event.

The next day's meeting with Jim Brown was about tax reform and my ongoing efforts to revive the issue in a legislature that was no more than lukewarm to it. We also spent some time talking about the new "row officers" who were to be inaugurated later in the month and about president-elect Clinton. While the conversation was mostly informal, these weekly meetings were valuable to me and kept me in the loop as to the governor's plans for the upcoming week. From Jim's perspective, I am sure they were mostly about keeping an eye on my activities.

There had been times when stray comments in the press or my public appearances were at odds with the course charted by the front office. Jim was cordial but direct when he conveyed the governor's displeasure to me. I was always grateful for his candor during those rare occasions. For the most part, it was a collegial convergence of purpose, and the meetings assured that the Casey/Singel team was functioning at a high level.

The Constitution of Pennsylvania requires that the General Assembly "shall meet at 12:00 o'clock noon on the first Tuesday of January each year." Since this first Tuesday followed an election year, it was swearing-in day for both the House and Senate. My duty was to preside over the Senate session and usher in a new set of faces to that chamber. We were also set to elect a new president pro tempore and establish rules for the 1993-94 session, which, for the first time in ten years, would be led by Democrats.

Normally these are ceremonial functions, but the tone for the rest of the year was set within minutes of my gaveling the Senate to order. The oath of office had just been administered to the new senators, and I had read a letter of resignation from Senator Jim

Greenwood, who had gotten elected to the US Congress the previous November.

That's when the fireworks started.

Even before we had established a quorum, before any business could be conducted, my colleague and sometimes adversary leapt to his microphone:

> Senator Jubelirer: *"Has the President of the Senate issued a writ of election to fill the now existing vacancy in the 10th senatorial district?"*
>
> The President (Singel): *"The chair would indicate that the paperwork is at the desk and the chair has not yet executed that writ."*

Senator Lincoln, the new majority leader, could see what was coming: the Republicans were about to make political hay over the fact that I was about to sign a document that would have set the special election for July 13. They wanted it much sooner to assure a full contingent of Republicans during what was promising to be a contentious budget fight and to begin their climb back to a majority in the Senate.

The problem was that Jubelirer was trying to force the issue before the Senate had even established a quorum. In an unprecedented parliamentary outburst, he ignited a two hour fracas dealing not only with the timing of the special election but (once again) the credentials of Senator Pecora to even be seated in the chamber.

It was not the first time that my own parliamentary skills were tested. The Legislative Journal for that day reads like a verbal boxing match that got personal at times. With a slim 25-24 majority in my corner, I was able to navigate through a maze of constitutional challenges, points of order, and direct attacks. All on a day that was supposed to be ceremonial!

I will always be grateful for the remarks that the new president pro tempore offered on that rocky first day of his own tenure:

> Senator Robert Mellow: *"I would like to extend my thank you to our Lieutenant Governor, Mark Singel, for the way he handled the proceedings here today. For his remarks of welcome to the Members of the Senate and our families and to our guests, and most, importantly, for just being Mark Singel, because Mark Singel has done an outstanding job under some extremely difficult times."*

What I would soon discover was that I was now squarely in the sights of the Republican minority and that I could expect a continuous barrage of invective coming especially from their leader, Bob Jubelirer.

For now, however, I dusted myself off and attended some receptions with new senators. I got back to my office in time to greet a visiting delegation of Chinese engineers and finished the day with a couple of radio talk shows.

The rest of the week brought a series of editorial board meetings in Huntingdon, Altoona, Lock Haven, and State College. While these were "official" events discussing the upcoming legislative year and the administration's position on issues of the day, it was also an opportunity to reconnect with editors and writers on my own behalf. The fine line I was walking involved being a loyal spokesperson for the governor while planting some seeds for my own candidacy in 1994. The governor and Jim Brown had made it clear that they were fully supportive of the former mission; they were not so much on board with the latter.

Senator Mike O'Pake from Reading was a savvy legislator who knew how to use the media to get his message out. My first introduction to him was when he visited Penn State in the early 1970s, and he insisted on staying in a dorm to connect with students. As it happens, he stayed on my floor with a buddy of mine, and we talked into the early morning hours.

On this Monday morning, January 11, years later, I was the guest on his TV show, which was produced by the Democratic Senate Information Office for distribution into his senate district. The issue was recycling and, more specifically, my role as the chair of the governor's task force on market development for recycled materials. Pennsylvania had scored a milestone victory with the passage of the strongest mandatory recycling law in the country, but we were now faced with growing mountains of paper, plastics, and glass that had previously simply been landfilled. My job was to figure out new uses for these materials.

It turns out that we did pretty well on that front. By the end of the Casey/Singel administration, we had created over 15,000 jobs in hundreds of small businesses that made products ranging from playground surfaces made from shredded tires, to park benches made from recycled plastics. One of my favorite recycling success stories was about an entrepreneur in Hazelton, PA, who owned a company called St. Jude Polymers. He received some grant funding to launch a business making bathroom stalls out of discarded plastics. I was enthusiastic about the project but a little hesitant about the brand name: "Hiney Hiders." The business actually prospered, and a few years later I enjoyed something of a small victory when I found myself in the Orlando airport answering nature's call. I looked up at the product name on the latch to the bathroom stall and saw it: "Hiney Hiders." St. Jude's had gone national in the toilet stall business!

Anyway, Senator O'Pake was, typically, knowledgeable about the issue of recycling. I was always impressed by his work ethic and his compassion. He was one of the "good guys" who died too young.

The taping with Flora Posteraro of WPVI-Philadelphia was for much broader distribution and was about the incoming Clinton administration. While I was known for candid answers to reporters' questions, I was always a bit leery of journalists from the rough-and-tumble Philadelphia market. I had learned to be casual but careful.

Her question was whether I was heading to the Clinton administration in some capacity. Given the strain between Casey and Clinton, there was no way that I could finesse the answer. While it might have been beneficial to keep the possibility open, it would not have gone over well in the front office. Besides, I was already focused on my own local race in 1994. The answer to Flora was a direct "No."

At a dinner at the governor's residence later that evening, Governor Casey remarked that he had seen the interview. He had a way of saying things in terse, no-uncertain-terms sometimes. "Good answer," was all he said.

Other business that week included some policy discussions with the PA Association of Home Health Agencies, the PA Public School Retirees, a PA Lottery contractor, a group of pediatric dentists, and several student groups and their professors. I was also continuing the drumbeat for property tax reform and had high level meetings with the PA State Education Association and the PA Chamber of Business and Industry.

On Friday, I found myself in the pulpit at the Messiah Lutheran Church in Harrisburg for their annual Martin Luther King commemoration. The governor had been invited but had some pressing issue that required me to fill in for him at the event. To me, this showed a good level of confidence in my abilities, and I never minded stepping up.

Also, I enjoyed church venues. I liked departing from ordinary talking points with an audience that was more pious than political. They seemed ready for loftier themes. I don't remember the exact sermon, but I do recall slipping into a rhythm that included a rousing conclusion to the message. I earned some "Amens" and "tell the story" shouts from the pews.

In a way, this was a warm-up to a much larger presentation scheduled for the following Monday.

While the lieutenant governor's office was closed for the Martin Luther King holiday, I was a speaker at Trinity Cathedral in Pittsburgh, where the National Conference of Christians and Jews was having their 8th Annual MLK Observance. This was more than perfunctory: on this day, Monday, January 18, 1993, for the first time, all 50 states observed the Martin Luther King Jr. holiday. It was not lost on me that the holiday was one week prior to the opening of a federal trial involving four police officers charged with civil rights violations in the Rodney King beating in Los Angeles. For now though, I was proud to talk about tolerance and justice in an almost religious forum.

This was a reaffirming moment for me. Stephen King once wrote that writing is telepathy. His art is all about reaching his audience with a clear picture of what is in his mind. Similarly, leadership, a key aspect of public service, requires connecting. Public officials need not transmit their views through writing or painting; they can reach their audiences directly through their spoken words.

With that in mind, I considered each speech a gift and an opportunity. This was particularly rewarding when inspiration struck and the words seemed to flow on their own. This is what happened in Pittsburgh that day.

I was traveling with Veronica Varga. She was not only my press secretary and a gifted writer but also a close friend to me and my family since grade school. We came from the same ethnic roots, the same church, and shared the same optimistic outlook on the value of public service.

She also seemed to have a much clearer path to the Deity than I had. She utilized her journalism training from Northwestern, coupled that with considerable natural talent, and then added a dose of inspiration that was ethereal at times. I know it was a source of frustration to Veronica and my whole staff, then, that I rarely read from the script. What they did not know was that their words gave me a base from which I could extend my reach beyond my grasp.

Something kicked in during the Martin Luther King services, and I came away feeling refreshed and invigorated. I like to think that the congregation also took something positive away from the speech, but I have no idea exactly what I said.

Part of that speech had to do with the need to unbridle the potential in all of us. There was a reason for that particular theme. Just prior to Martin Luther King Day, I had spent some time with the traveler.

Throughout my life, I have been fortunate to discover that wisdom comes from unexpected sources. For example, there was Mr. Mornin' from Washington, DC. As a young congressional staffer, I would pass him going to and coming from the office. His one word greeting was always served up with a wide smile:

"Mornin'!"

"Afternoon!"

"Evenin'!"

"Night . . ."

After a few weeks of this compact conversation, I sat with him to discover that he had a daughter who was a physicist with a PhD from Cal Tech. His son was an officer in the US Navy with three sons of his own. His wife had passed away, and he had lost contact with the rest of them. I gathered that they didn't know that he was living in a park in southeast Washington. Mr. Mornin' didn't really want them to know. He was content with gathering up a few dollars each day for food and alcohol and said this to me about his life:

"When I'm fed, my whole family's fed. When I'm happy, my whole family's happy."

In Harrisburg, there was a whole group of folks like Mr. Mornin'. I enjoyed their friendship and will keep them anonymous as they would prefer.

One such street person preferred to think of himself simply as "a traveler." He was willing to pause occasionally to share some thoughts with me. When I first met him, he was sitting on a bench looking at the Susquehanna River. An elderly black man with tight curly white hair and a salt and pepper beard, he looked up at me and said:

"What's next?"

Strange introduction.

Passers-by treated him like another urban nomad and did their best to ignore him. I never once saw him ask for money. He was just different than the panhandlers who hung out in doorways and by the Susquehanna River.

"Good morning," I said.

In Harrisburg, and everywhere I guess, white people don't always look black people in the eyes. This is something I'd noticed in my upbringing and political experiences, which was why I made it a point to be an exception to that generalization. I could see by his smile that the traveler appreciated it.

I was stunned when he went on to recite:

"Beauty is truth, truth beauty,—that is all
Ye know on earth, and all ye need to know."

"Keats?" I asked "'Ode on a Grecian Urn'?"

"There you go," he said.

The traveler seemed more like some kind of oracle to me, and I found myself watching for him on the streets.

Several months had passed since our first meeting. This time, it was a bitterly cold January morning by the river, and I must have seemed little preoccupied to the traveler.

"What's next?" he said, again with that peculiar greeting.

Without waiting for a response, he recited:

"Fie on't! Ah fie! 'Tis an unweeded garden
That grows to seed; things rank and gross in nature
Possess it merely."

"*Hamlet?*" I asked

"There you go," said the oracle.

Whether it was guidance from Mr. Mornin', the oracle, or any of the thousands of everyday people who share the planet, I was always grateful for their kindness.

It seemed to me that elected officials owed them something in return. Something like compassion and fairness.

Emerson spoke of the "infinitude of the individual." I am blessed to have seen that level of potential in Veronica, my family and friends, the good people of Trinity Cathedral, and thousands of people at political functions, and the oracle. "Government by the people, for the people, and of the people" has never been a scary proposition for me because I believed, and still believe, that greatness lurks in the lives of all citizens.

Soon enough, I was headed to the pomp and circumstance of the inaugurations of several new faces on the state and national scene.

The next day, three political leaders took their statewide posts. On January 19, 1993, Ernie Preate, the D.A. from Lackawanna County, was sworn in as attorney general; Barbara Hafer, a Republican from Allegheny County, became the auditor general; and Cathy Baker Knoll, a prominent Democrat from Allegheny County, took over as state treasurer. As I took my place on the dais and heard their first comments as elected state officials, I could not have known that all three would play a role in my own political drama and in Pennsylvania's history in the coming months and years.

More on them later.

For now, it was off to Washington for the historic inauguration of William Jefferson Clinton as the 42nd president of the United States.

On the eve of the inauguration, my wife and I had dinner with an old friend, Rick Welsh. Rick was a vice president at a large Pennsylvania bank, but I knew him from his younger days as a PA Senate staffer. He brought a group of prominent business leaders with him to a pleasant dinner in Georgetown for Jackie and me.

Later, we spent some time at the Mayflower Hotel with the Rodham brothers. I had spent some time with Tony and Hugh Rodham, Hillary Clinton's brothers, and we shared many pleasant days and evenings together on the campaign trail throughout Pennsylvania in 1992. They had some hopes of setting up shop to take advantage of their closeness with Bill and Hillary, and the Mayflower party was their own way of staking out some territory. Whatever the motivation for the event, it was fun. Loud music and alcohol fueled the kind of raucous party for which the brothers were famous.

US Representative Marjorie Margolies Mezvinsky joined me for breakfast the next morning. We had been personal and political friends for years. I was always impressed by her sparkling personality and her sharp mind. While we were simply touching base, I had it in the back of my mind that we could end up supporting each other in some kind of future endeavor. As expected, she was enthusiastic. In fact, there was an almost palpable energy, something I've found to be common when two ambitious politicians interact.

For example, this type of energy was present in an incident that occurred years before when I was serving as a congressional aide. On a walk across the US Capitol plaza, I was reading some papers and accidentally found myself sandwiched between two US senators reaching out to greet each other. I actually felt a jolt of electricity as Senator Ted Kennedy and Senator John McCain shook hands. I'm sure they didn't even notice the young staffer between them, but I was certain in that moment that there was something magical about political personalities. It confirmed my belief that I would run someday.

The electric vibe from Marjorie was just as compelling. She was a young congresswoman with an unlimited future. Little did we know then that she would soon be called upon to cast the deciding vote to enact President Clinton's economic reform package. The bill passed by the narrowest of margins and, in retrospect, was the key factor in reversing the economic recession of 1990-92. Marjorie Margolies Mezvinsky could have easily opposed the package and the assorted tax increases that it contained. Instead, she chose to put her own political career aside and performed an act of courage that may have saved the Clinton presidency—and the national economy.

While Marjorie did, in fact, lose her reelection bid, we would remain good friends for years to come. As fate would have it, another event occurred that was even more important in strengthening Marjorie's relationship with the Clintons. Her son, Mark, fell in love with and married Chelsea Clinton—a storybook confluence of two impressive political families.

Congressman Jack Murtha had provided good seats for the inaugural ceremonies, and we watched as Bill Clinton made history.

What I recall most about that day was the extraordinary weather. While it was brisk, there was not a cloud in the sky, and the robin's-egg-blue seemed to wrap around all of the participants. Maya Angelou spoke and Marilyn Horne performed. There was a strong sense of purpose that seemed to be endorsed by nature itself.

I remember thinking, "The good guys won." And if Bill Clinton's governing was as effective as his oratory, the country was in good shape. I didn't view Bill Clinton as one of the "rank or gross" leaders who merely possessed our "unweeded garden." I thought of him in that moment as someone who was committed to growing great things.

I skipped the parade and a few other afternoon events to reconvene at the Hawk and Dove Tavern on Pennsylvania Avenue with a bunch of old friends from my days as a congressional aide. Some of them joined us for the actual presidential ball at Union Station that evening.

It was an auspicious beginning to a year that would become more momentous as the months went on.

On many days, my early mornings were committed to spillover from the governor's calendar. Today, Monday, January 25, the event was a visit from the chief justice of the state of Bahia,

Brazil and an organization called PA Partners of the Americas. It was a reality that the governor was often over-scheduled, and it was also true that Casey did not see much value in these kinds of meet-and-greets. For me, it was usually a pleasant distraction and, sometimes, a moving experience.

Two brief stories:

Once, a delegation of businessmen from the Ukraine stopped by on their tour of American states. Having just shaken off the yoke of Soviet domination, they were gathering information on the interaction of government and private enterprise. This was new territory for the officials, many of whom had spent a lifetime under real oppression.

They also talked of their newfound freedoms of speech and religion and brought those topics up like children seeking an allowance from a very stern father.

As a descendant of Eastern Europeans, I felt an immediate kinship with this group. So much so that I shared my own religious upbringing in the Byzantine Catholic faith. This was akin to the Russian Orthodox faith that most of them had, until very recently, practiced in secret.

I thought I would try to bypass the translator by actually speaking in a tongue that they would recognize, and so I recited the "Otce Nas" (Our Father) and the "Bohorodice Divo" (Hail Mary) in Old Slavonic. I was amazed to hear them join in. It mattered to them that a Pennsylvania official shared their heritage and empathized with their political evolution. Several had tears in their eyes.

On another occasion, I may have contributed to some international confusion.

The lieutenant governor's physical office had undergone extensive historic preservation that had lasted about 18 months. One of the projects was to restore the portraits of the lieutenant governors that hung ceremoniously around the top of the walls. All but two had finally been returned to their place, and the remaining empty rectangles stood out like two missing teeth. As the month dragged on, it became annoying to look at those gaps every day.

On a Saturday of events in the York area, my press secretary, the indomitable and long-suffering Veronica Varga and I stopped at a gas station for a fill-up. As luck would have it, the station had a wide selection of truly horrible black velvet paintings featuring Elvis, Emmett Kelly's Crying Clown, and an array of voluptuous women and their pet tigers. It occurred to me that I could send a message to the preservation committee by filling the spots in my office with two of these treasures. I snuck into my own office with hammer and nails and put Elvis and Emmett alongside the grumpy looking public leaders.

The following Monday, a group of South Korean leaders came by. It was hard to keep their attention. The interpreter told me later that it was because they were whispering among themselves that they didn't know Elvis was from Pennsylvania!

The portraits were replaced with two resplendent former lieutenant governors the next day.

After the usual morning formalities, I spent some time with the Senate Democratic leaders. This was part of the Monday routine during session weeks. I appreciated the opportunity to keep in sync with their machinations and, occasionally, was asked to carry messages from the front office. Senator Bill Lincoln, the minority whip, was interested in my push for property tax reform but was realistic about reviving the issue. Instead, we were heading for some choppy waters on workers' compensation reform and other budget related items. They were awaiting the governor's seventh "State of the State" address and hoping for some signals from me on what to expect in the budget address.

Mike Hershock, the governor's budget secretary, kept things close to the vest when he was putting the $25 billion jigsaw puzzle together. Details would not be forthcoming for another month or so.

A quick visit back to the office to deal with correspondence, return some calls, and meet with one or two folks before heading back over to the Senate to preside over the session. These days were always busy, and by the time I stepped up to the president's chair, I had put in a full day—of which most of the senators were completely unaware. This is why the discourse in the Senate could strike me as being trite and sometimes grating.

Today, for example, the Republicans were firing some shots across the bow in anticipation of Casey's annual address scheduled for the next day. They were also continuing the Pecora saga in hopes of catching me in any constitutional or parliamentary gaffe that would bolster their cause or at least give them campaign talking points.

One of the last items of business on the calendar was to approve the resolution to meet in a joint session with the house to hear the governor's address.

When the governor made the actual speech, it fell to me to preside over the joint session. I gaveled the session to order and sat with then Speaker of the House Bill DeWeese in the chairs behind the governor.

A word about this ritual.

It is the lieutenant governor who is specifically designated to preside. Beyond the constitutional requirement, I always believed it was important visually to present the team performing their duties together. While the medical challenges that Casey faced in both terms of office are now well known, I found myself with a small issue just before the joint session one year. It happens that inflamed tonsils, adenoids, and cartilage in the back of my throat had become so bad that surgery was required. The operation was routine, but the recovery was problematic. I developed a tear in the cauterization in the back of my throat just when I was introducing the governor. I spent the next hour and fifteen minutes swallowing blood and praying for him to wrap it up soon! I have a picture of this event that hangs in my office today.

I mention this to make a point about service and loyalty. Yes, there were times when Bob Casey and Mark Singel were privately at odds. But I prided myself on demonstrating my full public support for the man and his mission—even if it meant stoicism as I swallowed my own blood. As soon as the cameras were off, I found the nearest bathroom and vomited an ungodly mixture of fluids.

This particular State of the State address was uneventful, except for an ambitious agenda that was going to run into the usual partisan wall. Sure enough, four different Republican leaders were conducting their critiques in the hallway before the governor was settled back in his office.

My staff and I had developed our own State of the State address. After some deliberation about the propriety of adding our comments to the governor's, we released it to the press. Here's a part of what we were espousing in 1993:

Here in Harrisburg, as in Washington, with our executive and legislative branches working together for the first time in a decade, we have both the responsibility and the opportunity to break the gridlock that has engulfed our legislature, and to act boldly to chart our state's future.

But our power to do so is tenuous: The Senate stands only one vote from deadlock, and that deadlock may soon return.

That means that my role as President of the Senate is of unprecedented importance this year. I am faced with a unique challenge—and opportunity—to keep legislation flowing and progress growing in Pennsylvania.

I intend to grasp that opportunity, and to meet that challenge head-on.

Because of this unprecedented responsibility, I am today taking an unprecedented step for a lieutenant governor: I am reporting to the people of Pennsylvania as their lieutenant governor on the State of the Commonwealth as I see it and the directions I intend to pursue in the coming year.

In the short run, of course, it is essential that we enact the agenda laid out yesterday by Governor Casey:

- *We must expand our efforts to bring jobs into our most desperate urban and industrial centers. And we must build on the successes of our high-tech investment efforts like the Benjamin Franklin Partnership that I helped author a decade ago.*
- *We must act swiftly to reform our workers' compensation system and roll back the crippling rate hikes.*
- *We must fight for a comprehensive health plan to make medical care available to every family, and we must enact Family and Medical Leave so that no Pennsylvanian ever has to choose between their job and their family's well-being.*
- *We must strengthen our support for HIV and AIDS treatment, prevention, and education.*
- *We must enroll more doctors in our Healthy Beginnings program to provide prenatal care to low-income women; we must reach out to enroll more children in healthcare programs through medical assistance; and we must expand health, nutrition, parenting, and job offerings in community schools.*
- *And, most of all, we must adopt a new and equitable system of financing public education, so that children everywhere in our state receive the best schooling possible—and we must again increase college scholarship aid so that every Pennsylvania student can go on from there as far as his or her abilities will take them.*

We build on a foundation that Bob Casey and his generation are constructing, but we must recognize that it is only the foundation for our further work—and not the ceiling on our aspirations.

INDUSTRIES OF THE FUTURE

We must begin with the world that today's students will work in tomorrow—a world of new industries, with a new economy. If we do not look ahead toward how that economy will differ from today's, then the next generation will simply be left behind.

The Pennsylvania of tomorrow will include not just the "greene country townes" of William Penn's dreams, and the roaring steel furnaces of Pennsylvania's industrial revolution. It will be a world of high-speed rail lines, fiber optic communications, software engineering, and other advances in technology occurring almost daily. It will also be—and must also be—a world of environmentally friendly technology, a world in which economic advance and environmental degradation are no longer seen as inevitable companions but are instead recognized as incompatible.

We must muster our collective experience and talent to recapture Pennsylvania's and America's competitive leadership, and build an environmentally sustainable economy.

Our state's priority must be developing the correct infrastructure, training network, and funding capabilities to become a prime location for industries that will remain competitive in the next century. More and more, these industries of the future will be not just "clean" industries, but "green" industries—companies and technologies that help other industries protect, and even clean up, the environment.

Germany and Japan are surpassing America as leaders in these technologies. We must work to bring these industries to Pennsylvania—both because they will help keep our state clean, and because they will help keep it "in the green," as investments in these technologies soar in coming decades. Later this year, I will produce a detailed plan for attracting these environmentally productive businesses and jobs of the future to Pennsylvania.

But we have already demonstrated what can be done: The Recycling Market Development Task Force I chair has helped promote the recycling industry in this state by developing markets for recycled products. The result: Not just a cleaner environment, but 10,000 additional jobs.

That is why I am also calling for an innovative new program of "recycling manufacturing zones." This initiative—similar to our current Enterprise Zones—would use economic and tax incentives to promote the recycling industry by encouraging all facets of recycling, from sorting to manufacturing, in one accessible location. This is but one example of how we can identify and nurture Pennsylvania growth industries that also preserve our state's unequaled natural inheritance.

GOOD ENVIRONMENTAL POLICY IS GOOD ECONOMIC POLICY

Another step we can and must take is to further embrace public transportation as a means of unclogging our highways and preserving our environment. Making mass transit more available and affordable as a commuting option will result in more people using it. Our recent $2 million investment in high speed rail research and development is a clear example of where I want to take Pennsylvania's transportation future.

We must also offer an economic benefit for companies to adopt environmentally responsible production techniques, with the cost burden borne by the worst polluters. The best policy, where possible, is to adopt market-based environmental policies that reward good environmental citizens and businesses, rather than using costly regulations to police their behavior.

EDUCATION FOR THE FUTURE

Ultimately, however, it is not enough simply to build the economy of the future without preparing our people for it. Quite simply, education is the most fundamental building block of the future— both for individuals and for our society as a whole.

We can start to build the educational system of the future by implementing the new learning outcomes recently approved by our State Board of Education: It's imperative that the focus of education in Pennsylvania shift from how we teach to how students can most effectively learn. Learning outcomes offer school districts greater flexibility and represent the same basic insight as school choice programs: While the state has a duty to identify the base of knowledge students must possess in tomorrow's world, parents, teachers, and local officials can best determine what particular educational program meets their needs in achieving those ends.

In fact, children's best teachers are often their parents—and that is why I support a state program similar to the one in Arkansas begun by Hillary Clinton, to help teach parents of Head Start-eligible children how to better teach their own children.

At the same time that we recognize that school management and educational choices should be exercised in smaller, more individualized units, we are also recognizing that responsibility for financing education must be more broadly shared.

That is why I wholeheartedly support Governor Casey's call for a more equitable school finance system. All Pennsylvanians recognize that the quality of a child's education should not depend on the property values of his neighborhood. This will be a long, difficult process, however, and will require cooperation and understanding. But one relatively easy place we could start is by basing state reimbursements of school districts' Social Security and retirement contributions upon the equitable statewide school subsidy formula—ESBE—rather than providing grants to districts regardless of financial capability.

CITIZEN SERVICE

We must also heed the renewed call from Washington for citizen service nationwide, for a new generation of leaders that asks what they can do for their country. Let's make that aspect of America start here, too, with a public service college finance program where student loans are forgiven for community service following graduation, and a tuition credit program for students who perform community service in college or to enter college.

WELFARE REFORM

A renewed social contract must form the basis for welfare reform in Pennsylvania, as well. Welfare in its origins was an unwritten contract, and if we are to correct the abundant problems in the welfare system today we must return to this concept of a contract as our guiding principle.

I believe we can save money without hurting individuals unnecessarily, and we'll strengthen our state's economy as well as our human spirit. One of the most effective things we can do to improve the economic condition of poor children—while at the same time reducing the welfare load on our taxpayers—is to further strengthen Pennsylvania's leadership in enforcing child support. We must make sure that parents never forget: You've got a family in Pennsylvania.

I would add one item to Governor Casey's initiatives to strengthen child support enforcement in this state: Last year, we gave our courts the discretion to order that noncustodial parents with health insurance include their children under that coverage.

31

This same sense of responsibility must infuse our entire approach to welfare: We as a society must be more responsive to those who need help, but those who need help must assume responsibility themselves. Next month, I will announce a broad package of legislative and regulatory reforms to achieve these goals. They will include changes to regulations that currently discourage marriage, savings, work, and mandated educational efforts by welfare recipients. I will also press for an innovative new program to save administrative costs and reduce fraud by replacing the traditional maze of bureaucratic welfare paper with an individual computer card like that now used in places like Michigan, Texas—and Reading, Pennsylvania.

But one simple step we can take to slash welfare costs and improve service is to contain the rising costs of medical assistance through managed competition. I support Governor Casey's attempts to bring these reforms to all Pennsylvanians—but we can easily start to persuade the cynics by implementing managed competition statewide for medical assistance beneficiaries, just as we do now in parts of Philadelphia.

REALITY CHECK ON AIDS

We must also recognize, once and for all, that HIV/AIDS is one of the key issues of our time in terms of the scope of the disease and its impact on an already burdened health care system. For all of us, it's time for a reality check on AIDS.

This epidemic demands the attention of a united front: Political leaders and community activists, teachers and clergy, corporate and labor leaders, parents and health care workers. There is far too much to be done in education, prevention, and care for any of us to remain silent or to sit on the sidelines. I have advocated realistic, workable, and effective HIV/AIDS policies for Pennsylvania, and I will continue to do so.

LOCAL TAX REFORM

If our state government is to be any good at doing all this, however, then we need a government that is truly as good as its people. We must therefore begin today to return our government to the People.

And the first place to start is property tax reform and property tax relief. I have taken the lead in pushing for enactment this year of a local finance system that is easy to understand, easy to administer, fair to all Pennsylvanians, and will provide real property tax relief for years to come.

Most importantly, my proposal calls for mandatory reductions in property and nuisance taxes at all local government levels, a moratorium on property and nuisance tax increases, and a requirement that any net revenue gain be channeled exclusively into increasing public safety or fighting drugs.

Yesterday, Governor Casey announced that he is considering signing such a program if enacted. This is wonderful news for Pennsylvania taxpayers, and I pledge to work with the governor to ensure passage of this landmark legislation.

"REINVENTING GOVERNMENT"

We cannot stop there. Later this year, I will be announcing further initiatives to restructure government, including possible reforms in our business tax structure to help attract investment in Pennsylvania, eliminating outdated regulatory efforts, and "reinventing government" to de-emphasize traditional programs and bureaucracies and re-emphasize the provision of service.

CAMPAIGN REFORM

And finally, we must act to bring campaign finance reform to Pennsylvania. Specifically, I would like Pennsylvania to implement public financing of statewide elections through an income tax check off similar to that for presidential campaigns.

Let's establish and enforce campaign spending limits and let's return some fiscal sanity to the entire election process.

This week, we lost a towering figure in our Nation's recent history: Justice Thurgood Marshall. Marshall was a personal inspiration—a man who rose from poverty and obscurity to sit on the highest bench in the land. But he was more than that, for Thurgood Marshall's work elevated us all.

In one of his last public appearances, Marshall spoke in Pennsylvania on Independence Day. "America can do better," he told us, and then added, "America has no choice but to do better" because, as he observed, "our futures are bound together."

As we stride into that future together, we must keep advancing the torch of human decency that Thurgood Marshall and others of his generation carried so long. That torch is being passed every day. The obligation for those of us in the generation who assume it now is not only to pass it on when the time comes but

*to ensure that the next generation is prepared to carry it even
further forward.*

While we were careful not to contradict any positions that the
governor had laid out, the statement raised eyebrows in his office.
I am sure that I was not the first lieutenant governor to release his
own version of state affairs. It was like an understudy clearing his
throat in anticipation of a singing role. On the other hand, and with
the benefit of hindsight, I probably would not be pleased with my
own second-in-command making such a bold pronouncement. In
retrospect, I can fully understand that the governor's annoyance
with the statement—and he was annoyed.

During that last week in January, PEMA Executive Director
Joe LaFleur briefed me on several small emergencies that needed
attention. I say "small" to differentiate them from life-threatening
incidents that we faced about once every ten days. It was to Joe's
great credit and to the credit of the clear-thinking, steady emergency management personnel that the overwhelming majority of
those incidents were handled and mitigated without drama.

The rest of the week included some appearances on cable TV.
Senator Allyson Schwartz wanted to talk about the governor's
agenda; Senator Mike Dawida wanted to push out a message on tax
reform; Senator Bill Stewart, my hometown senator, did a segment
on emergency management. I was pleased to help each of them out
with some "talking head" discussion and even more pleased that
they thought I was enough of an expert to have on their shows. The
PA Newspaper Association was also looking for some information,
and at their Harrisburg conference I did a Q & A with them on the
administration's plans for the coming year.

Thursday was Board of Pardons day.

At that time, the pardons board met on a monthly basis in
Pennsylvania. The lieutenant governor chaired this body alongside
the attorney general and three citizens (appointed by the governor) with some expertise in the criminal justice system, psychol-
ogy, or victims' rights. The board considered the circumstances of
a prisoner's life history and incarceration to determine whether
clemency or an actual pardon for the original crime was in order.
The board first conducted a merit review to determine whether an
individual's case should be heard. After an actual hearing and a
recommendation by a majority of the board, the governor could
take action.

It is notable that the governor could not act alone to commute sentences or pardon criminals. The Board of Pardons needed to make its recommendations first. This check on gubernatorial power was established in the late 19th century in an era of considerable corruption at all levels of government in Pennsylvania. The board was, in part, a way to ensure that governors could not pardon or commute with a mere stroke of a pen. There had been reports of the buying and selling of pardons, and the Board of Pardons eliminated that possibility.

The board also provided a safety valve for the criminal justice system in those instances where judge and jury simply got it wrong. While rare, there were cases where prisoners and their advocates could actually prove that the facts of a case were incorrect, or times when exculpatory evidence came to light years after incarceration. The board could recommend justice to those who were wronged by the system.

The board's main purpose, though, was to temper justice with mercy. In the overwhelming number of cases, the facts were not in dispute. The question was not whether the state should reconsider guilt or innocence, essentially retrying the entire case, but rather to determine whether prisoners were entitled to a second chance.

In the Pennsylvania Constitution, there are only two duties spelled out for the lieutenant governor. "The lieutenant governor shall preside over the Pennsylvania Senate and shall chair the Board of Pardons." For me, the preparation and hearings as chair of this board were the worst parts of my job. The case files of applicants included every possible type of crime ranging from shoplifting to murder. Poring over the horrible details of the violent crimes took hours every month. Wading through the hearings was like slogging through a swamp.

I remember the very first case file I opened involved a brutal gang rape of a woman that ended with her murder. She was impaled with a broomstick.

On my way to one pardons hearing, one of my top aides made this cynical comment: "Just vote NO." While a natural political instinct is always to avoid the risk of future embarrassment, I was determined to exercise my duties according to the letter and spirit of the pardons statute. In addition, there was something deep inside of me that viewed compassion and forgiveness as essential qualities. I suppose it had something to do with those "Hospodi Pomilujs" that I recited endlessly as a boy. Translated from Old Slavonic as "Lord, have mercy," this phrase was repeated over one hundred times in every liturgy. My religious and family upbringing valued mercy toward one another—just as we hoped for it from the Divinity for ourselves.

As repulsive as many of the cases were, I considered myself duty bound to provide an actual opportunity for mercy in those rare cases in which it was warranted. In fact, I was so annoyed by the staffer's comment that it crossed my mind to fire him on the spot. I didn't, and years later, his words proved to be prophetic.

In the meantime, one remarkable thing I discovered about the pardons process is how affected I was by the actions of people I had never even met. One of them was Richard Klinger. A convicted murderer, Klinger sought a commutation of his life sentence and came before the board in 1989.

One prosecutor argued that Klinger should never be released because of the "cold-blooded murder" he committed. My response to that was: "We are aware that he is guilty. The question is: Does he deserve mercy?"

Ernie Preate, a Republican who had just won election for attorney general on a "get tough on crime" platform made his position abundantly clear and did some grandstanding with regard to mine: "Your heart is bleeding all over the place," he said to the audience and the reporters in the room.

We exchanged some words in public and privately, but the tone and the actual proceedings of the board had already been affected. I made sure that outbursts and political posturing by board members would be done in executive session, but Ernie had stirred up the media interest enough that it became necessary to take actual votes in public. I had serious reservations about subjecting the citizens on the board to that exposure. I also believed that it might impact the actions of political leaders who might use the board as platform for their own ideology rather than focusing on the life and death realities facing the applicants themselves.

While the January 1993 session of the Board of Pardons produced no reverberations, I was still able to act honorably and objectively when considering applicants. As I told the staffer who advised a politically correct "NO" on all serious cases, the Board of Pardons brings a different level of pressure and responsibility with it. On any other board or commission, with almost any other legislative or executive decision, you may pay for a mistake with lower polling numbers or a lost election. It was my opinion that shirking your duty on the Board of Pardons may cost you your soul.

On a brighter note, the board did assist in the reconstruction of some lives.

However, the name of Frederic Jermyn would surface and inject a pang of soul searching for me at a time when life was already spinning quickly. As acting governor, I would sign a warrant for his death in September 1993. I remembering looking at my chief of staff, Eric Schnurer, and saying: "I may have just stepped on the path to hell." He thought I was joking. I can't remembering being more serious in my life.

But the most profound story of colliding fates came to me in the form of one Reginald McFadden.

The board had recommended McFadden on a 4-1 vote. (Preate had abstained but wrote a supportive letter saying that McFadden was a good candidate for clemency, but he needed more time to adjust to society).

That board vote was the dropped stone in a pond that rippled through the lives of thousands. The commutation application would sit on the governor's desk until the spring of 1994 when Casey signed it. McFadden was released, mistakenly, into the streets of New York by state prison officials. I say mistakenly because the recommendation of the pardons board specifically called for a halfway house and a mentor who would take responsibility for McFadden's gradual return to society over a period of several years.

Instead, officials in New York freed McFadden prematurely and he went on to commit several heinous crimes in October 1994. The timing of those crimes would have a direct impact on politics at the state and federal level. Long after the events of 1993, long after the McFadden crime spree of October 1994 and its impact on the victims and their families, long after the election results of 1994, I remained bewildered by the consequences of all of those events. The McFadden story is one that will be told in full someday, but for now, at the Board of Pardons hearing in January 1993, my focus was where it always was: performing the delicate balancing act of tempering justice with mercy.

Friday was supposed to be a day of media contacts in the Pittsburgh area. Ostensibly to discuss the Casey/Singel agenda, I had penciled in some important meetings alongside the TV and radio interviews. I was to meet with Mayor Sophie Masloff, a Pittsburgh legend and an ally; and I was especially looking forward to participating on the highly rated Ann Devlin show at WTAE radio.

As soon as the plane hit the tarmac in Pittsburgh late on Thursday, though, I got the call about Three Mile Island. It turns out that a deranged man had crashed the gates of Three Mile Island in a beat-up station wagon. He had somehow managed to hide himself in a section of the plant that was, thankfully, apart from the nuclear reactors and other critical operational components.

It was my job to coordinate the state's response and to project a calm, in-control demeanor for the citizenry. The state plane made an about-face and headed back to the EOC (Emergency Operations Center) in Harrisburg. After a methodical search of the plant, and after determining that the threat was minimal, I was on site at the power plant itself, briefing reporters on the incident.

Given the historic incident at TMI in 1979, we were obsessive about safety at the plant and at critical facilities statewide. After a long two days of interactions with levels of federal and state officials, and after asking some tough questions about access to the site and what improvements were indicated, we were able to put the incident to bed. There were, of course, after-action reports and follow-up hearings. By and large, however, a potentially explosive incident was defused by the capable folks at PEMA and General Public Utilities.

At the end of January 1993, while we in PA government were caught up in a whirlwind with the beginning of a new year, the rest of America enjoyed watching Michael Jackson and Mariah Carey dominate the 20th American Music Awards and the Dallas Cowboys thrashing the Buffalo Bills in Superbowl XXVII.

FEBRUARY

The new month brought an opportunity to present some ideas on job creation to the PA Chamber of Business and Industry conference at the Harrisburg Hilton. I had developed some expertise in this area from my days as minority chair of the Senate Community and Economic Development Committee. I was anxious to inject some new thoughts into the discussion but careful not to step too far in front of the Casey messaging on the subject. This was always a challenging balancing act, and I made sure that every speech began and ended with my commitment to the team.

Other folks in the office that week included mental health and children's health advocates, and some testimony before Senator Mike Dawida's ad hoc committee on tax reform. This subject was a recurring theme for me in the early part of 1993 for two reasons: One, it was desperately needed in Pennsylvania; and two, we had come close to meaningful tax reform just a few years earlier, and I thought that it could be revived if I was persistent enough. The reality is that the issue was quicksand.

While everybody agreed that seniors faced an unfair property tax burden, efforts to change it quickly degenerated into partisan distortions that twisted reform into "tax increases" to the average voter. The issue of tax reform had been simmering for many years. While we were still grappling with it in 1993, it actually came to a full boil in the waning days of 1988. A little flashback on this issue . . .

One of the most exhilarating experiences I had on the Senate floor had to do with property tax reform. Casey had made it a key issue for his first term and there was a full court press to get something done as the 1987-88 session came to a close. In fact, just prior to the sine die adjournment (when the session officially ends "without a date" for reconvening and with all unfinished business left to die in committees), we had managed to get to an actual final vote on a property tax reform package in the Senate. It was the eleventh hour of the last day of session.

To capture the intensity of the legislative action, I wrote the following for the *Pittsburgh Post-Gazette* regarding that evening:

REFLECTIONS ON LOCAL TAX REFORM ENACTMENT

On November 20, 1988 the Senate finally passed a tax reform package initiated by the governor and needed by local governments for over thirty years. The following are my recollections and reflections on the legislative path of Senate Bill 442 on the final evening of the 1988 Senate session.

At 9:00 P.M. the Senate broke for dinner after debating for several hours to compare notes with the House on pending legislation and end-of-session requirements. Still working on the previous day's calendar, Sen. Joe Loeper, the Republican floor leader, gave assurances that we would return by 9:30 P.M. to dispose of all formalities and move to the last calendar of the session which contained the House-amended version of Senate Bill 442, Governor Casey's property tax reform proposal.

During the break, I consulted once again with the governor, who had made personal calls to the majority of Republican senators during this final session day. We knew that Sen. Jack Stauffer had left his written instructions and, as a final act of statesmanship that typified a career that would end at midnight, had broken with his own caucus to support the governor. We had also heard that Sen. J. Doyle Corman, a local government expert and GOP leader in the tax reform movement, would vote with us—even on procedural votes, another rare act of legislative courage. We had some rumors of other defections if we could get the bill in a position for a vote.

10:10 P.M.—The Senate officially recognizes the November 30 calendar and begins work on the final legislative calendar of the session. Final hurdles before that issue can be addressed include four other bills.

10:15 P.M.—After preliminaries, Sen. Ed Zemprelli calls up S.B. 442 and the Republicans object to jumping it ahead of other bills. Some debate occurs on the official record and negotiations at the rostrum have become tense.

10:30 P.M.—Loeper asks for a recess of the Senate. Zemprelli moves that the recess last only 15 minutes and the motion slips through on a voice vote. I am determined to reconvene at precisely 10:45.

10:45 P.M.—The GOP offers a proposition: move ahead with some items on the agenda and we will take "some action" on S.B.

442 at 11:15 P.M. This causes concern: Will they prolong debate? Will they insist on long roll calls? Even if we get to tax reform, will there be time for debate, expected motions, roll call votes, and signatures in the Senate and House in 45 minutes? The word we receive is that the GOP mavericks will have been released only after 11:15 P.M. This means that forcing any vote before that time could be disastrous. We decide to take the deal.

11:17 P.M.—After moving at an auctioneer's pace, we completed most major legislative items. True to his word, Loeper calls up S.B. 442 but, by agreement, we move the CAT fund legislation first. Both sides want to make sure that this bill doesn't get lost in the shuffle but the chill of reality is that the GOP doesn't believe we will finish by midnight.

11:18 P.M.—Loeper moves to table S.B. 442. This will be the key procedural vote. A vote to table is a vote to kill the tax reform proposal. The roll call identifies the players and the motion fails 23-26. We now know that we are working with the slimmest of majorities—thanks to four GOP senators who are "with us" on procedure.

11:25 P.M.—A new tactic: Loeper moves to suspend the rules so that amendments can be offered at this late hour. A new match point for tax reform. Sen. Zemprelli moves the previous question, a precedential motion that could get us to resolution in two votes.

11:27 P.M.—The GOP makes a point of order that the rules tactic must be dealt with first. I rule that the previous question motion takes precedence. Loeper appeals the ruling of the chair, forcing a roll call vote. The GOP senators voting with the democrats hold and there is still hope.

11:34 P.M.—Yet another ruse: The GOP petitions to have the entire bill read before the Senate in length. This is a desperate maneuver that is extremely rare and completely dilatory at this time. I rule it out of order, Loeper appeals the ruling of the chair forcing yet another roll call vote. The ruling stands: 26-23.

11:40 P.M.—The decibel level on the Senate floor increases as Sen. Frank Salvatore demands recognition. He launches into a castigation of the bill which is not yet before the body. He is out of order, tax reform is almost out of time, and the senator is gavelled down.

11:43 P.M.—I call for the vote on the previous question amid uproar and charges of "gag order" and heavy-handedness. The clerk calls "Afflerbach," and when the senator responds, the roll call is enjoined and cannot be interrupted. Since no other motion—even adjournment—could interpose between the previous question and the final vote, this was the signal that we were about to punch this football into the end zone. Vote on the motion, 26-23.

11:47 P.M.—We move right to the up and down vote on S.B. 442 itself. "Will the Senate concur in House amendments placed in S.B. 442?" On the question, the final tally, at 11:53 P.M. is 31-18. Preemptively, Zemprelli calls up another bill on the calendar. In the din surrounding his remarks, I sign the legislation and it is whisked to the House by Rep. Dave Sweet, the House mover of the legislation, who delivers it directly to the speaker of the house.

11:56 P.M.—The GOP wants a reconsideration of the bill. They learn that it is in the House and demand that it be recalled for "further action" in the Senate. The recall motion is debatable, and in another fitting irony, Sen. Jim Kelley, the preeminent stickler and orator in the Senate, makes his farewell speech on the Senate floor and talks the motion to death.

12:00 Midnight—Sen. Clarence Bell makes the point of order that, as of midnight, the speaker is no longer a sitting senator, the session having expired. Bell is correct, the session is over, and the tax reform package is on its way to the governor. The hour of midnight, November 30, 1988, having arrived, the 1987-88 session, complete with a tax reform victory, came to a close.

As exciting as the legislative arena was that night, we were in for a delayed disappointment. In the time-honored tradition of Pennsylvania political maneuverings, the Republicans had insisted on a clause in the bill that required a public referendum on the issue at the following May election. This is known as a "poison pill." The level of misinformation about the reform package and the outright distortions allowed the opposition to defeat the package handily in the court of public opinion.

Casey immediately moved on from the issue, and it was only now, in 1993, that the legislature was beginning to reassess the matter. Maybe it was too soon or maybe it was just too high of a political mountain to climb, but the matter, more than twenty years later, remains unresolved. Property taxes are still too high and seniors are still paying too much for school services that they stopped using long ago.

I realized that I was banging my head against the wall shortly after the Dawida hearings. The governor was asked to comment on remarks I had made on the issue, and he said off the cuff: "Sounds like a tax increase to me."

I was stunned by the remark. Bob Casey had taken a direct shot at me and stopped any further discussion of property tax reform in its tracks. Whether it was deliberate or not, I decided that I should focus my energies elsewhere.

One of those areas remained economic development. To that end, I was involved with a number of industrial development organizations throughout the state including one that showed great promise in western PA. Representative Mike Veon introduced me to the Beaver County Initiative for Growth. This was a consortium of local leaders who would invest public and private funds in job-creating projects. While it seemed like a good idea at the time, Mike would come under fire later for his role in obtaining and allocating those public funds.

For the most part though, there was a surge of creative investments throughout the state that was the result of a more cooperative climate at the highest levels of government. I served on the Governor's Economic Development Partnership, and it was a wellspring of ideas that nurtured this revitalization.

We also continued to emphasize alternative energy, recycling, and new technologies, and there were regular press conferences to announce substantial grants and loans to further those causes.

Photo-ops that week included my presentation of the governor's proclamation on National Dental Health Month with the PA Dental Association; a presentation to AARP; and some remarks to the Huntingdon County business leaders at their annual dinner. I also joined Representative Gordner in honoring his state champion Berwick Area High School football team.

On the energy front, Jan Freeman, executive director of the Pennsylvania Energy Office and I (as chairman of the PEO) paid a visit to top executives at Ford, General Motors, and Chrysler in Detroit. The mission was to learn from the Electric Transportation Coalition about each company's plans for deploying electric vehicles. Pennsylvania was a potentially huge market for the vehicles if we could help with appropriate power stations and consumer education. Detroit was in the research and development phase of battery technology that could extend the range and lower the cost of such vehicles. We left Detroit with visions of millions of electric vehicles on the road, dramatically reducing American dependence on foreign oil. Regrettably, the industry faced larger economic problems in the years to come that interrupted this adventure.

With the dramatic harnessing of natural gas in PA in recent years, and with the world class research and development capabilities that we have, I believe that Pennsylvania can and should regain its preeminent status in alternative fuels.

I landed in Pittsburgh at the end of that week in time for the PA Jaycees banquet and black tie event and returned to Harrisburg for remarks at the United Steelworkers of America 35th Annual Conference. Labor had always been supportive of me, and I was a natural supporter of working families. I came from one and grew up with the steelworkers, mineworkers, and garment workers in the Johnstown, PA mills and factories. It was always fun being with my good friend, President Andrew "Lefty" Palm. At the apex of my own run for governor, I would say to him that he would be an excellent secretary of labor and industry in PA. And I meant it.

The governor's budget address is always scheduled for early in February. I joined him at dinner on the eve of the joint session address and again at breakfast for two different sets of legislative leaders. While the specifics were to be released in conjunction with the governor's speech, the broad strokes indicated that there would be balance between revenues and expenditures. This was due, in large part, to an infusion of new revenues that occurred after the infamous Casey/Singel tax increases of 1991. While there had been much grandstanding and rhetoric surrounding the budget of 1991, the reality is that a tax adjustment was necessary. It was *the* only time in eight years that Casey proposed a substantial tax increase. Despite partisan attacks, it put Pennsylvania on a solid fiscal path for years to come. It also meant that 1993 was going to be relatively smooth sailing on the budget front. I had learned, however, that there were always ancillary issues that complicated things. One Senator had prepared me for this with a bit of wisdom: "We can't pass a Mother's Day resolution around here without ten amendments!"

While the legislature was beginning the review of the governor's budget plan, I was about my normal duties for the remainder of the month of February. These included a visit from the PA Insurance Federation and PA Farmers Union, a presentation to the PA Association of Housing and Redevelopment Authorities, press conferences on energy and recycling, and support for the governor's education initiatives at several venues.

I also filled in for Casey on his regular "Ask the Governor" radio show. I enjoyed the challenge of taking on listeners' questions. Casey was not as comfortable with my style, though. "Tone it down a bit," was the message that Gubernatorial Chief of Staff Jim Brown conveyed on more than one occasion.

In between official functions, in the second week of February I managed to squeeze in some events that had political overtones. Lynne Abraham, a good friend and a determined prosecutor, was running for district attorney in Philadelphia. I attended a fundraiser and some private meetings on her behalf. In Philadelphia, I made the rounds of local talk shows and spent some time with another good friend, Mayor Ed Rendell.

The mayor had launched a number of environmental initiatives in Philadelphia, and we joined forces at an event highlighting industries that were benefiting from recycling initiatives. Ed, whom the press had dubbed "America's Mayor," was a perfect fit for Philadelphia. He was smart and politically savvy. Together with his brilliant chief of staff, Dave Cohen, he charted a course for a Philadelphia renaissance that has been the envy of big cities everywhere. Ed was in my corner in every one of my political endeavors, and I was pleased to return the favor when he ran successfully for governor in 2002.

Every statewide campaign runs through Philadelphia. The sheer percentage of votes and the concentration of serious political contributors makes it a mandatory early stop on candidates' agendas. In 1993 (and still today) much political strategy emanated from the offices of the Campaign Group. This company featured the irascible Neil Oxman, who annoyed candidates until they figured out that he was usually right; and the redoubtable Thomas "Doc" Sweitzer, the go-to Democrat counselor who would show up in national, state, and local races all over the country.

Doc and I attended Penn State together and remain good friends. It was my turn to visit Campaign Group on the off chance that they would be interested in abetting my candidacy for governor in 1994. Let's just say that Doc and Neil were lukewarm at the time. This was due in part to the bad track record that lieutenant governors had in succeeding their governors and also their own preference to keep their options open until other candidates surfaced.

I wasn't offended by their hesitation. In fact, my reaction was to make a mental note to shop around when the time came to engage a firm. While the Campaign Group was the gold standard for state-wide campaigns in Pennsylvania, that didn't mean that some new talent could not be recruited.

Jim Baumbach said the same thing at the Palm Restaurant later that day. Jim had been an insider for many years, and I respected his insights and political knowledge. He was friendly, as always, but candid about the challenge that lay ahead. Could I raise $5 or $10 million (at that time a record amount for Democrats)? Would Casey support me? Where were the unions? Were Doc and Neil on board? Legitimate questions that made me understand that I needed a lot more time to answer them.

The early political soundings continued in Pittsburgh and other areas.

Dennis Roddy, a political reporter for the *Pittsburgh Post-Gazette*, wanted to pin me down on my own political plans. "Too soon," I told him. But I was back in the Pittsburgh area lining up early support. On this trip, Allegheny County Sheriff Gene Coon was helpful, and the Black Ward Leaders looked me over at their monthly meeting. Tim Uhrich, a key worker for me in the area, introduced me to some of the key elected officials and operatives.

Straight back to Philadelphia for more political prospecting with some members of city council: Ron Donatucci, the well-connected register of wills; and my buddy, City Controller Jonathan Saidel.

On this trip, though, I would also continue my own education on a subject that was about to burst into public view. At the insistence of my assistant, John Lord, I was attending and keynoting the Mid-Atlantic Regional Federal AIDS meeting. Hundreds of AIDS patients, as well as leaders of the gay community, were there to let me know, in no uncertain terms, that government officials needed to address the growing AIDS epidemic. Most advocates are dedicated to their cause for various important reasons. These AIDS awareness leaders had a passion that derived from the fact that we were talking about a life and death issue that affected them personally.

John Lord had taken it upon himself to spearhead my office participation in the movement, and he was intolerant of any hesitation that I may have shown. (Remember: In 1993, AIDS and the scourge that it presented to the gay community was still a controversial matter; however, the issue being of personal significance to John Lord, he would simply not allow me to "sit it out.") With his guidance, we issued an unprecedented report to the governor and the media on the need for an action agenda on AIDS, and I came to understand the community and the devastation caused by the disease.

After a prolonged battle that shriveled his own body and tested his faith, John announced to his family that he was "ready." He asked them not to follow him upstairs. He closed his eyes and died of AIDS. The best gift that I received from John Lord was his example of courage and commitment. I like to think that my team honored his memory by keeping the issue on the front burner throughout my service in government.

The loyal opposition was back to its feistiness in the Senate. One of the most routine functions is to grant "legislative leaves" to senators who were not available to vote in person because of other duties in their district. Even this routine function could be twisted into a verbal attack—particularly if the target was Frank Pecora.

Senator Jubelirer: *"I challenge the granting of leave for Senator Pecora."*
The President (Singel): *"The chair would entertain a motion at this point to move that legislative leave be granted for Senator Pecora. That would be the appropriate motion at this point."*
Senator Lincoln: *"Mr. President, I so move."*
Senator Jubelirer: *"Mr. President, may we be at ease for a moment?"*

Being "at ease" usually meant that one side or the other was gathering its wits or counting votes. Clearly, Senator Jubelirer had not expected to get to a motion and a vote so quickly and was preparing to drag out this drama.

Senator Lincoln: *"Mr. President, is this a debatable issue?"*
The President: *"The chair is in somewhat uncharted territory here because the question comes up so rarely. The chair would, however, indicate to the members that it is his opinion that there is limited debate allowed on this motion, and the chair stresses 'limited debate' as to the propriety of the leave itself. And only on that subject would the chair allow limited debate."*

Senator Lincoln produced the letter requesting the leave of absence and entered into the record Senator Pecora's complete schedule of legislative activities for the day. He railed against the pettiness of the minority and warned that it could come back to haunt them when they had similar requests.

The reality, of course, is that without the senator present to vote on his own leave request, the Chamber was deadlocked at 24-24. This forced a vote from me to break the tie, and in my Republican colleagues' estimation, aligned me with the "nefarious" Frank Pecora. Which was exactly what they wanted. It was one of many legislative squeeze plays that would occur in the months ahead.

Two weeks into the month I had the pleasure of returning to my hometown to present a lottery check. Bob and Mary Lou Carruthers went to St. Mary's Byzantine Catholic Church—my own parish in Johnstown. They, like my own relatives, were hearty Carpatho-Russians who believed in God, hard work, and their community of faith and friends. I presented a check of $6 million to them in their favorite local tavern. When the press asked them what they would do with the money Mary Lou responded that she could finally get her Chevy Nova fixed.

Here's a shout out to the parishioners of St. Mary's Byzantine Catholic Church in Johnstown, Pennsylvania. Thank you all so much for teaching me about faith in God, commitment to duty, and the need for humility in all circumstances. No amount of money could shake the foundation of what makes these folks exceptional.

Other events on the schedule included the formal hearing on the intruder incident at TMI and an actual NRC-monitored exercise at the Susquehanna Nuclear Power Plant. Since the accident at TMI in 1979, states with nuclear facilities were required to participate in emergency preparedness drills. As the chairman of the PA Emergency Management Council, I was in charge during natural or man-made crises. We treated drills like the real thing, and I believe that Pennsylvania has developed an emergency response and management capability that is second to none.

One incident is worth noting here.

On September 30, 1987, Governor Bob Casey was taken to the hospital to undergo multiple bypass surgery. Dr. David Leaman of Hershey Medical Center was quoted in the governor's press release that: "Except for the duration of the surgical procedure and the immediate post-operative period, the governor will not be incapacitated or disabled." This statement, drafted in conjunction with Bob

Grotevant, the governor's press secretary, was meant to send reassurances that it would be business as usual for the state with little or no disruption. The truth is that no one recovers speedily from heart surgery. In addition to the surgery and post-operative period, Casey spent several days out of commission.

It was at the precise moment that the governor was under anesthesia, when he truly was incapacitated, that PEMA reported an incident on the heavily traveled Schuylkill expressway. A tanker carrying a full load of toxic material had overturned. There was a danger to nearby residents of poison fumes if the tanker was breached. Nearby residents totaled about 3 million people!

This made for a long night in the emergency operations center. We received continual updates from the state police on the scene and from all state and local health care resources preparing for the worst. The essential executive decision that had to be made was whether or not to evacuate residents who were in the "plume" of the toxic cloud. These evacuations were always dangerous. The logistics—particularly in a densely populated area—were daunting. Moving frail or bedridden folks, for example, would almost certainly result in casualties and deaths.

Weighing all of the risks, I was prepared to issue the order to evacuate until the governor's legal counsel weighed in, one member saying, "You can't do that. Only the governor can issue such an order."

"But he's incapacitated at the moment," I'd replied.

"It does not matter," he said. "Since there has been no formal transfer of power, you would be committing an illegal act by ordering an evacuation."

The dilemma was clear: sign the declaration and face civil or criminal punishment or don't evacuate and risk the lives of millions.

"Draw up the papers," I said.

And then, as we were managing traffic and providing appropriate alerts, *deus ex machina*: the weather changed. When the temperature dropped below freezing, the toxic cloud crystallized and particles of frozen acid were simply swept off the highway. The immediate potential health crisis and the public policy crisis was averted.

The experience gave rise to some soul searching in both the governor's and lieutenant governor's office. We agreed that the Commonwealth should never be exposed like that again. Henceforth, any hospital stay that required anesthesia for the governor or any incident that caused even short-term incapacitation would generate a transfer of power document according to the 25th Amendment to Pennsylvania's Constitution. This approach would be followed later in the summer of 1993, and it would be repeated in subsequent administrations.

By the end of the month it was back to Philadelphia to continue discussions with Ed Rendell. The official event was a luncheon with US Commerce Secretary Ron Brown and business leaders. It gave me a chance to cement my friendship with two key leaders. The rest of the day was spent reaching out to the minority community: a live interview with Rotan Lee on WHAT Radio, a celebration of Black History Month at a local community center, and a Citizen Action Awards Dinner at the Hilton.

After a breakfast meeting with key black leaders, I sat in on one of the final governor's health care hearings at a recreational center. Casey, like President Clinton, was committed to finding some way to lower health care costs and providing universal health care coverage. The president had established his wife, Hillary, as the point person for the national discussion; Casey embarked on hearings of his own in the state. I found myself going to both sets of health care fora and hearing much of the information twice! Still, it was important to lay the groundwork for substantial health care reform—which did not really occur until the Obama administration twenty years later.

February ended with a whirlwind weekend of political activities.

The Association of Township Officials convention in Carlisle.

The Arab American Leadership with my friend, Marwan Kriedie, in Camp Hill.

The Allegheny County Democratic Committee Endorsement meeting.

While it was an "off year" with no state races, that didn't stop the Allegheny County Democrats from slugging it out over their favorites for judge, mayor, city council, and local offices. I attempted to schmooze with all of the factions—and to steer clear of the intramural hostilities. I have to admit that politics at the ground level were always an education and an exhilarating experience for me.

Watching the Pittsburgh pandemonium reminded me of another impactful scene. My political foray in 1980 was for the 35th district Senate seat in PA. This district included hardscrabble Johnstown and working class communities in Cambria County. The "boss" of the Democratic Party in that county was a warrior whose experiences went back to Franklin Roosevelt. In fact, he loved to share tales of working with Harry Truman, Hubert Humphrey, and the Kennedys. On the state level he served as the secretary of labor and industry under Governor Milton Shapp and was regarded as one of the most effective—if somewhat unscrupulous—chairmen in the state. His methods for cajoling funds for his political machinery from state workers had already earned him some jail time, and he was nothing if not controversial.

My first encounter with him came in 1978 when I, all of 25 years old, ran against his machine for a state House seat. The obligatory visit to the chairman's home was actually going quite well. Sally Torquato had baked cookies, and John (Mr. Torquato, of course) was regaling me with a fascinating series of stories. I was enjoying them thoroughly, but I remember feeling relieved that we were not being recorded! After an hour or so, the chairman said:

"Son, I like you. You're going to be a star."

"Thank you, Mr. Torquato," I said. "Can I count on your support?"

"No, Mark," he said. "I am going to have to cut your throat."

Lesson from the professional pol: Don't mess with the organization! It was a clear and honest message that actually saved me a lot of time. I didn't spend one more second calling any ward leaders! Metaphorically, he fulfilled his promise that year.

Two years later, having actually beaten that same machinery in the primary race for state Senate, the circumstances had changed. The voters had spoken, and even the burly, boisterous John Torquato was ready to embrace me. He was a party man through and through, and I was now on the team. At the packed House dinner of Democrats in the fall of 1980, I was nervously going over my remarks in my mind. These were the same folks who did me in two years earlier. How do I convert them? How do I get them enthusiastic about the campaign?

It was John Torquato who gave me the answer.

Just before I was introduced, he pulled me aside.

"Son," he said. "Do you see that crowd?"

I looked over the eleven hundred people. Mostly ward leaders, committee people. Most had figured out how to score a free ticket to the dinner or the chairman had shaken enough money trees to cover the costs. It was sea of faces chattering away in a ritual that they repeated every election season.

"I just want you to know," said the chairman, "that I've taken that *garbage*." He hesitated as he waved his beefy arm over the crowd, "And I've turned into pure *slime*."

New message from John Torquato: "Don't worry about Cambria County; I can mold them any way I want." That "slime" was malleable; he could shape the local Democrats into whatever he chose! For the record, that's not how I perceived the local workers. They became my friends and I enjoyed their company and support.

Crudeness notwithstanding, I came to appreciate his candor and loyalty over the years. He was followed by his loyal sidekick, William Joseph, who proved to be equally effective in delivering the vote in Cambria County. It has only been in recent years that the Republican Party has come anywhere near breaking that hold on the electorate.

When John Torquato died, a slew of FBI agents attended his funeral. They wanted to document any public officials with ties to Torquato. The chairman had helped countless aspiring politicians, but I was the only elected official who showed up to pay respects.

Bill Joseph had an even more interesting demise. He was right in the middle of one of his famous rallying-cry speeches for a slate of Democrats when his heart exploded. He died amid all of his friends and followers with bombast and pride.

One more political war story that needs to be told: Late October 1986. Bob Casey and Mark Singel are in the final stages of a rough-and-tumble campaign for governor and lieutenant governor. An issue that had arisen was drug indiscretions by a youthful Bill Scranton (the then lieutenant governor and candidate for governor). Bob Casey had instructed me and his entire team to steer clear of the issue.

I found myself in a van with several reporters who were embedded for the "inside stories" of the campaign.

"What about this drug issue?" came the question from Bob Zausner, the *Philadelphia Inquirer* reporter.

I was on script: "The candidate has given us explicit instructions that the issue is off limits."

Bob: "Does that mean for surrogates and supporters as well?"

"That means for anybody associated with the campaign."

Just then the van arrived at a nondescript hall that was hosting two large ward meetings. I was there to rally the troops, but it turned out that feisty old Representative Bill Rieger beat me to the task. Just as the reporters and I walked into the hall, we heard Rieger bellowing at the top of his lungs: ". . . and you certainly don't want no fucking drug addict for governor."

"Shit," I said audibly.

Zausner just shrugged and said: "That's Philly politics."

Back to February of 1993 . . .

This is the month that Michael Jackson was at the peak of his reign in popular culture. His appearance on the Oprah Winfrey show drew a 90 million person audience. Eric Clapton won a Grammy for "Tears in Heaven," a paean to his infant son who died in a tragic accident. In a precursor of awful things to come about a decade later, the World Trade Center was bombed. Seven people were killed by a bomb placed in the parking garage. There was some discussion about a murky group of radical Muslims behind the attack. Americans would be introduced more formally and brutally to Al-Qaeda and Osama bin Laden on September 11, 2001.

MARCH

At the beginning of March, Pittsburgh turns its thoughts, as always, to hockey. In 1993, they were pinning their hopes on Mario Lemieux and cheering on their beloved Pittsburgh Penguins to victory. However, my visits to Pittsburgh, much like Philadelphia, were the prerequisites to a bona fide gubernatorial campaign.

The first of the month I convened a group that we called the Future Focus Breakfast. Steve Wray, a bright staffer who would go on to run the Pennsylvania Economy League, helped construct these mini think tanks in various regions of the state. I enjoyed hearing points of view from folks outside of the Harrisburg bubble. It didn't hurt that they were prominent in their communities, and for the most part, potential political supporters.

Official functions that followed included a labor leaders meeting, a speech to the Energy 93 Conference, another speech to the North Hills School district, and a meeting with some executives from Waste Management.

Office meetings and calls predominated the next few days, followed by another western PA trek to Indiana University of Pennsylvania at the invitation of a political science class that I was able to couple with a grant presentation at the Allegheny Ludlum Corporation. They were good partners in an education initiative that was Secretary of Education Don Carroll's baby. Don was a dedicated public servant committed to educational excellence, and it was kind of him to let me share the stage.

Education was also one of my passions, and I was attentive to the needs of districts like Greater Johnstown. They were struggling, and Dr. Richard DeLuca, superintendent, came to make a case for fairer funding.

My staff was convinced that public exposure on any and every topic was desirable. It was not unusual to have eight or ten talk shows, editorial conferences, and reporter calls every week. The topics were usually about energy, PEMA, my role on the pardons board, or the hot legislative topic of the moment. I kept myself informed, but it was truly an attentive and aggressive staff that got me through.

Joe Powers ran my Senate office and lieutenant governor's office with a kindness for the troops that was remarkable; it was this gentle touch that got the best out of all of them. Veronica Varga was the press secretary and "message meister" who wrote beautifully and on deadline. Tom Haertsch and Joe Leighton shared research responsibilities and always knew their stuff. Bonita Truax, Karen Stefanic, and Jennifer Glass handled thousands of constituent matters and communications with grace and patience. Jean Brannon, my executive assistant, kept a close eye on my calendar and office details, including various matters down to filing procedures and the steady flow of paperwork. Michelle Maley administered the lieutenant governor's home and personal functions for the Singels.

Gina McBean did double duty as a caseworker in my office and as a personal assistant to Jackie. She, more than most of the staff, became a family companion and a new "aunt" for my children. Chris Wakeley was a bright policy wonk whose work was always top rate.

We beefed up the team as the year wore on. Tony Barbush came in to help Joe with the growing workload. Eric Schnurer, who had worked as a key staffer for several congressmen and governors, came on in anticipation of building an even stronger team as 1994 approached.

All in all, they were the finest group of public servants I have ever known.

Second week in March and we were on the road again.

A Levittown radio station, the editorial board at the *Bucks County Courier Times* and the *Daily Intelligencer*, and a rare personal indulgence: lunch with a good friend. Walter Conti and I served together on the board of trustees at Penn State. He was a charming, caring individual who owned the famous Conti's Cross Keys Restaurant in Doylestown. The lunch was outstanding, and the company could not have been better. On a politically-related note, Joe Conti, Walter's son, inherited his dad's easygoing style and would win a state Senate seat of his own in 2002.

Next stop: Washington, DC. The spring meeting of the National Conference of Lieutenant Governors. After a pleasant meeting with my friend and colleague, US Senator Harris Wofford, I settled in for the opening luncheon with my lieutenant governor peers. This was an impressive group that featured some folks who were already stars: Ann Richards of Texas, Mel Carnahan of Missouri, Jim Folsom of Alabama, and Doug Wilder of Virginia to name a few. Many others would go on to be governors and senators—and presidential contenders.

I am a character witness for Dr. Howard Dean. He was the lieutenant governor of Vermont at the time, and I had a friendly relationship with him. In fact, I was seated beside him when I saw him put his medical training to use.

The luncheon speaker was US Senator Richard Lugar of Nevada. He was downing some lunch and making conversation when some food lodged in his throat. I was the first one to notice that he had gone silent and, in fact, was turning a light shade of blue.

"Aren't you a doctor?" I said to Howard Dean.

"Yes," he said noticing at the same time Lugar's problem.

Dean jumped up and performed an efficient Heimlich maneuver on the senator. I literally watched Howard Dean save Richard Lugar's life. We didn't keep in touch as much as I would have liked, but I always place Dean in the category of one of the good guys.

For now, I had to get back to Pennsylvania for the statewide PSEA conference followed by an interesting meeting in State College with Dr. John Leathers of Penn State. The latter was a planning session for a trip to Great Britain to initiate cooperative academic programs between Penn State and Kent County, England.

What met us on the way back from State College was the blizzard of 1993. The week of March 15 was interrupted by record snows and ice conditions all over the state. I found myself at the Emergency Operations Center surrounded by the various emergency management personnel from each of the appropriate agencies. One computer-driven projection screen already had situation reports from all over the state. Another was tracking weather patterns in real time, and a third had a punch list of "unmet needs" that would likely need to be addressed soon. The electronic displays and the individual glass cubicles for each agency were innovations of which I was very proud. We had taken the PA Emergency Management Agency from white boards and grease pens to a state of the art facility connected to all 67 county EOCs. In fact, the PEMA team led the effort to establish a statewide 911 system and made sure that even the most remote areas benefited from computer connections to the state system. Many of these changes were the direct result of lessons learned from the 1979 Three Mile Island incident. Governor Thornburgh and my predecessor, Bill Scranton, began the overhaul of our emergency response and management capabilities, and we continued to upgrade into the late 1980s and early 1990s to make the PA system the best of its kind in the nation.

An under-reported fact about Pennsylvania is that, because of its geography, extensive network of roads and bridges, and wide variety of rural, suburban, and urban realities, the state faces incidents on a daily basis. About once every ten days we experienced something that could be life-threatening on a large enough scale to activate the EOC. I had already been through the Camp Hill prison break, numerous floods, toxic spills on highways, plane crashes, and even the occasional earthquake or tornado. Industrial strength disasters like oil spills, chemical plant explosions, and even nuclear incidents were not unusual.

This blizzard was a good example of technology and well-trained state employees meshing to address a real time, life-threatening situation. PennDOT was reporting a number of fender benders on main and secondary highways relating to the first coating of surface ice. They were also nervous about coping with the record snowfalls projected for the evening. Travelers were likely to be stranded on roads throughout the state, endangering their own lives and making it even more difficult to get roads cleared and salted.

The situation worsened as the minutes ticked on. It was time to get into response mode.

I looked around the conference table at the folks from the various departments and asked for suggestions.

It was State Police Commissioner Glen Walp who stepped up. Glen was rock-solid, physically. He was also a well-respected leader of what I still believe is the best law enforcement team in the country.

"Close the highways," he said.

I believe that my initial reaction, which was probably not recorded anywhere, was: "Are you crazy?"

"Seriously," Glen went on. "We can give PennDOT a fighting chance of keeping this cleared for the morning traffic if we get all non-essential traffic off the highways now."

This was an unprecedented action, but PennDOT loved the idea, and I agreed.

It was after 3:00 p.m., but we still had time to get motorists to safety before night fell at about 5:00 p.m. We needed the governor to issue the proclamation soon, and we needed to get the message out as quickly as possible.

I called the governor and told him the idea.

"Are you crazy?" was his initial reaction. I talked him through the closure plan, positioning state police at limited highway entrances to enforce the order, and even ways to reach out to the hospitality industry to prepare for some unexpected guests at roadside inns.

The governor approved the plan, and we went immediately into public announcement mode. This included a hastily organized press conference at 4:00 p.m. and deployment of hundreds of state troopers to enforce the 5:00 p.m. curfew.

It worked.

No lives were lost in the blizzard of 1993, PennDOT did a remarkable job in cleaning up a 3-4 foot snowfall, and the hotels and motels in Pennsylvania had their best night of the year! Just one of dozens of stories of the quiet competence of state and local responders.

After that, things quieted down a bit, and I was back to the routine. This included a pleasant visit from two hometown friends. Charlie Neuhoff of H.F. Lenz Engineers, and Dan DeVos of a new company called Concurrent Technologies, had come from Johnstown to discuss some energy innovations that they were working on. H.F. Lenz was a premier firm known for its creativity. Concurrent Technologies got its start working on government opportunities developed by the hardworking and well-connected Congressman John P. Murtha. This was a heads up about several projects that might require some state assistance. I was always pleased to support the Johnstown folks and delighted to work with Murtha. My relationship with the congressman went back to my days as a campaign volunteer in high school. It was rare that I attended events that were purely social, but there were many evenings that featured some official business in pleasant surroundings with good friends.

Jackie particularly enjoyed our interactions with the Penn State Board of Trustees. Governor Casey had appointed me as his representative on the board, and it turned out to be a perfect perk. Dr. McCollister Evarts, the CEO of Penn State's Hershey Medical Center, entertained the entire board at his home. The business leaders, scholars, and philanthropists on that board were some of the most accomplished and pleasant people I have ever known. The unifying factor was our collective love for Penn State and the huge impact that it had on the commonwealth. I have been fortunate to associate with presidents like John Oswald, Bryce Jordan, and Joab Thomas. Outstanding leaders all.

The board met at the Hershey Medical Center, and typically it fell to me to address the state funding plan for Penn State and higher education in general. While the governor's plan increased funding slightly, Penn State enthusiasts argued loudly that it was not nearly adequate given the number of students served or the return on that important investment. It was difficult for me to convey that we had a host of priorities with an equal claim on tax dollars. I got the annual board "grilling," but it was always good-natured.

Back in Philadelphia for a taping of the *Issues and Answers* show at WPVI studios and a quick return for a political event. Bill Titleman, a major fund-raiser with the PA Trial Lawyers, was hosting a dinner for Chairman of the Democratic National Committee David Wilhelm. David was in town to speak at the Democrats' state organization, and it fell to me to introduce him to the troops. David and I connected during the 1992 presidential campaign, and he was an effective cheerleader for President Clinton and the Democratic agenda.

Mid-March brought about a break in the action for some family time.

Career Day at my daughter's sixth grade class. If there is a lingering regret about my public service, it is that I did not spend nearly enough time watching my kids grow up. We did try to have breakfast together each day, and we scheduled brief vacations when we could. But it is a fact that, especially in the hectic days that were to come, I was on the job and away from home more than I realized. Still, Allyson, Jonathan, and Christopher were patient and beautifully behaved during staged events and official functions, and we made the best of our private time together.

When Christopher entered first grade, he was asked what his father did. For reasons that had to do with too much television and an overactive imagination, he replied: "He's an international man of mystery."

I tried to describe my career for Allyson's class, but I think the kids still found my functions a bit mysterious.

Other items on the schedule that week included the PA State Association of Boroughs, the PA Catholic Conference, and the PA Community Bankers. Events like these were often my part of helping with the governor's schedule. If he couldn't attend, the organizations were gracious enough to accept me as a surrogate. I always enjoyed the public speaking part of these occasions, and I was happy to schmooze. Some newspaper once wrote that I would rather campaign than eat. I suppose that is true. I know that it derives from my honest affection for most people.

A quick side trip to Reading to help negotiate the positioning of a new highway. More specifically, Route 322 was being rerouted in such a way that it would have a crippling impact on the old Reading Inn. I was pleased to bring together Secretary Yerusalim of PennDOT and other key officials with my old friend, Jack Sheehan, the owner of the inn. We were able to accommodate the needed safety improvements and the economic concerns of the inn and surrounding businesses.

I was also able to squeeze in a visit to the Easton Area High School. My friend Sal Panto, the mayor of Easton, had invited me to help kick off the fund-raising campaign for the school band to participate in the 1994 Rose Bowl.

The end of March was another foray into the Philadelphia political scene. Breakfast with some key contributors followed by a rapid succession of meet-and-greets. Lunch with the editors of the *Philadelphia Inquirer*. The afternoon was dedicated to transportation issues. Happy Fernandez was an outstanding member of the Philadelphia City Council, and this was my first of several sessions on key issues with her. I was grateful for her insights and impressed by her breadth of knowledge on transportation and many other issues.

No rest on the weekend, but an enjoyable trip back home.

Richard Burkert, the director of the Johnstown Area Heritage Association, was opening his new headquarters in a revitalized old building that had served as a brewery and then as a paper company. This was Richard's specialty: taking a piece of Johnstown's heritage and transforming it into a new purpose. He had done wonders with the transformation of parts of the steel plants in the area and was the driving force behind the Johnstown Flood Museum. Richard was one of the most talented innovators in the preservation field. He struggled mightily to revitalize a community caught in the rust belt. It was a pleasure to return home to give him a boost.

Since I was close, my team had scheduled me as the speaker for the annual luncheon of the Italian Sons and Daughters of America at the Pittsburgh Hilton. More accurately, Tom Castelli, a dear friend and my roommate when I first arrived in Harrisburg as a state senator, insisted on it. Tom was fiercely proud of his heritage and was intent on having me adopted as an honorary Italian. Since he was a statewide official with ISDA, I got invited to many of their events.

I should mention that Tom Castelli was also a lifelong friend of my father. They were at each others' weddings. Tom went on to be the deputy treasurer in Pennsylvania. It was no accident that we were roomies. I believe that my father arranged it so that Tom could keep me in line and away from the distractions of Harrisburg.

Two stories from my Italian friends and hosts:

The local ISDA chapter bestowed their Man of the Year award on Tom Castelli in 1986. I was a state senator already engaged in the campaign for lieutenant governor. I was honored to be the keynote speaker at the event, although it came on a Friday evening after a brutal week on the campaign trail. I was also thinking about the christening of my son, Christopher, who had been born just a few weeks before. We had arranged for the event to occur that Sunday at my hometown parish, St. Mary's Byzantine Catholic Church, with the parish priest, Father William Sabo, who had nurtured me since childhood, officiating.

The problem was that I hadn't been to confession in many months, and I felt a need to unburden myself before I received Holy Communion. Father Balestino, he of Italian fervor equal to Tom Castelli, was on hand at the event to give the invocation and benediction. I told him of my spiritual challenge and he had a solution.

"Let's take a walk," he said.

He meant right through 200 couples doing the Tarantella.

"Just speak in a regular voice and nobody will pay attention," he said.

"Bless me father, for I have sinned," I began and proceeded to offer my first confession on a dance floor.

The other story involves a prelate who was legendary in Pennsylvania. Cardinal Anthony Bevilacqua was charismatic and imposing. He provided both spiritual leadership and savvy political direction to the Philadelphia flock in a way that drew the attention of his peers and of the Vatican itself.

We found ourselves seated next to each other on a dais honoring ISDA's Man of the Year at a lavish banquet on Society Hill. The honoree happened to be the redoubtable Senator Vincent Fumo, who was loved by many and reviled by a few—in the Pennsylvania Italian community, he was almost as revered as the cardinal himself.

Over the salad and main course, Cardinal Bevilacqua couldn't resist applying a bit of a moral spanking to me on the issue of abortion. He was, of course, insisting that I align my position with the Catholic Church. The way he put it was: "You should be more pro-life—just like Casey." Discussion ensued about *Roe v. Wade*, and my genuine respect for the Blackmun decision. Even if he was listening to me, he wasn't, unsurprisingly, budging on his stance.

Since we had ventured into controversial topics and since it was just two guys talking off the record, I asked him about a canonical pet peeve of mine.

"What about celibacy, Your Eminence? In the light of all of the problems the church is facing, how can we justify this archaic position?"

"Mark," said Bevilacqua. "You have to understand the Gandhi-esque commitment to our calling. We set earthly things aside."

Perhaps impertinently, I continued. "C'mon. You're an attractive guy with, I assume, natural tendencies. How does it benefit anybody for you to live an entire life with those in check?"

His response was: "I can look upon a beautiful woman with appreciation; not lust."

I swear that as he was finishing that sentence, a young Italian woman with stunning eyes and jet black hair approached the dais. "Good evening, Your Eminence," she breathed, her rather prominent breasts pushing upward against a dangerously low neckline. She shook his hand and moved on.

"Well, Your Eminence," I said, noting that he wasn't oblivious to the woman's ill-concealed curves. "Tell me, was that appreciation or lust?"

In the next moment, it was clear that there was some common ground that would seal our friendship.

"You got me there, Mark," he replied.

The drumbeat of normal assignments continued.

Jesse Bloom from Williamsport was having a problem with a landfill operator in her area; the PA Coal Association was in town for their annual convention; my good friend, Bill Greenlee, a savvy Republican operative and key lobbyist in Harrisburg, brought an oil company client to talk about their innovations in alternative fuels; St. Francis College in Loretto had me in for a leadership training seminar; two dinners with key legislators; and a bill signing in the governor's office.

Meanwhile, in other world news at that time, Ezer Weizman was elected president of Israel, and Intel accelerated information technology with something they were calling the Pentium processor.

I spent the final day of March in 1993 at Dulles airport preparing for a trip to London and a half dozen other cities in Europe to promote academic ties with Penn State and to pursue some international trade deals that were in the works.

APRIL

The European trip was the result of some masterful scheduling and preparation from the folks at Penn State, my own staff, and the PA Department of Community and Economic Development. Andy Greenberg was the DCED secretary, and he was joining me to help lead the trade aspect of the trip. It was a rare opportunity to bring my wife along, and we both found that the hospitality and social activities were as enjoyable as the array of contacts and friendships we established.

The official schedule was demanding:

Jack Worms was the director of PA's European office, and he proved to be extremely well connected with public and private leaders. He coordinated an event with the British-American Chamber of Commerce and several key meetings in London. These included a British technology group seeking a beachhead in Pennsylvania, and top officials with British Airways on the possibility of direct flights between Heathrow and Pittsburgh International.

Our travels would take us to Warsaw for the signing of a bilateral coal agreement between Mr. Sheldon Wool of Custom Coals and his Polish counterpart, Dr. Roman Ney. We would also spend some time with Mr. Kazimierrz Pazgan, president of Konspol International Ltd.

We also touched base with some investment groups based in Brussels and folks from the Antwerp Port Authority who were already doing substantial business with our Philadelphia ports.

On the academic side, we established a strategic alliance between PSU and the University of Kent, thanks to the efforts of Dr. John Leathers and Penn State's Assistant Dean of Agriculture, Dr. Don Evans.

We squeezed in a visit to the "Chunnel" project, which was in mid-construction at the time.

The need to present a serious, cooperative tone was important—especially to the British. It was far less formal one evening at a pub in Brussels, where Trooper Bob Schott, Jackie, and I found ourselves defending the good old USA with a gaggle of high-spirited students.

The particular spirit they were enjoying was a national favorite—Duval beer. The "devil's brew" was about twice the alcohol content of American lagers, and our Belgian friends didn't think we were up to its challenge. After some international trash talking, Schottie, a proud American and a bruising 6' 4" specimen, asked if he could be off the clock. Since we were within walking distance of the hotel and since Jackie was the designated adult for the evening, he and I both defended Pennsylvania beer drinkers!

Let's just say we held our own.

On the walk back, we passed a magnificent cathedral bathed in a golden glow of spotlights. We took a moment, and much to Jackie's amusement, had a bizarre discussion about whether this was what the pearly gates looked like—and whether we could get in given our present condition.

Not to worry: We were both at our posts the next morning.

Back home, construction was beginning on the Cleveland Rock and Roll Hall of Fame. This was noteworthy to me because I had led a short-lived campaign to locate the facility in Johnstown. My hometown, it turns out, was the birth place of Allen Freed, the disc jockey who coined the phrase "rock and roll." It was also a community in dire need of some new attractions following the implosion of the steel industry. The staid bankers and businessmen of Johnstown were not buying into the concept, and the state economic development guys were equally skeptical. Too bad. In my opinion, we missed a huge opportunity for commerce and for commemorating some of my boyhood musical heroes Pennsylvania style.

In early April, the United States launched something called STS-56, better known as Discovery. This was a Star-Trekkian probe that would eventually reach the outer limits of the solar system.

In sports, NC State beat Michigan for the NCAA championship, and the Pittsburgh Penguins were wrapping up an NHL record 17-game winning streak.

Monday, April 12 was the day for the official debriefing on the European trip. The press conference was scheduled for 1:00 p.m., but I had two interesting encounters to attend to before that.

In the lieutenant governor's office that morning, I connected with Freddie Mann Friedman. A Philadelphia philanthropist whose family had donated millions to cultural causes, Freddie had run a short-lived campaign for US Senate in the previous year. Unfortunately for me, it added to the diversion of votes in the "year of the woman" that contributed to my loss in that primary election. I had no idea what she wanted until the end of the meeting when she announced, "If I had known you better at the time, I would never have run for Senate." While it didn't change my belief that the Democrats squandered an opportunity in 1992, it was a very kind thing for her to say.

Next was a planning meeting with Danielle Ammaccapane, LPGA star and recent champion of the Lady Keystone Open, which was held at Hershey Country Club. Jackie and I had housed Danielle and several of her professional golfer friends for years during tournament week. She was in town to plan another LPGA exhibition, and it was great spending some time with an old friend.

The press conference on Europe was noteworthy. After Andy Greenberg and I outlined several million dollars' worth of commerce and academic initiatives that we had helped advance, the press seemed interested in any negative angle they could find. What did the trip cost? Who benefited from the deals? I actually enjoyed jousting with the press, but there were times that it was clear that they were interested in dirt rather than successes. On behalf of well-intentioned politicians everywhere, I can only quote Langston Hughes, who wrote in his poem "The Wrassler:" "Thou knowest his fall; thou knowest not his wrasslin'!"

As always, there was no time for further discussion because there were places to go and people to meet.

Pittsburgh had become something of an obsession of mine. With Philadelphia as the only exception, I spent more time in official meetings and in political outreach in the 'Burgh than anywhere else. In fact, some reporter caught me in a candid moment and asked if I was preparing for my next campaign. "Yes," I joked. "I've just rented an apartment in Squirrel Hill." Unfortunately for me, it appeared in one of the Pittsburgh papers, and I had yet more explaining to do to the governor!

The agenda included a speech to mortgage bankers, a round-table with business reporters mostly interested in British Airways, a public service announcement with the Pittsburgh Steelers' Greg Lloyd, and a dinner with executives from Westinghouse.

I couldn't help but note that this was a great stretch of governmental and political education for me. Governor Casey and his close advisors had the burden of day-to-day decisions affecting the state, and I was free to explore new concepts and new connections. Yes, my staff had constructed a packed schedule designed for my own needs, but I viewed the schedules I kept throughout that early part of 1993 as helpful to the Commonwealth as well. I felt that I was learning at a fast pace and that I was putting myself in position to handle the responsibilities of governing—whether that meant after 1994 or, God forbid, should something happen to the governor before that.

It was with the same motivation that I had embarked on an "intramural tour" of all of the Commonwealth departments. In both the first and second terms of the Casey/Singel administration, I met with each cabinet secretary and their top staffs on their turf in an informal setting to discuss real-time issues and objectives. These meetings opened my eyes to the array of challenges that public servants at that level faced daily. The Department of Public Welfare was, literally, a lifeline that prevented hunger and disease in poor families. The Department of Transportation went about the business of maintaining 43,000 miles of roads and 46,000 bridges under some of the worst weather conditions in the country. The Department of Labor and Industry dealt with about $1 billion of "pass through" federal funding affecting everything from workers' compensation payments to labor/management relations.

Two of the most outstanding officials came from L&I. Harris Wofford, the governor's eventual choice to replace John Heinz as a US senator, was a statesman. Highly educated and professionally accomplished, Harris mastered the job of secretary of L&I and went on to be a thoughtful and distinguished US senator. His deputy, Tom Foley, had an equally interesting resume that included active participation in Irish politics and a burning desire to contribute to the public discourse. When I did my second drop by to L&I, Tom had replaced Harris and didn't miss a step. He was just as competent and dedicated as his predecessor, and I had already made a mental note to figure out a way to work with him in the future.

Joe LaFleur, the executive director of PEMA, was another standout in the all-star team of officials with whom I interacted. Joe and I had several meetings and regular phone calls every week. He had successfully focused information gathering to the point where PEMA had immediate knowledge of any incident that could put citizens in danger anywhere in the state. This week's focus was on the Nuclear Regulatory Commission and a briefing we were preparing for county emergency management directors.

Mid-April was when we took the governor's show on the road. Casey had developed a program called "Capital for a Day," wherein the governor, myself, and the entire cabinet swooped into a Pennsylvania town and focused on real life concerns. We actually operated out of that locality for 48 hours with official proclamations, bill signings, grant awards, and town meetings.

This time it was in Donora, PA, a small community in Fayette County less than 30 miles from the West Virginia border. This was the home of our good friend, Senator Bill Lincoln, who was serving as the minority whip at the time.

We handled a variety of local concerns relating to energy, the environment, local education efforts, and drug prevention issues. The governor came prepared to dole out "goodies" like highway funding and grants to local health care facilities. The town meetings that capped off the events were always informative, but they could be excruciating. Governor Casey insisted that we all join him on an auditorium stage somewhere in town, and citizens were invited to talk about any and every subject on their minds—and they did. Casey deflected many of the technical or specific cases to the appropriate secretary (food stamps to agriculture; heating assistance to public welfare; class sizes to education). It was remarkable, though, to watch the governor dive in to even the smallest of concerns with a thoughtful response that showed clear mastery of the matter and of the processes of government to address it.

At this particular town meeting in Donora I was struck by another realization.

The governor just didn't look well.

I made a note to bring that up with Jim Brown at our next off-the-record discussion.

Archbishop Thomas Dolinay was laid to rest on Monday, April 19, 1993. The funeral service at the Holy Spirit Byzantine Cathedral in Pittsburgh included dozens of bishops, priests, deacons, and cantors intoning the lugubrious "Vicnaja Pamjat" (Eternal Memory) in four part harmony. The solemn, beautiful liturgy was a remembrance of many such services from my youth. Unlike most Christians, Byzantine Catholic children were brought up amid the centuries-old music of Russian composers. We sang "Blahoslovi Duse Moje, Hospodi" (Bless the Lord, Oh My Soul) to the music of Tchaikovsky; we sang the vespers of Rachmaninoff.

We were brought up with a reverence to God that included daily Mass before school and extensive rituals during high holidays like

Christmas and Easter. It was a great honor, when I was deemed old enough, to accompany my father to nocturnal adoration. I remember kneeling for an hour with the men of St. Mary's in complete silence as they prayed and thought in the presence of the Blessed Sacrament at 2:00 a.m. These were thin men in dark suits and narrow ties who had spent much time washing coal dust or blast furnace residue off their skin so they could perform as worthy sentries of the Lord Himself in the wee hours during Lent.

They would emerge from the barely-lit church to smoke cigarettes and make some quiet conversation. They seemed strong and sure of themselves to me. And why not? They had just spent some quality time with God Himself.

My first memories of music and art, faith and family, all came from church.

"Vosklinite Hospodevi vsja zeml'a," "Shout joyfully to the Lord all the earth," was the first musical phrase I ever heard—sung by sopranos who sounded like angels to me. The basses and tenors followed with booming voices that filled the hearts and minds of everyone in the pews, all under the watchful eyes of the saints on icons throughout the church. By the time we reached elementary school my brothers and sisters all could sing the Divine Liturgy in Old Slavonic in four- and five-part harmony.

My grandfather insisted on hearing the prayers in Old Slavonic: "God doesn't listen to English," he said.

The Carpatho-Russian culture allowed itself the presumption of proximity to God.

"S'Nami Boh" (God is With Us) was the chant that rang from the choir lofts during holidays. It was also a bit of a password with my family that got us through difficult times.

This closeness to God also engendered great humility. As I mentioned, the phrase "Hospodi pomiluj" (Lord, have mercy) is uttered over a hundred times during Sunday Mass.

The idea of mercy as a divine gift was never lost on me.

A great moment for me occurred when I posed for pictures with Archbishop Kociosko, then Bishop Dolinay, and my father in my Harrisburg office at my inauguration. We were actually holding up the inaugural ceremonies for Governor Casey a bit, but he understood the magic of the moment.

Tom Dolinay was a parish priest when he married my parents. Father Tom and his successors helped chart a steady moral course for all of the Singel family, and I joined in full-throated musical appreciation when his casket was wheeled down the aisle.

From this lofty spiritual plane back to the Senate sandbox.

I arrived just in time to resolve a dispute about the proper consideration of a bill to allocate fuel tax funds.

What was unusual about this particular spat was that I found myself siding with the opposition. As thin as the Democratic majority was, and as much as I wanted to secure the bond with my own team, I took my responsibility to the Constitution and to the rules of the Senate very seriously. Specifically, Senate rules required that bills that affect revenues or expenditures be considered by the appropriations committee. SB 428 had been brought directly to the floor in an effort to expedite payments to localities. While the goal was noble, the rules were clear.

> The President (Singel): *"Senator Jubelirer . . . you are raising a point of order that the bill before us really cannot be considered for third consideration inasmuch as it violates Rule XIII, Section 16 (b), of the Senate rules."*
> Senator Jubelirer: *"That is precisely the case, Mr. President . . ."*
> The President: *"The chair appreciates the gentleman's point of order, and with all due respect to my colleagues in the majority, I agree with the gentleman from Blair. The chair is forced to rule that the bill is out of order for consideration at this time and should, in fact, be re-referred to the committee on appropriations for review."*
> Senator Lincoln (after a brief period "at ease"): *"Mr. President, I really do not agree with the ruling of the chair but because we, the chair and I, work together very well, I really do not believe that I should be appealing any of the chair's decisions. I will accept the chair's decision, and I move that Senate Bill No. 428 be referred to the committee on appropriations."*

If there was any recognition of this non-partisan gesture it was not conveyed publicly or privately to me. It did, however, seem to have a positive impact on another controversial bill. Senate Bill 1, the long awaited, much debated Workers' Compensation Reform package, mustered enough support that same day to be sent to a conference committee for some final wordsmithing.

The truce was short lived. It wasn't long before the next volley of political fire would occur.

For now, there was more business to tend to in Pittsburgh.

District Attorney Bob Colville was kind enough to invite me to a presentation of his anti-crime package. After being turned around to assist with the fallout from the 1993 TMI incident the last time I had been invited, I finally appeared on the *Ann Devlin Radio Talk Show*. I took some shots from some anti-politician callers in her audience. All in all, though, it was in this week that we ratcheted up our political presence in Pittsburgh a bit.

A young staffer by the name of Bill Peduto took charge of and coordinated some important events. These included the Devlin show, the *John Cigna Show*, a high-end fund-raiser with my high school friend and entrepreneur extraordinaire, Mike Zamagias, and a strategy session with Jeff Craig, an investment counselor and close friend who had been in my corner since my first election campaign for state Senate.

A word about Bill Peduto: Indefatigable.

No one worked harder in 1993 and, more importantly, throughout 1994 in my political pursuits. In fact, Bill had signed on early as a political activist in my short-lived run for US Senate in 1992. In the heat of the campaign for governor in 1994, Bill was serving as my western PA coordinator. I admit that the pressure of the campaign and the sheer volume of activity had gotten to me and I blew off some steam with my top campaign staff.

I was trying to make a point about carrying too much of the campaign load.

"It's like we're in an Iditarod race," I bellowed. "And all the dogs are riding while I'm pulling the sled."

The staff wasn't used to me melting down, and there was stunned silence in the room until Bill Peduto finally gave the retort: "I don't ride no fucking sled!"

The street-cred defiant tone broke us all up and became a rallying cry for the entire team for the duration of the campaign.

Work ethic and sheer talent like Bill Peduto's comes along once in a great while. He went on to be a first-rate Pittsburgh city councilman and, inevitably, the mayor of Pittsburgh—with a still undetermined political destination endpoint!

The weekend was like most others. If there was some downtime, it was usually mixed with official functions.

Jackie and I thoroughly enjoyed participating in the Bat Mitzvah of Stacy Kessler, daughter of Mr. and Mrs. Alan Kessler of Philadelphia. A prominent lawyer in Philadelphia, Alan and his entire family starred in my political commercials for lieutenant governor. We stopped in Reading on the way home to join another good friend, Mayor Warren Haggerty, to kick off his city-wide beautification project.

The last Monday in April brought me back to the Senate for more trivial pursuits.

Yet more bickering over legislative leaves.

At one point in the proceedings, Senator Jubelirer questioned whether or not Senator Frank Lynch from Philadelphia actually attended the meetings for which his absence was approved. While it is certainly within the rights of the leaders to monitor leaves, it was beginning to fray the normal collegiality of the Senate. Granted, the 25-24 majority of the Democrats was tenuous, and the Republicans had every right to make sure that all votes on all issues were legitimate. This particular request had a more mendacious tone. Senator Lynch was in poor health, and the unstated reason for the challenge was that he just might be recovering at home or in a hospital somewhere. It turned out that this was a glimpse of an ugly scene that was to occur when both sides were rounding up critical votes on the budget in the next month.

That evening, though, the Pennsylvania Travel Association Dinner provided some much needed respite. Hundreds of legislators and a thousand businesspeople in the tourism and hospitality industry crowded into the Hershey Lodge and Convention Center to show off the commonwealth's second largest industry. The food was elaborate and the audience was perfect for political leaders. For some reason, the governor deferred to me on this occasion, and I made the brief remarks before dinner.

The remaining days of April had me back at the desk, but as I had learned, there was always an interesting flow of visitors. Jack Ham, a good friend and Steelers hall-of-famer, stopped by with Paul Cooney, a large coal operator from my home area. Dan Hilferty introduced me to the Delaware County Chamber of Commerce at their "Harrisburg Day" luncheon. The fourth grade class from Brecht Elementary School in Lancaster and their state representative, Jere Strittmater, stopped by for the appropriate proclamations. The Board of Pardons met without incident.

My team sent me back to Philadelphia and Johnstown for some editorial board meetings.

Back in my home area, I was pleased to participate in the ground breaking ceremonies for the Colver Power Plant. We had nurtured this and other innovative co-generation energy projects in that same area. The Pennsylvania Energy Office, which I chaired, really did play a key role in transforming the entire region from a declining coal industry to a power-producing area that one reporter eventually called "power alley." It felt good to play such a direct role in providing desperately needed jobs back home.

At the end of April 1993, a few incidents occurred that affected or would soon affect all of us.

A jury reached a guilty verdict in the federal case against the cop who assaulted Rodney King. There had been some concern that a "not guilty" verdict would have caused race riots to erupt nation-wide—an eerie foreshadowing to what actually did occur after Ferguson, MO and New York City incidents in 2014 and in Baltimore, MD in 2015.

A sect known as the Branch Dravidians ended a 51-day stand-off with federal agents by committing mass suicide.

Russia elected Boris Yeltsin as its leader, and something called the World Wide Web was born at the CERN technology center.

These kinds of events reminded me that my world probably amounted to what Conrad Aiken called "trivial acts." Still, there was "terrific action" behind those acts.

The first four months of 1993 were busy but manageable for me. I had participated in events too numerous to mention, and I had begun what I thought was to be a two year process leading to my eventual ascendance to the governorship. The pace was about to quicken, though, and I was about to find myself at the middle of the maelstrom.

PART TWO — THE QUICKENING

MAY

May began with the usual variety of events. First, a keynote speech at the PA Recycling Conference followed by a presentation to the Hempfield Senior High School State Government Seminar. Senator "Buzz" Andrezeski and I had been doing this annual class since 1981. Rich Redmerski, a wonderful teacher and chaperone for the visiting students brought the "best and the brightest" from the high school year after year. Years later, it was a shock to Buzz and me when one of the participants made the remark: "Yeah, my mother attended this seminar when she was in school."

The Pittsburgh Steelers' Franco Harris was in town to assist with the Great Pennsylvania Work Out Day. We had attended Penn State at the same time and remained friends. The two of us held a press conference and jogged around the Capitol.

The Senate was well behaved and routine matters were the order of the week.

Here was a change of pace: I attended the Red Mass homily at St. Patrick's Cathedral. Sponsored worldwide by the St. Thomas More Society, the ceremony brings public figures, attorneys, judges, and others together for an intermission of reflection. For me it was a chance to offer some remarks about subjugation to a Higher Power and the real role of politicians—to serve. I got some warm feedback from my colleagues and the clergy attending the event, but alas, I had to return to the Senate floor for its relatively mundane activities. This was not my first appearance at the Red Mass. In 1989, I was honored to be the one to deliver the actual sermon in front of the distinguished list of public servants, jurists, and attorneys. Here is the text of those remarks:

Statement of
LIEUTENANT GOVERNOR MARK S. SINGEL
The Red Mass
St. Patrick's Cathedral
Harrisburg, Pennsylvania

Tuesday, April 4, 1989

Bishop Keeler, Monsignori, Very Reverend and Reverend Clergy, Venerable Sisters, civil officials, advocates, counselors, and friends—

Two years ago I sat in this magnificent cathedral and participated in a ceremony that was, for me, both moving and momentous. The new administration's inaugural Mass featured choral genius, rhetorical brilliance, and a congregational faith that seemed to wrap around me like an overcoat.

Bishop Keeler was kind and gentle in his admonitions to the new governmental leaders, and I felt close to this parish and to my faith.

In the warmth of that commencement I remember focusing on a single phrase that the celebrant offered during the consecration. It is a short petition that speaks volumes about the human condition and about why we are here today:

'. . . May we come to share in the divinity of Christ who humbled Himself to share in our humanity.'

What can be more abject and more preposterous than humankind?

This species that thinks and dreams and governs also lies and steals and wages war on itself. This species that has been given dominion over creation itself has squandered its inheritance and survives only because our God is merciful and must have an eternal sense of humor.

I suspect that, when most of us face judgment, there will be some serious plea bargaining going on.

Yet, Christ himself did join us in this puny pageant, and by example, showed us a path to the sublime. This Carpenter, this Teacher, this Lawgiver, this Politician, this Fisherman spent His time on earth serving others.

Emerson spoke of the infinitude of the individual—the chance for mankind to approach divinity through self-awareness and introspection. Wordsworth had 'intimations of immortality' through his art. They were both wrong.

As laymen, our best hope—our only hope—of even a glimpse of godliness is to serve humanity. In this gathering of judges, lawyers, politicians, and officials, the most exalted are those who can truly call themselves public servants.

I stand here two years into my venture as lieutenant governor convinced that the rewards for that calling are infinitely more substantial than margins of political victory or billable time.

To the jurist who renders mercy; to the attorney who defends the oppressed; to the public official who looks beyond the next election to generations unborn, our Ultimate Advocate says:

I will raise him up on eagles' wings
Bear him on the breath of dawn,
Make him to shine like the sun,
And hold him in the palm of My hand.

Bishop Keeler was a close friend and an unusually pious man. It is easy to be cynical about priests and politicians—or anyone who follows a calling. Most of us are skeptical of folks who are committed to truth or to justice, or to just living an honorable life. William Keeler was one of the shining examples of a man infused with the goodness of a Higher Power. We spoke for a few minutes after Mass, and the conversation inevitably turned to abortion.

While we did not linger long on the topic it was clear that Keeler, like other Catholic leaders, believed passionately in protecting the unborn. He was also interested in my nuanced position on the subject and on the implications it had for me spiritually and politically. Simply put, he wanted me to reject the logic of *Roe v. Wade* and join Governor Casey in complete opposition to abortion and to a woman's right to choose.

Because of my admiration for Keeler, who today is one of the Church's most worthy cardinals, I wish we could have lingered and talked through some of the arguments on both sides of the debate.

While I didn't pretend that I had the language committed to memory, I got the gist of the Blackmun opinion:

This right of privacy, whether it be founded in the Fourteenth Amendment's concept of personal liberty and restrictions upon state action, as we feel it is, or, as the District Court determined, in the Ninth Amendment's reservation of rights to the people, is broad enough to encompass a woman's decision whether or not to terminate her pregnancy.

We, therefore, conclude that the right of personal privacy includes the abortion decision, but that this right is not unqualified, and must be considered against important state interests in regulation.

Also, directly from the opinion:

". . . the fundamental right of single women and married persons to choose whether to have children is protected by the Ninth Amendment, through the Fourteenth Amendment."

And this interesting discussion from Blackmun on the notion of "quickening." He points to philosophical, theological, civil, and canon law concepts and notes that:

> These disciplines variously approached the question in terms of the point at which the embryo or fetus became 'formed' or recognizably human, or in terms of when a 'person' came into being, that is, infused with a 'soul' or 'animated.'
>
> Christian theology and the canon law came to fix the point of animation at 40 days for a male and 80 days for a female, a view that persisted until the 19th century; there was otherwise little agreement about the precise time of formation or animation. There was agreement, however, that, prior to this point, the fetus was to be regarded as part of the mother, and its destruction, therefore, was not homicide. Due to continued uncertainty about the precise time when animation occurred, to the lack of any empirical basis for the 40-80-day view, and perhaps to Aquinas' definition of movement as one of the two first principles of life, Bracton focused upon quickening as the critical point. The significance of quickening was echoed by later common law scholars and found its way into the received common law in this country.

So here is the essence of *Roe v. Wade* from Blackmun's opinion:

> (a) For the stage prior to approximately the end of the first trimester, the abortion decision and its effectuation must be left to the medical judgment of the pregnant woman's attending physician.
>
> (b) For the stage subsequent to approximately the end of the first trimester, the State, in promoting its interest in the health of the mother, may, if it chooses, regulate the abortion procedure in ways that are reasonably related to maternal health.
>
> (c) For the stage subsequent to viability, the State in promoting its interest in the potentiality of human life may, if it chooses, regulate, and even proscribe, abortion except where it is necessary, in appropriate medical judgment, for the preservation of the life or health of the mother.

What I wanted to know from the good bishop was: "Does this not represent clear and reasonable thinking on the issue? Is this not a fair compromise between protecting life—particularly the life of a "quickened" fetus—and assuring that we did not intrude on the constitutional rights of all the women in America?"

Yes, I was a Catholic; but I was an American first, and I could not, in good conscience, argue against Blackmun's logic or his defense of the Constitution. I supported women's rights to choose based on the guarantees of the Constitution, but I agreed with the decision (and with Casey) that states had the right to impose reasonable restrictions.

While I considered my position rational, Casey believed it was based on political convenience and viewed it as an act of personal disloyalty to him. I, however, couldn't interpret the Constitution any other way. Casey couldn't align that aspect of the Constitution with his opinion of truly protecting life, as he saw it beginning at conception. The closest we ever got to closure on the issue was a conversation that compared "pro-choice with restrictions" to "pro-life with exceptions." Even Casey had to agree that those thoughtful positions were closer ideologically than the zealots would allow.

Years later, as I look at the "pro-life/pro-choice" chasm that still exists in our state and nation, I regret not being able to do more to draw the sides closer together. I know that the folks on the pro-choice side are, in no way, supporting a culture of death—they are simply assuring that those most affected can make this most wrenching decision without fear of prosecution. Similarly, those who are pro-life are genuinely concerned that abortion impacts the most vulnerable in a dramatically brutal way. Both sides are right, but we won't have a consensus until we put the sloganeering behind us and let reason prevail.

As I headed back to the Capitol, I was struck by how the issue, and particularly the idea of "when life begins," really matters. Also, for some reason, this notion of quickening resonated with me as a metaphor for my own political life. After five years as a congressional staffer in Washington; six years as a Pennsylvania senator; five statewide campaigns; and, by 1993, six years as lieutenant governor, I felt strongly that my own political gestation was just now starting to accelerate.

A new addition to my calendar was phone time. While it was only May, we began to steal an hour or two each day to begin the outreach that would be necessary for a statewide campaign. As with any fund-raising campaign, at this point it was not so much about money as it was about securing relationships. The intense dialing for dollars would come later.

I was let out of the calling cage to join Jackie for the Governor's Awards for Excellence Ceremony followed by an appearance at a Democratic State Committee event for prospective judicial candidates. Jackie was patient with all of the social and political demands on our schedules, but it was on these days, when we both would return home at 10:00 or 11:00 p.m., that she had a sense of my daily grind.

Some travel the next day to a health care forum, a tourism event with the Pennsylvania Travel Council, and a pleasant interlude with the fourth grade class of Villa Maria Academy. The latter was the result of a commitment I had made to the good Sisters of St. Basil the Great. These were the nuns who provided my early education, and I always felt close to the order.

On Thursday, it was back to Philadelphia for Temple University's nurse recognition, a luncheon with the publisher of a local newspaper and savvy leader in the African American community, Jerry Mondesire, then to city hall to pay some respects to Councilwoman Jannie Blackwell.

I had to get back to Harrisburg in time for a taping of *The People's Business*, a statewide cable television production that was just building its viewer base. This was the precursor to PCN, which, to this day, does an outstanding job of displaying state government at its best and worst.

On Friday, May 7, the government of South Africa agreed to multi-racial elections. The name of Nelson Mandela was beginning to appear in newscasts all over the world. It was not lost on me that earth-changing developments like these were occurring at the same time that I was tending to much smaller campfires.

Still, I was able to participate in meaningful events that mattered to family and friends.

The 42nd commencement of St. Francis College on Mother's Day, 1993, for example. A school nestled in the pines of western PA, the institution stressed faith and strove to emulate the humble piety of the founder of the Franciscan order. Gerry and Rudolph "Boots" Schonek received honorary degrees for their philanthropy to the school. They were my wife's aunt and uncle, and we both developed a strong affection for them. Over the years, Gerry and Boots provided a warm embrace for the Singel family. They treated our children like their own grandchildren. It was a special honor to say some nice things about them at the commencement.

Later that evening, the good parishioners of St. Andrew's in Johnstown celebrated the 50th anniversary of their pastor and my friend, Monsignor Joseph Fleming. A devout man who brought several generations of schoolchildren and their parents closer to God, the monsignor was also a savvy fund-raiser. His claim to fame was paying off a multi-million dollar mortgage on a new church, school, and auditorium complex in a few short years with a continuous schedule of carnivals, fish fries, raffles, and, of course, bingo. His closest buddies knew him affectionately as "Casino Joe."

By the second week in May, the legislative discussions on the state budget were beginning in earnest. This was unusual since the process was normally conducted in breakneck fashion at the absolute end of the fiscal year deadline of June 30. In fact, we had drifted past the deadline several times—once into late August. This was all a function of partisan positions on issues and all players performing their respective roles in the process.

Two things seemed to be different this year. The governor was letting it be known that he wanted matters resolved by the end of May if possible. While most chalked this up to his desire to be effective and efficient with the public purse, there was also a hint of something more personal—like the governor was looking for some real downtime for some reason.

The second difference was that the Democrats controlled both chambers. They had already proven that they could break the logjam on key issues with those majorities, and it was in their interest to demonstrate that they could handle the heavy lifting of budgeting as well. May was the new June, and it was important to keep an ear to the ground in Harrisburg.

This did not mean that my office and travel schedules were curtailed, however.

My team had a full day of meetings set for Erie on Thursday. An editorial board meeting with the Erie Times, some give-and-take with a talk show on WLKK radio, and a press conference with officials at the Hamot Medical Center on prospects for expanding health care coverage beyond the current CHIP program were the assignments. There were a few other stops before I made my way down to the Community College of Beaver County to deliver the commencement address.

The western PA swing ended with me checking into the Nittany Lion Inn in State College just after midnight. The board of trustees was meeting the next day—I always found that to be a pleasant duty. The last broadcast of *Cheers* on NBC had aired earlier that evening, and I caught a rerun of it as I was dozing off.

I was able to catch my son's tee-ball game on Saturday, but Jackie and I were soon off to two black tie events. No Sunday off either: I was in Philadelphia to speak at the Jewish Community Council's celebration of the 45th anniversary of the state of Israel and to bring greetings at the Gala Celebration of the life of the legendary Georgie Woods. Woods was a music impresario, media personality, and community leader and a joy to be around.

Monday, May 17, the day before the primary election, I had the opportunity to meet with First Lady Hillary Clinton. She had flown in to do some last minute fund-raising for the Democrats and invited me to a brief lunch at the Philadelphia Airport just before she took off for Washington. I had met her previously and I remained impressed by her vast knowledge of Pennsylvania politics. Among the issues we discussed was Bob Casey. What could they do to bring him around? I assured her that the governor supported the president, but it was probably not ever going to be a close friendship. She seemed prepared for that response, and we reaffirmed our own friendship.

I caught the last part of a PEMA Council meeting and made it in time for the retirement dinner of Sergeant Robert Basile of the Executive Detail of the Pennsylvania State Police. Sergeant Basile ran the detachment that was responsible for the security of the governor and lieutenant governor of Pennsylvania. I remain convinced that the Pennsylvania State Police is the best trained, most effective state law enforcement organization in the country. The Executive Detail troops were and are the best of the best.

We looked forward to the detail's annual picnic at our home at Indiantown Gap. Putting twenty or so off duty troopers and their spouses near a pool and kegs of beer could be very entertaining. Let's just say we were happy to help them blow off some steam on occasion.

And they had good reason to let their hair down. My schedule averaged 12-14 hour days. This meant that the trooper attached to me had preparation, driving, and paperwork duties that were absolutely exhausting on a daily basis. The troopers assigned to the governor were even more pressed.

One or two anecdotes about the Executive Detail:

Early on in the administration, I was, quite typically, running late and rushing down the turnpike to an event. A tire blow-out going 60 miles an hour caused a few out-of-control moments that ended with us on the highway shoulder and hopelessly late for the next event. Not to worry: Mike Donley, a young, personable trooper who was to become a close friend, was up to the task.

"Time me," Donley said.

I tried to help, but he had the jack in hand and fully deployed within minutes.

He spun the lug nuts off of the wheel with the blown tire like he was in the pits at the Indy 500. Spare on; blown tire in the trunk; and Donley back behind the steering wheel.

"Three minutes and 48 seconds," I said.

"I'll do better next time," said Donley.

Another favorite of mine was Colonel Butch Saunders. An imposing, athletic, silent type, Butch didn't suffer fools. It took awhile, but we became very close.

Saunders had an infatuation with old spy shows and insisted that Mike Donley call him "Black Falcon 6." The detail didn't actually have code names for anybody, but Mike became "Hawk 1" when the two of them communicated by phone or radio. Saunders couldn't stop himself from naming me "The Sparrow."

"What?" I said. "I don't want to be the Sparrow! How about Eagle or Raven?"

"You're the Sparrow," said Butch. And that was that.

The detail was invaluable to me and my family. I recall a rare dinner at the kids' favorite restaurant—the Olive Garden outside of Harrisburg. One of the guys (who had been waiting patiently in the car) came bursting in and escorted me to the vehicle and directly to the governor's mansion. He explained that a prisoner had escaped and was heard to be looking for the lieutenant governor. Apparently, he had applied to the Board of Pardons several times and held me responsible for his rejection. The Executive Detail took no chances and made sure my wife and kids were secure before I was whisked to the safety of the troopers on duty at the governor's residence. They caught the prisoner, by the way.

Another event that was handled with cool detachment was the Gap bomber incident. I was traveling home on the small twin-engine Navajo that was operated by PennDOT. We were making an unusual landing at the Indiantown Gap airstrip. To our surprise, we were waved off just as the wheels touched down. The pilot gunned the engines and we landed at Harrisburg International Airport twenty miles away.

The local police had identified an intruder on the base, and he was parked just off the runway. At the exact time my plane was landing, the Executive Detail trooper on duty at the residence approached the man who was mumbling something about: "They're coming. I'll stop them. I can stop them."

Clearly deranged, the man was convinced that "the enemy" was about to land. The trooper restrained him and checked the vehicle to find a trunkload of AK-47s, M-80s, and enough firepower to take out six planes.

The troopers assigned to this detail were not just occasional drinking buddies or fodder for nostalgic stories. They were tough and smart. And they may have saved my life on more than one occasion.

Still, to them I remained the Sparrow—at least for now.

On Wednesday, May 19, the day after the primary election day, the Dow Jones closed above 3,500 for the first time. There was considerable chatter about that lofty number at the Capitol.

With no session scheduled, I combined business with pleasure and joined a local business leader, Mr. Ted Lick, at the Pro-Am Golf Outing prior to the LPGA Open at the Hershey Country Club. One of my favorite places, the Hershey Country Club has a history that includes Ben Hogan as a former club pro, and champions like Byron Nelson, who won the 1940 PGA tournament there. The West Course features a short hole that rolls right up to the Milton Hershey Mansion.

We played with Danielle Ammaccapane, who won the tournament the year before. She was fourth on the LPGA money list at the time and had a beautiful swing. Danielle and her golfing buddies were thoroughly fun people and skilled athletes. Danielle and her friend, Nancy Harvey, loved our kids and actually taught them about hip-hop music whenever they stayed with us—although I was a little dismayed to hear my seven year old performing a popular lyric of the day: "I like big butts and I cannot lie."

The girls also shared some of the funniest stories that I used (with some discretion) on the campaign trail.

Dennis Owens, a local TV reporter, came out for breakfast and did a nice interview with Danielle and me. Conversation was light, but neither of us rapped for the camera.

Back to business. I always had an interest in alternative energy. As the chairman of the PA Energy Office, I was determined to apply clean coal technologies so that we could make better use of our indigenous resources. John Rich stopped by to discuss an innovative approach to convert coal to liquids, and we worked with him to get his project off the ground.

It was a given that any downtime would be filled by outreach calls. Noreen Wert, who had worked diligently on the Senate campaign in 1992, was picking up where we left off. The Friends of Mark Singel had rented space within walking distance of my lieutenant governor's office, and all political calls were made there. Her job was to lash me to a chair and phone with a call list whenever possible.

Oddly, I didn't mind these sessions. For one, the heavy lifting of asking for big dollars hadn't really begun. I was just in the schmooze phase of keeping my supporters close at hand. Secondly, I was not averse to making the pitch for money. For me it was reminiscent of my early days when it was possible to go door-to-door in a relatively small district. Since I was now spread statewide, these thirty-second calls were the closest thing to retail politics that I had. For a people person like me it was a sales pitch, not an ordeal.

On Friday, we snuck in a political day. There was, of course, an official function—in Allentown, relating to a new energy product—but we shot directly down the turnpike for more of Operation Philly.

Some important pols had lunch with me. This was followed by a press conference with local notables Councilmen Joe Vignola and Herb DeBeary on the issue of welfare reform. A coffee break at the Bellevue with Councilman Angel Ortiz, followed by more coffee with two key supporters at the Palm, followed by two separate law firm visits with their key partners. On the way out of the city, the staff had penciled me in at the Pan Asian Association of Greater Philadelphia 9th Annual Awards Banquet.

Another 8 a.m. to midnight day, but I had to admit it was interesting.

The following Monday I realized: This was going to be another long week.

A series of meetings in and out of the office was the precursor to what would turn into a marathon week on the Senate floor. Added to the routine was the death of Senator Jim Ross, who was a gruff but kind-hearted man who took me under his wing when I first arrived in the Senate. His viewing was scheduled for that evening.

First came some volleys in the Senate.

The never ending Pecora war was still raging.

Senator Melissa Hart had just outlined her proposal to enact a constitutional amendment to tie state spending to federally-reported economic growth. It aroused some spirited debate, and Senator Pecora couldn't help but chime in:

Senator Pecora: *"Mr. President, you know it is amazing sitting here listening to the conservatives who wish to have fiscal responsibility. It brings back memories of when I sat in the Senate on the highest tax increase in Pennsylvania's history and wanted to read the budget and the gentlemen and ladies on the other side of the aisle voted against me postponing the vote of the budget to make recommendations on cuts. So some people speak with forked tongues, or they are playing politics and are not sincere."*

This was the first time Pecora had taken to the floor in many weeks, and the Republicans had little tolerance for his tone or his perspective.

Senator Jubelirer, the Republican leader, was often grumpy, but when it came to Frank Pecora, he was apoplectic. He sneered back at Pecora and made a direct public reference to his party switch and to his place of residence in one swipe:

Senator Jubelirer: *"Mr. President, it is rare that I agree with the Democratic gentleman from Allegheny, or Southeastern Pennsylvania, Senator Pecora, but I agree, sometimes people do speak with forked tongues."*

Senator Fumo, the Democrats' appropriations chair, put a knife in the arguments of the Republicans in his usual blunt style:

Senator Fumo: *"Mr. President, the way to do a budget is not based on last year's income as reported by the federal government. We all know that. It is silly. It sounds nice. We can argue about taxpayers and all the rhetoric we want, especially when we are running for reelection. We can wrap ourselves in the flag. We can do whatever we have to do, but today we are going to do the responsible thing and beat this amendment."*

Fumo, of course, was correct: the goal of the Republicans, as the debate on the PA Budget for 1993-94 was about to begin in earnest, was to position their members as guardians of the public purse. More importantly, it was to set traps for Democrats and force them to put anti-taxpayer votes on the board. It was no accident that the vote on this particular amendment was 24-24. Yes, the president of the Senate could have weighed in: An "aye" vote to uphold the Democrats' position, which would be spun as anti-taxpayer. A "nay" vote to slap my team in the face and be viewed as opportunistic. It was one of many no-win situations that the minority party concocted to generate some material for their opposition research on me, specifically. I stuck with the Ds.

The partisan guns were lowered a bit when Senators on both sides moved to a discussion on SB 1, the long-awaited workers' compensation reform package.

The session concluded early enough for a commercial flight to the Ross viewing. I returned at midnight again and in the process had missed another of my son Jon's baseball games.

The governor had scheduled another "Capital for a Day" for Hazelton. The timing was particularly bad for me given the wheeling and dealing that was occurring in the general assembly over the budget. Both chambers were beginning to move the relevant bills into place, and the Senate fully intended to push the bills to the governor's desk by the end of the week. This meant that there was going to be at least one marathon session soon.

Hazelton turned out to be a nice diversion, however. I had my typical assignments: a local radio talk show, high school class lecture, luncheon with the governor and state employees, and a private meeting my good friend, Mayor John Quigley.

The town meeting was mercifully brief. The residents seemed to be a little more docile than those in other towns we had visited. This meant I could get back to the battle in Harrisburg.

It happens that the session lasted well into the evening and we needed to make some adjustments on the calendar. Specifically, we canceled on the president of the United States, who was headlining a fund-raising event for US Senator Harris Wofford in Philadelphia.

It was necessary, though, because the Democratic leaders were prepared to move the budget bill and related items to a Senate vote. The session, of course, featured the usual amount of sniping over procedures. I had ruled out of order an amendment from Senator Mike Fisher that had to do with welfare reform. The Rs appealed the ruling of the chair, and some interesting comments are recorded in the Senate Journal:

Senator Lincoln: *"I will be persistent in my efforts to make sure that the debate is centered strictly on the rules in a scholarly manner, and I think the parameters set by the chair should be adhered to."*

The President (Singel): *"The chair thanks the gentleman and again is grateful for that guidance. . . . In the interest of hearing everybody on the subject, the chair would also suggest that we be concise and cogent, collegial, cooperative, and quick."*

The parliamentary maneuvering went on for a few more minutes, but we got to final consideration of the budget a full month before the fiscal year deadline.

Since there was a vacancy (the special election to fill the Greenwood seat was still six weeks away), 25 votes constituted a majority. The Republicans had already signaled that there would be NO votes from their caucus for SB 815, that year's general fund budget bill. Senator Frank Lynch's physical condition had deteriorated to the point that he was bedridden. Under normal circumstances, the leaders would agree to some kind of a humanitarian arrangement so that Lynch's vote could be recorded in absentia.

Instead, the Republicans insisted that Lynch appear in person on the floor of the Senate to vote. Few things shock those of us who have been in the political arena; this one was a shocker. The Ds had no choice but to bring Lynch by medical transport to his post in Harrisburg. They set up a trauma center in his Senate office complete with bed and monitoring equipment. When it came time for critical votes, we all watched as Senator Lynch made his way gingerly to his desk. He uttered "Aye" as defiantly as he could.

Between votes, Lynch drifted off to sleep at his desk. During the evening of May 28, I called upon the sergeant-at-arms twice to make sure that he was breathing!

The budget passed only because of Senator Lynch's twenty-fifth vote. Both Lincoln and Fumo made note of his sacrifice:

Senator Fumo: *"I want to thank everyone who worked hard to get this done, and in particular, I want to thank the gentleman from Philadelphia, Senator Frank Lynch, who went above and beyond the call of duty to be here today because his vote was needed . . ."*

Senator Lincoln: *"The remarks made about the gentleman from Philadelphia, Senator Lynch , are just hard to put into words, the respect for him."*

Senator Frank Lynch passed away four days later.

JUNE

Following some much needed downtime on Memorial Day weekend, I was back at the phones on the first day of June. There was still work to be done on priority bills that the governor wanted passed alongside the budget now sitting on his desk, and there were several official functions to attend to, but the political whitewater raft I was on felt like it was picking up speed. I felt like something was coming, and I was hoping that it wasn't a cliff. The best I could do was to continue paddling.

I made sure that I was back for a rare dinner date that evening—Jackie's 40th birthday. We celebrated with a handful of close friends at the Maverick Steakhouse. The restaurant was a favorite hangout for Harrisburg politicos because of their discreet, friendly service and because of the sheer quality of their steak and seafood. The restaurant is gone now, but I am happy to report that we have never lost touch with the friends we encountered there.

On Thursday, June 3, we buried Senator Frank Lynch. The Mass of Christian Burial was at St. Timothy's in northeast Philadelphia. This part of town, like Frank himself, was fiercely middle class of Irish ancestry. Frank was never a sparkling orator or a deep thinker but he was a hardworking party loyalist who had an irrepressible sense of humor and a solid moral compass. Given the circumstances of his last days, there was some bitterness at the funeral—particularly when the Republicans filed by the casket.

It also complicated relations between the parties in Harrisburg and between me and the loyal opposition. We now had two vacancies in the Senate. The count was now 24 D-24 R, and it was up to me to schedule the election for Frank's vacant seat.

Unlike the vacant seat in Bucks County, this one was presupposed to remain Democrat. I could have scheduled the seat for the summer or waited until the November election. Much depended upon what the Democrats wanted to accomplish in the next few months.

The Republicans continued to fire off letters and lawsuits to change the July 13 date of the 44th Senate district election, and I couldn't blame them. They viewed the date as a crass maneuver to keep the Democrats in control through the budget process. I said publicly that that was exactly right, and I felt vindicated in my decision because of the solid, no-tax-increase budget that had just passed. There was also some cleanup work to do, and we had a month and a half left in the Democrats' season of governing.

I opted to set the election for the Philadelphia seat to concur with the November elections. This would save taxpayers the expense of a special election, and it, I believed, allowed candidates to emerge and campaign for the spot.

The next question was when would both senators be sworn in and begin occupying their seats on the Senate floor. This became a subject of heated correspondence between Senator Bob Jubelirer and me, and it set the stage for some interesting events that would occur in November.

For now, I was back at both political and official pursuits.

I confess that I left the funeral and went directly to two law firms to do some prospecting.

The next day I met the mountain man.

Jim Cunningham was a bearded, bear of a man with a folksy style as homespun as Jack Daniels bourbon. He was proud of his Kentucky roots and brought another flannel-clad operative with him by the name of L.A. Harris. L.A. didn't have a first name—just L.A. Together, they were making a name for themselves as fund-raisers and strategists for Democratic candidates all over the country. We met at an inn in Hunt Valley, Maryland, halfway between Harrisburg and their Washington, DC office in order to discuss the particulars of my upcoming fund-raising strategy.

While I had been through numerous campaigns, and while my staff and I had charted a course that we thought was inching us closer to the kind of support that we needed to launch a gubernatorial campaign in our own right, Cunningham was having none of it.

"If it ain't money or media," he said of any extraneous activities, "it don't matter."

He had a clear sense of the cost of campaigning and he was talking about raising money in terms that were downright frightening. The "buy-in" by December 31—a year away from election day— had to be $2 million, cash-on-hand. If the primary was contested, think in terms of another $2.5 million. Keeping competitive with the Republicans after that would cost another $5 million.

"How do you plan to raise that kind of money?" I asked.

"I can't raise you a damn dime," was the odd response.

He went on to describe the Cunningham/L.A. method for pressing the candidate into continual fund-raising mode. They would cull all of my contacts, organize the call room, focus on prospects, and operate a relentless follow-up system that left no target off the hook.

"You," Cunningham said, "will raise the money by direct calls."

I liked the honesty of the meeting and the reality that they were injecting into my own political awareness. It was clear that they would energize the fund-raising aspect of my potential campaign. It was equally clear that I would be signing up to do the heavy lifting.

Before the meeting broke up, Cunningham provided another dose of reality.

"Let's say we gather all of your names, get the focus sheets in place, and strap you into a call room by August 1," he said. "That leaves about 300 working days to hit the numbers. You have to expect to raise $30,000 per day for the next 16 months."

I left the meeting reeling but clear-eyed about the road ahead. I had to think about it, and we promised to get back together within two weeks.

During the weekend, I snuck down to the office for some alone time. The mountain to climb was daunting, but it seemed preferable to me than biding my time. As I was considering this, who walked into view on State Street just outside my office window but the traveler. I rushed out to talk with him.

"What's next?" he asked. Not "What's up?" or "How are you?" Strange.

"Good question," I said, thinking more about my current state of mind than anything else.

Here's what the traveler, Art, had to say at that moment:

"Don't underestimate the value of doing nothing."

"Who said that?" I asked.

"Winnie the Pooh," said Art. "There you go."

Back to work on Monday. The Senate was in session but catching its breath following the unusually early passage of the budget. There were related bills to consider, and this week was about that cleanup. There were also some big ticket items like workers' compensation reform, technology deregulation, and funding the state's environmental programs through the proposed Key 93 bond financing. That would be coming a little later.

For now, both sides had lowered their guns a bit as these and other items worked through the committee process.

My office calendar was still filled with meetings. Roger Mecum from the PA Medical Society stopped by with the society's company line on several issues. The task force on recyclable materials, which I chaired, met. I spoke at the PA Federation of Democratic Women.

The Tuesday morning meeting with Jim Brown was different.

For one, he brought Dick Spigelman, the governor's legal counsel, with him. Eric Schnurer, my chief of staff, sat in on the meeting, and we both sensed that something was up.

"Am I in trouble here?" I asked to lighten the mood just a bit.

"Not at all," said Jim, and we went on to discuss some mundane items like the upcoming legislative agenda, the budget, and some appearances that they wanted me to cover for the governor.

Then, Jim Brown let me in on the Secret: Casey was ill. Dangerously ill. Since his bypass surgery in 1987 he had lost 50 pounds. And, while he maintained that he felt great, the governor was dogged by reporters following rumors that there was something else going on. I recalled one of the more impertinent scribes shouting out during a routine bill signing ceremony: "Do you have cancer?" It was outrageous, and I was struck by the constant intrusions that this very private man tolerated.

It wasn't cancer, but it was a mysterious disease of the blood called amyloidosis. This was affecting the governor's organs, and in particular, his liver. Oddly, former Mayors Lou Tullio of Erie and Dick Caliguiri of Pittsburgh had died of the exact disease.

It turned out that Casey had known about the diagnosis for two years. He accepted the fact that there was no known cure and that he simply was going to do his job until the disease started shutting down his organs. This was shocking to me—and more than a little disturbing.

"Why didn't you tell me sooner?"

Either they didn't know or they were under strict orders from the governor not to share the information with anyone—I never got an exact answer. In that instant, I had a completely different perspective on the governor's hesitation to assist in my own endeavors. He was sick and he knew it, and he didn't want me straying too far from home.

I had a vivid recollection of a conversation with the governor from as far back as 1991. He had been agonizing over the name of a replacement for US Senator John Heinz, who had died in a tragic plane crash. I admired John Heinz and would have loved to pick up that mantle in the US Senate at the time. Everybody seemed to like the idea except Bob Casey. After weeks of agonizing over the issue, we finally had a direct conversation in which he told me that he would not be appointing me to the spot.

Our good mutual friend, Jim Haggerty, who was serving as the chief counsel at the time, sat in on the meeting. I made my case that I could be useful to him and to the commonwealth as a US senator, and I was truly confounded by his hesitation.

Here's what the governor said to me: "I wish we could have a different conversation about this, Mark."

The comment was too cryptic for me, and I got a little heated.

"What the hell does that mean?" I blurted out.

"I need you here," was all that he told me.

The way Jim and Dick were presenting it today, however, was with optimism. Dr. John Starzl from the University of Pittsburgh Medical Center was doing some pioneering work on transplant surgery. He and the governor had already been in touch about the possibility of a liver transplant, and Casey was to report for a checkup at UPMC to determine his suitability for the operation. What was promising about all of this was the possibility of dealing with the amyloidosis head-on. That is: remove the affected organ altogether and replace it with a healthy one.

This, of course, depended on the governor's health to sustain the operation, and a donor of the organ. Still, Jim Brown was upbeat:

"We may have found a way to save the governor's life."

We agreed to keep in close touch on the governor's trip to Pittsburgh. Jim would be with him and would contact me with any news. In the meantime, the governor would have a full-blown press conference to discuss the amyloidosis and inform the public about a possible miracle cure.

The rest of the week's activities seemed somewhat trivial now. I didn't cancel anything, but I must admit that my thoughts were with the governor and what might lie ahead. Still, it was important to carry on. I had learned that when there was uncertainty, it was up to those in leadership positions to move forward with steadiness. Here were a few items that needed attention at that moment:

Joe LaFleur and the PEMA deputy director had some incidents to report on, though none that rose to the level of activating the Emergency Operations Center; commencement addresses at the

York County Vo-Tech and the Richland Senior High School; and a string of meetings with community leaders in my home area, just keeping in touch.

At one point in the week, Senator Bill Stewart, my successor in the 35th Senate district, brought in a constituent by the name of Rob Gleason. A key Republican leader in Cambria County, Rob had actually been my opponent in my first race for Pennsylvania Senate in 1980.

Today was about Rob's potential appointment to the PA Turnpike Commission. This was one of the plums of Pennsylvania politics, and governors found themselves conferring the position on well-connected supporters and deferring to legislative leaders for some partisan balance from the other party. In fact, Gleason had been nominated previously by then-Governor Thornburgh for the same position. I had just gotten elected as senator and was none too pleased that I was being asked to accommodate my recent opponent with a consolation prize. I also had serious concerns about his potential business conflicts, and I didn't need him second-guessing my actions in Harrisburg from such a prominent perch. I invoked that informal privilege of "senatorial courtesy" and sent the nomination back to the governor.

Gleason's ambition was not to be denied, however, and he campaigned for the post with leadership and with key staff in Governor Casey's office.

Senator Stewart was supportive of the nomination, and by that time, I didn't view Gleason as a threat in any way. Moreover, the governor saw this as a way to make some peace with the Republicans, and I had to admit that it wouldn't be bad to have another Johnstowner in a prominent post. It was time to focus on the road ahead, and I was glad to declare a truce.

Friday was a long day of events in Philadelphia.

A talk show on WWDB radio; a visit to the law firm of Pepper, Hamilton & Scheetz, where my good friend, Dave Sweet, had become a partner; two health care centers for continued discussions on the president and governor's plans; and a visit to leaders of the Korean community.

I was able to sneak in a pleasant lunch at the Palm Restaurant with my friend, Mark Segal, a leader in the Philadelphia gay community and the publisher of the *Philadelphia Gay News*. Given the similarity of our last names, we often received one another's phone calls. Hence, these meetings always had a friendly tone to them. We called each other "cousin" and he made sure that I was supported by the gay community. Mark was also a savvy political operative, and I was grateful for his counsel and friendship.

I was exhausted after the end of a long and emotional week and wondered how the governor's checkup was going.

On Saturday, I got the first call.

"Mark, this is Jim Brown."

"How are you? How's the governor?" I asked.

He went on to explain that the situation was dramatically worse than they thought. The physical exam revealed that the governor's liver and heart were in bad shape. One doctor described it like a football that had hardened to the point that it was just barely compressing with each beat. While the liver had to be removed, the heart would not sustain the trauma of the operation.

The solution: a rare, double-organ transplant that would insert both a new heart and a new liver as soon as possible. At that point, the procedure had been done only six times in the entire world!

As dramatic as it sounded, the alternative was worse. The governor's organs were failing, and the doctors had already decided not to release him until a donor was found to proceed with the operation.

"Is the governor OK with all of this?" I asked.

"Here," said Jim. "You can ask him yourself."

"How are you doing, Mark?" asked Bob Casey.

"Are you kidding?" I responded. "How are YOU?"

He told me that he had agreed with the UPMC staff's prognosis and the medical plan. There was a steely calm about the conversation. It was similar to what I heard in his voice dozens of times before when he was sure of a particular cause or when he held his ground against opponents. This time he faced his toughest opponent, and I had the sense that the famous Casey determination (stubbornness?) would pull him through. In one of the simplest and most poignant comments I have ever heard, Bob Casey gave me my instructions: "When the time comes, do a good job."

He handed the phone back to Jim Brown, and I peppered him with questions.

Do we have any idea when we will find a heart and liver donor?

Is this a process that takes weeks? Months? Years?

Will he operate with key staff from his bed in the meantime?

How did they want me to proceed during the protracted absence?

For now, nobody really had the answers to those questions.

On Sunday evening we already had one answer:

A donor had been located. A young man caught in the crossfire of a drug deal had been shot and killed that morning. His blood type and other markers were a sufficient match to the governor's to give the medical team enough confidence to operate.

Given the dire condition of the governor's heart, the landmark double-organ transplant was scheduled for the next morning.

"We found a donor," Jim Brown said, calling from Presbyterian Hospital. It was 3:30 a.m.

I asked about the young murder victim and learned that his name was William Michael Lucas.

William Michael Lucas was a 36-year-old African American man who had been dragged from his home on June 6 and beaten severely in an incident that authorities were saying was gang related. He was pronounced brain-dead just hours after Casey was told he would require a heart and liver transplant. Lucas, by coincidence was a good fit for Casey since they had the same body proportions (they were both 6 foot 2 inches tall). They also shared the same blood type: O-positive.

I also had some questions about the process. How did this happen so fast? I was under the impression that patients waited months and even years on organ transplant lists. Evidently, the fact that Casey's heart and liver were deteriorating moved him ahead on that queue. I was moved by the dignity of William's mother during the whole episode. She braced herself and attended the press conference with Governor Casey's doctors. They wanted to put to rest any suggestion that the governor received any special treatment or that the Lucas family was mistreated in any way. Frances Lucas, William's mother was asked what her son would have felt about the whole donor process. "He would feel very good about it," she responded. In fact, William Michael Lucas saved at least three lives. The governor received his heart and liver and two others received his healthy kidneys.

Another question that I had to ask was: How long would he be under anesthesia? This was an important matter since we had already learned that any incapacitation required invoking Article 4 and transferring powers. I was concerned that the governor and his staff might try to tough it out and bet on a quick return even after such a dramatic procedure.

Not this time.

The governor had already conferred with his own legal team and was prepared to issue the letter devolving powers.

When?

5:00 a.m., Monday, June 14, 1993.

Any idea how long he would be out of commission?

No idea.

The letter was on my desk when I arrived in my office just after 7:00 a.m. that day:

To the General Assembly
Commonwealth of Pennsylvania
Pursuant to 71 P.S. section 784.1, I hereby declare that effective 5:00 AM, June 14, 1993, I will be temporarily unable to discharge the powers and duties of the Office of Governor, and that in accordance with Article IV, section 13 of the Pennsylvania Constitution such powers and duties shall be discharged by Lieutenant Governor Mark S. Singel, until such time as I transmit to the General Assembly a declaration to the contrary.

Sincerely,
ROBERT P. CASEY
Governor

By 8:00 a.m., all hands were on deck in the lieutenant governor's office. We didn't have time to linger over details. I must say that everybody was attuned to quick, efficient actions that would become the order of the day in the weeks to come. We selected 10:00 a.m. as the time for the press announcement. The idea was to send a visual and verbal message to the people of Pennsylvania that we were not skipping a beat. Susan Woods, my press secretary, ran a media advisory down to the Capitol Press Corps on the second floor, altering them to the time and place.

We decided against a formal statement for fear of appearing "too prepared." The last thing I needed was to charge the stage with the zeal of an understudy with over-rehearsed lines. As important as the event was, I still decided to wing it.

The location mattered. A ceremony in the governor's reception room—where the governor bared his physical challenges to the world just a few days before—would look callous. We would do the press conference in my own office. In fact, with few exceptions, all official public functions would be performed there. Our preparations continued in the staff room attached to the lieutenant governor's office so that the press could set up cameras and lights in the main office. We moved my desk into a corner and set up a dozen chairs facing a podium in front of the ornate fireplace.

Jim Brown joined us with the information that the governor's surgery was underway. He was prepared to join me in a show of unity between our two offices, and I knew he would be sincere and effective.

Then, a new development. We all received word that US Senator Arlen Specter was taken to a Philadelphia hospital for surgery on a brain tumor. In a coincidence of historic proportions, the governor and the state's senior US senator were officially out of commission. One staffer couldn't help but speculate about worst case scenarios: What if both were to die on the operating table? What are the constitutional implications? What are the prerogatives of the newly-minted acting governor?

I saw Jim Brown wince, and I shared his revulsion at the speculation. "We're not going there," I said. "Our prayers are with both Governor Casey and Senator Specter, and we expect them both to make a full recovery," was what I thought I would shortly say to the people of Pennsylvania.

It was time to step into the glare of the Klieg lights and the shrub of microphones that sprouted from the podium. The murmur of several dozen reporters, cameramen, staff, and elected officials crammed into the office dropped to a dead silence. I took a deep breath as I took my place behind the podium and remember feeling that my suit coat suddenly felt heavy. Oddly, I had a palpable sense of weight that had settled in on my shoulders. I believed then and I believe now that I was feeling the responsibility for 12.8 million Pennsylvanians—not merely as their constitutionally designated leader but as the surrogate father to a huge family. I felt it to be a deeply personal and sobering role.

On the other hand, there was a reassuring instant of clarity that occurred when the lights went on.

A déjà vu moment took me back to an experience from high school. Like this moment, I was standing behind a podium waiting for the lights and microphone to come on. Unlike this moment, I was then just a student council president.

My role was to introduce the topic and the guest speaker of an assembly to the nearly 800-person student body. It was the Thanksgiving Assembly, and I was at peace. I was doing well in school both academically and socially. I was grateful for strong family support, a wonderful girlfriend, and a spiritual bent that was always reflective at that time of year. I felt open to some life force that I didn't even understand and had no idea what I was about to say.

Suddenly, brightness from a spotlight poured down on me like a blessing. I remember feeling like time slowed down enough for me to actually see the rays flow from the lens of the light itself to where I was standing. When I was bathed in the light, I sensed another thing—comprehension. My mind seemed to be open to a different level of understanding. It seemed only right to take advantage of this enlightenment to explore this phenomenon.

I found myself looking into the faces of everyone in front of me. My mind seemed to be racing from student to student, row after row, with the incredible sensation that I was understanding everything there was to know about each of them—past, present, and future. The experience was so real that I recall pausing on four individuals with a sense of concern. With apologies for how absolutely strange this must sound, all four of those students died early deaths. To this day I have no idea why I singled out those individuals who shared such an unusual fate.

On balance, though, the millisecond or so that I spent with this awareness was more than extraordinary—it was life changing.

The incident in the lieutenant governor's office on June 14, 1993, was not as mystical. I did feel a transformation of sorts. It was like an airplane moving from the taxi lane to the runway. The engines were louder and preparing for a journey. I retain some indelible memories from that moment.

The faces in the room were familiar. The wire reporters from AP and UPI were in the front row. Correspondents from every major newspaper had their pads out. Television reporters stood close to their equipment and nodded to the "sticks" to begin rolling.

Jim Brown stood directly to my right, and my wife, Jackie, was on my left. A somber line of legislators who had arrived in Harrisburg early that Monday stood close by.

Senator Bob Mellow, the Senate pro tem, and Senator Bill Lincoln, the majority leader, were there. Both had befriended me from my first day as a senator. It was reassuring that they had my back now.

Senator Leonard Bodack from Pittsburgh was there as well. Leonard was a people person with an irrepressible sense of humor. In the millisecond that I glanced over at him, I recalled an incident from our days together in the Senate.

The leader, in a closed-door caucus, was looking for a consensus on a difficult social issue. The Democrats, as usual, were all over the map on the subject.

"Jesus Christ," exclaimed the colorful and beloved Ed Zemprelli. "You guys can't agree on ANYTHING! Just go to the floor and vote your conscience!"

To which Leonard Bodack retorted: "Wait a minute—what about us guys without a conscience!?"

Bodack's closest buddy in the Senate, the wily, aw shucks J. Barry Stout from Washington County couldn't let that go. "Leonard," Stout said. "You could fit your conscience in the navel of a gnat and still have room for three caraway seeds!"

As I was about to make the most important presentation of my life, I was distracted for a moment by some wonderful memories like that.

Others in the room included Senator Roy Afflerbach from Allentown and a dear family friend from Harrisburg, Representative Pete Wambach.

The press included Bob Zausner from the *Philadelphia Inquirer*, John Baer from the *Philadelphia Daily News*; stringers for local papers from Johnstown, Scranton, and Erie; Tim Reeves from the *Allentown Morning Call*; Joe Serwach, Carmen Brutto, and Jeannette Krebs of Harrisburg's *Patriot News*; and Sean Connelly and Pete Shelley from the *Pittsburgh Post-Gazette*. I always found this group to be fair with me, and it was clear that they were giving me some additional deference on this day.

The letter I received earlier already had the effect of devolving all powers from the governor. Still, it was important that a picture of a smooth transition be conveyed to the people of Pennsylvania. In fact, I said that we were "not looking to make waves" but rather to "set a tone of competence." I made it clear that I was fulfilling the role of *acting* governor and that I fully expected the governor back in power sooner rather than later.

Some unusual questions ensued:

Would I move into the governor's mansion?

No.

Would I take over the governor's office?

No. I would function right here in the lieutenant governor's office for the duration of the governor's absence.

How do we address you? Governor? Acting Governor? Lieutenant Governor?

Mark, I said, would be fine.

Immediately after the press conference, I convened the cabinet in three separate groups. This was partially to avoid any violation of the Sunshine Act that required public notices to be issued before a quorum of appointed officials could meet to transact business. It also made for groups small enough to encourage questions or to raise any sensitive issues during this extraordinary moment.

There was nothing but support and cooperation in all three groups. Let me state for the record right here that the cabinet assembled by Robert P. Casey was one of the best in Pennsylvania's history. I keep an official portrait of this group and to this day remember with great fondness every one of them.

In the next few hours, there were three items that demanded immediate attention.

First, a $176 million bond issue to raise funds for the construction of a new prison in Greene County needed one more sign-off from the governor before it was presented to the investment bank in New York. The deadline for the paperwork was 12:00 noon on that date. Missing this deadline had bond rating implications for the state.

While Casey and his budget secretary were all familiar with the details of the deal, I was not. In fact, I was uncomfortable with the sole source nature of the legal and financial concerns involved. I was also not familiar with the novel capital leveraging that was a part of the package. At 10:30 a.m., I asked Eric Schnurer to draw up a short list of appropriate questions for the budget secretary. It was important to me that we had done at least some cursory vetting of the process. I intended to have something in writing for my files.

While I in no way intended any disrespect for the governor's staff, and while I was confident that the entire transaction was legitimate, I wanted some coverage for myself. One or two folks in the front office took it as a direct slap with possible legal ramifications. One of them said to Eric: "You have pointed a loaded gun directly at my head."

Thankfully, Eric was able to calm everybody down. Budget Secretary Mike Hershock did his usual superb job in answering the questions, and we all felt comfortable transferring the documents with my signature to New York—at 11:55 a.m.

There was also the matter of expanded gaming. It was widely known that I was in favor of bringing slot machines to a limited number of venues in Pennsylvania. We were getting our economic clock cleaned by the casinos in New Jersey, and it just seemed logical to me to keep some of that gaming revenue in our state. It took all of an hour and a half for the first call to reach my office.

A lobbyist for one of the state's horse racing operations called. The good wishes soon turned into a question that went something like: "Should we be drafting legislation to expand gaming at the tracks?"

The subtext, of course, was that Casey was incapacitated so now would be a good time for them to, ahem, place their bets. I told him that expansion of gaming in any way would be off the table as long as I was the acting governor and carrying on with the business of government in Casey's stead. To do anything else would have been a huge breach of loyalty and a demonstration of hubris that I was not willing to make. Slots at tracks would have to wait until I was governor in my own right.

There were two certificates of approval relating to bonds issued by the PA Higher Educational Facilities Authority that required the governor's signature that day. I signed off on $7.5 million for the PA College of Podiatric Medicine and Duquesne University.

There were also several memos entitled "Bills Awaiting Governor's Signature." While I had decided to wait a day or so before actually signing my first bill, the form and names on the memos are worth noting.

I had the benefit of a talented group of staffers from the governor's office who augmented my own staff and kept a stream of due diligence memos on recently passed bills coming. Typically the memo was drafted by Dick Spiegelman or Andy Sislo in the general counsel's office. Copies were shared with Walt Carmo, legislative secretary; Pat Beaty, legal counsel for legislation; Eric Schnurer, my own chief of staff; the cabinet official whose department was affected by the legislation; and someone from the governor's press office.

I mention this to emphasize the level of cooperation that existed at that time between the lieutenant governor and the governor's office. I also benefited from a variety of perspectives on every topic from individuals who will always have my respect and admiration.

By the time I emerged from my office to make the short walk to preside over the Senate, I had already dealt with three separate cabinet meetings, extraditions, proclamations, some administrative duties, and one major financial transaction. I had also set a direction on key issues that I believed were in keeping with Casey's outlook.

And one more reality check greeted me in that time frame. Within days of Casey's surgery, the House Democrats sent over two very good friends as emissaries on a sensitive issue. Representative Pete Wambach of Dauphin County and Representative Bob Belfanti of Schuylkill County came to talk to me to make the case that they were overdue for a legislative pay raise. I wasn't expecting that hot potato, at least not that early in my tenure. Instinctively, though, I knew I had to drive a stake through the heart of that idea. I told them in no uncertain terms that I was not interested in some pay raise deal and that I would veto it if it came to my desk.

In the hallway outside of the lieutenant governor's office, I encountered John Baer of the *Philadelphia Daily News*.

John was a reporter who came with a career's worth of attitude. Specifically, he was the communications director for Lieutenant Governor Bill Scranton in the Casey/Scranton battle of 1986. He was known for lobbing written grenades at candidates and office holders, and I was no exception. He also had perfected the art of lurking. That is, after all of the broadcast media and his fellow journalists had completed their questions at a formal press conference, John would lag behind and isolate you to get his own scoop. On the day of the transfer of power, he had asked what I felt when I first heard the news that Casey was going in for surgery.

My mind was buzzing with the events of the day. I was also thinking about all of the events of my life that led up to that moment. Most of all, I was thinking about Casey facing life-threatening surgery.

I recall telling John that I spent the better part of an hour talking with my wife. In the still of that very early morning we discussed fate, God, politics, duty, our children, and of course, what the whole Casey family was going through. I told John than it was a "real Maxwell House moment" meaning that, like the television commercial, two humans were connecting on a human level over coffee. Unlike the commercial, however, this was for real; we were gathering our strength for what we knew was going to be a tsunami.

In a book about Pennsylvania politics, here's how John Baer later reported that encounter:

"I'm sure I cringed even as I took notes because I know I was thinking, not good; Pennsylvania won't like this . . . Too flip. Too commercial. Too made-for-TV."

It was a total misread of what I was thinking and feeling. It also showed a complete lack of awareness of the quickened pace of life that I was now facing. We would have some frank words about those comments at a later date.

For now, another ambush question was about a rumor that a pay raise was in the works for the legislature. He had been fed the story from someone in the House leadership and wanted to know if I was going to seize the moment to ingratiate myself with folks who would be important to me in the coming months and years.

He did not know about the meeting with two key House Democrats that had just concluded. He also was probably not expecting the response I gave him:

"There will be no pay raise. If the legislature is foolish enough to send me one I will veto it immediately."

Baer was expecting something nuanced like: "We're talking about it," or "Let's see if we have room for it in the budget that was just passed." My instinct was that anything less than a flat-out "NO" would be taken as a sign that this was negotiable and that I would be malleable as acting governor. More importantly, as I told the House Democrats, I was not interested in being the one who opened the cookie jar to them.

The Philadelphia headlines were dramatic: "Singel Play – Acting Governor Shuts Down Pay Raise." While the incident caused some ruffled feathers with my friends in the House and Senate leadership, it was clearly the right thing to do.

It was also a lesson for me about communications at the gubernatorial level. Not only was it important to be clear; it was also critical to be quick. Any hesitation at all with just one reporter could have had lasting negative impacts for me, and whether they knew it at the time, the legislators themselves.

The pay raise issue and the confrontation with the gaming interests needed immediate closure. While the duly-elected governor could reasonably ask for time to reflect and negotiate, the acting governor was being tested. Vacillation would give folks the false impression that the ship of state was rudderless and open to all manner of piracy. The events of the first morning and the pay raise ploy made it clear to me that my stint as acting governor, no matter how long, was going to be faster-paced and more consequential than any previous roles.

A side note to the pay raise dust-up: One reporter, Bob Swift, who was then writing for a statewide news service, speculated that Bill Lincoln and I had concocted the whole thing. Bob wrote:

"One wonders if more went on behind the scenes. Is it farfetched to ask if Lincoln floated the pay raise idea just so Singel could shoot it down?" After all, he went on: "Lincoln owes Singel for helping Senate Democrats hang on to their precarious control of the Senate."

Bob did accurately report my response: "Singel says you need a devious mind to think that."

For the record, there was no such chicanery.

Thankfully, my colleagues in the Senate were reserved on the day I became the acting governor. I appreciated the fact that they were giving me some breathing room and forgoing the usual parliamentary hijinks—at least for one day.

Just to make sure that our bases were covered, I had asked Dick Spiegelman to prepare an opinion on the rights and obligations I had as both the acting governor and president of the Senate. If the Republicans had any intention of challenging the legal status I had to perform both roles, my good friend Senator Craig Lewis of Bucks County headed them off by inserting into the record the legal opinion, addressed to me, which read, in part:

"Pursuant to the Art. IV Sections 13 and 14 of the Pennsylvania Constitution the Lieutenant Governor continues to exercise the powers and duties of the office of Lieutenant Governor in the circumstances when the duties and powers of the office of Governor have devolved upon the Lieutenant Governor. . . . Under the plain language of the Constitution, you may simultaneously perform the powers and duties of Lieutenant Governor and Acting Governor . . ."

The Senate broke for caucus meetings and did not return until much later that evening for some clean up that did not require my presence. This allowed me to tend to a business-as-usual series of events that I had scheduled previously.

It happens that Corporal Butch Saunders was assigned to that day's events in Philadelphia. But there was something different on this trip: A second trooper was in the vehicle and there were two others waiting for us at the event. At my request, the detail for me had been as small as possible. Usually one trooper did all of the advance, driving, and logistics on our jaunts. Butch let me know that the protocol had just been changed.

Along with that change was a noticeable difference in tone. While the Executive Detail was always professional, we allowed ourselves some personal banter during long trips. This time, I had Gina McBean of my staff in the vehicle with me and she had already collected a stack of paperwork that needed attention during the car ride. We also needed time to prep for the events.

This was to be the new pattern: little or no time for personal research or writing; I had to trust my team to prepare talking points that I could review en route. And now there was certainly little, if any, time for the pleasant distraction of conversations. The quickening of the pace for me had already become similar to a lawyer preparing his case as he walked into each courtroom.

The two events that evening were a town meeting on crime and drugs at a church in north Philadelphia followed by a sit-down with key ministers and political leaders. Prior to each event, I encountered a gaggle of reporters with cameras and microphones peppering me with questions about the governor's health, the day's agenda, and what the future might hold. I did the best I could to continue the tone I had set earlier in the day: calm, steady stewardship with deference to the ailing governor's policies.

Councilman John Street and I connected in a more personal way than we had ever done before. He was planning to run for mayor and until now had viewed me as irrelevant to that endeavor. Today, he was the one reaching out for a deeper connection. We had crossed paths before, but this time but we both felt that this encounter was more than just a photo op. US Representatives Chaka Fattah and Lucien Blackwell interrupted their own schedules to join me along with several key ward leaders. I'm sure I would not have drawn the attention of such luminaries twenty-four hours before.

The troopers deposited me at the lieutenant governor's residence at 11:45 p.m. that evening. I had been up since 3:30 a.m. and I remember Jackie saying when I walked into the bedroom: "Are we having fun yet?"

"Fun" was certainly not the correct word for it. I was used to the workload, but it would take a little time to get used to the gravitas of actually being the acting governor.

Butch Saunders had his own way of adjusting to it. I heard him radioing in to the detail's command post as I was entering the house: "Eagle Two is back at the nest." I was the Sparrow no more.

My notes on the next few days are fuzzy. This is because the normal routine had been disrupted dramatically, and I was now balancing the schedules of five personae: governor, acting governor, lieutenant governor, president of the Senate, and potential candidate for governor. There was no time for carefully-scripted schedule cards, which I usually carried in my suit coat pocket; instead, we had to ride a wave of events that could change instantly.

The once obscure actions of the lieutenant governor were now being recorded in the glare of an unblinking press. For the first time ever a lieutenant governor/acting governor signed bills into law. Among these was a strong anti-stalking law that addressed the murder of a young girl named Laurie Show. Her parents, as well as the legislative sponsors, were on hand for that bill signing.

Another bill required local governments to allow for citizen comments at meetings, and a third was an appropriation to operate the workers' compensation program for the coming fiscal year. By the week's end, I had signed more than 150 letters, proclamations, budget-related documents, and other official actions that came with the territory.

One of the more substantial actions on that day was sandwiched in between all of the other activities. With the help of the intrepid Pat Halpin Murphy, a senior Casey advisor and a breast cancer survivor, we launched the PA Breast Cancer Coalition. It has gone on to be an invaluable premier fund-raising and educational organization After 23 years, Pat still leads the organization.

The second day after I assumed the governor's duties was historic in another way.

The Senate was about to put the finishing touches on a workers' compensation reform package that had been years in the making. Pennsylvania had one of the highest workers' compensation rates in the country, and businesses had just seen a whopping 24% increase in their premiums in December. To get things under control, a bipartisan group of leaders recommended cost reductions and limitations on some benefits. It was the first overhaul of workers' compensation in forty years.

Joe Serwach reported in the *Harrisburg Patriot News* that: "Since Gov. Robert P. Casey underwent a heart-liver transplant Monday, lawmakers and administration officials have been trying to be more polite to each other, uniting in a time of crisis."

Not exactly. The AFL-CIO was not happy, calling the package "the biggest rip-off to workers and employers in the last 30 years to the exclusive benefit of one special interest in Pennsylvania, the insurance industry." Some Democrats agreed and voted with labor while some Republicans thought that the package wasn't stringent enough.

With razor thin Democratic majorities in both chambers, the leaders had learned to strike while the legislative iron was hot. Even the Republicans acknowledged that the tenuous coalition on this issue would fall apart if it drifted even one more day. The debate went late into the evening but passed the Senate by a vote of 34-14. The House followed suit.

In an odd bit of reality at the time, my signature appeared on this landmark law three times: when it passed the Senate on June

16; when the Senate approved the final conference committee version on June 21; and, ultimately, when it was signed into Act 44 on July 2, 1993.

There was no time to savor the win since I had a long-standing commitment to deliver the commencement address at Souderton High School in Montgomery County that evening. This event had been arranged by Jim Maza, a prominent local attorney and a buddy of mine from our undergraduate days together at Penn State.

It was appropriate that I would encounter Jim in the middle of this whirlwind. He had been involved in all of my political endeavors. We had been to each others' weddings, and we remain close confidants. I have a lifetime of stories about our adventures together.

Here's a snapshot or two of Jim Maza.

We arrived at Penn State in 1971. I headed toward the liberal arts and interspersed my English lit and history classes with an active social schedule with dormmates, a generous amount of poker, and beer. Jim arrived as an activist, angry at Nixon's handling of the Viet Nam war and determined to do something about it. He tells the story of his one-man protest lying spread-eagle at the intersection of College Avenue and Atherton. Penn State is not exactly a hotbed of radicalism, and Jim's Tienanmen Square moment didn't last long. He was escorted off the street by a local traffic cop while the stoners on the famous Penn State wall raised their doobies in a foggy "far-out, man" tribute.

His other activities on campus were much more effective. Jim led and energized the academic assembly and tried mightily to raise the level of discourse on all issues of the day. We remained in close touch after college and agreed that we would try to save the world in our individual ways.

His was law school and a possible political career; mine was plunging into government as a congressional aide. We hung out in Washington together when he clerked for the US Supreme Court, and we prepared for life's adventures. We would make sure that we never drifted too far apart.

Just before the commencement address at his high school alma mater, Jim asked me:

"So how does it feel?"

He could always cut right to the heart of anything with me. His candor and humor had a therapeutic effect on me. I understood that he wanted to know what the mantle of power was like. It was something to which we both aspired.

"It feels right," I said.

"Yeah," said Jim. "I thought you'd say that. It's like what Oliver Wendell Holmes said: 'the best generals do not need bigger tents; they need command.'"

The level of respect and friendship that he conveyed in that moment is a gift that I will never forget.

At the end of an eventful week, I visited Pittsburgh for a presentation to a bond financing seminar. I also added a media event to encourage organ donations in Pennsylvania. This took on poignancy given that the governor's life was saved with donated organs just days ago. There was also a PennDOT event involving some dramatic new traffic message board on the top of Mount Washington.

But the real reason for the Pittsburgh visit was to spend some time with Governor Casey's family at the University of Pittsburgh Medical Center. The governor was just three days out of intensively complicated surgery, and we all decided to let him rest. The visit with Ellen Casey and several of her children, though, was moving. Ellen was her usual steady self. She was always a model of grace and composure; she welcomed me like her own child. I deeply appreciated the warmth that I received from the entire Casey clan. I tried my best to convey the good wishes for the governor and all of them that I was feeling from every corner of the state.

Within a few days, the press had already begun its analysis of the Singel interregnum. Most of it was fair and respectful of the burdens that we were all carrying.

Tim Reeves quoted Jim Brown and me in *Pittsburgh Post Gazette*:

"We're certainly in good hands," Brown said. "Our staff and everybody in the administration is ready to go to work with the lieutenant governor, whom everybody respects a lot . . ."

As far as previous tensions between the offices were concerned, I meant it when I said:

"The lieutenant governor's office and the governor's office may have had some differences over the years, but this is the kind of thing that makes them pale. As far as I am concerned, we are in this together and there is a very harmonious, close working relationship."

Reeves asked what Casey told me just before his surgery. My response was: "He said, 'Do a good job'; and I intend to."

Dennis Barbagello of the *Greensburg Tribune Review* wrote two interesting stories from completely different angles. One was a recitation of Pennsylvania history:

111

"The last lieutenant governor to assume the chief executive's job was John Bell Jr. of Philadelphia, who became governor when Gov. Edward Martin resigned on Jan. 2, 1947 to become a US Senator. Bell served as governor for 19 days pending the inauguration of then Governor-elect James Duff. The only other record of a Pennsylvania lieutenant governor assuming the governorship was William Freame Johnston, a Whig, of Westmoreland County, who took office on July 26, 1848, following the resignation of Gov. Francis Shunk, a Montgomery County Democrat."

The other article called out the Senate Republicans for exploring succession options even before Governor Casey lay on the operating table. According to Barbagello:

"It was less than an hour after Gov. Robert Casey announced he may undergo liver transplantation surgery that Senate Republicans reportedly activated an old file. It's a file on succession to the governorship." Barbagello called the action "ghoulish" and "vulturous."

Just as inappropriate was speculation about my political future. It was simply not the time and place for that discussion, and frankly, my hands were full with other matters.

Still, that didn't stop one political pundit from speculating that: "Taking over the duties of governor, for whatever period of time, should put Lieutenant Governor Mark Singel in a better position to run for that position in 1994." Michael Young, a political science professor at Penn State made the remarks and went so far as to speculate presciently that "Singel will likely find himself in a Western Pennsylvania contest with US Representative Tom Ridge of Erie County."

Mike Young and I were, and remain, close friends, but the political analysis was a bit too much too soon.

In fact, I thought it was appropriate to send a message to my nascent political campaign team that things had to be put on hold for a while. I believed that it would have been inappropriate to do political fund-raising at this moment. I also just didn't have the time to make those calls and visits.

I remember getting Jim Cunningham and L.A. Harris on a conference call to get them to stand down.

"Are you frickin' kidding me?" was Cunningham's reaction. "Your stock just went up. You're like the bull in the barnyard and the cows are all callin' yer name!"

Loved that guy. In terms of countrified wit, he was second only to J. Barry Stout.

I stayed out of the political barnyard for the rest of the month. I had no idea what the governor's prognosis was. My own interests could wait until that picture cleared up a bit. The political operation shut down, but the team made me promise to revitalize it in July.

By June 22, the state government was moving steadily along its tracks. The depot for this huge train was now the lieutenant governor's office.

This morning featured an array of items that required executive attention. First up were a number of documents to wrap up details relating to the close of the 1992-93 fiscal year and to allocate funding now available for the 1993-94 fiscal year. This included $15 million in inter-agency transfers that shifted some surpluses to those agencies that were coming up short as the end of the fiscal year loomed.

I also:

- authorized payments to key departments totaling $30 million
- distributed just under $300 million in federal funding
- authorized about $2 billion from special funds to the treasurer for expenditure
- approved a tax anticipation note of $400 million
- authorized about $20 million in capital and housing projects
- announced the distribution of federal funds for the snow removal emergency that we faced the previous January

Just as I was putting down that pen and picking up the gavel in the state Senate, I got a friendly call from my wife:

"How is your day going?" she asked.

"You know how you don't trust me to balance our checkbook?" I responded. "I think I just spent about three billion dollars!" The reality, of course, is that the heavy lifting of accounting and financial operations was spread around among experts in various departments. It was only upon their guidance and recommendations that I could act with confidence.

The next morning I dealt with an interesting mix of executive actions. Many of these had been lingering awhile in the governor's office.

Some were routine but important, like the flood of greetings that went to state employees who chose to retire at the conclusion of the fiscal year. I actually knew many of them and paused to add a personal note of thanks on some of the letters.

Other transactions included interstate arrest warrants, extraditions, visa requests for a number of foreign doctors who required sponsorship from their state of destination, citations for student achievements and high school bands, anniversaries, and sports champions. This was not unlike the casework and commendations that I issued as a senator and lieutenant governor. The difference was the volume. It was like someone had replaced a garden hose trickle with a high-pressure fire hose.

I was also struck by the number of life-changing actions that I was called upon to take. On this morning, for example, I signed commissions for appointments to boards and other government entities for twenty people. Prothonotaries for Blair and Westmoreland Counties; district justices for Elk and Westmoreland; the coroner for my home County of Cambria; and a dozen court of common pleas judges to benches in Philadelphia, Allegheny, Montgomery, and Franklin Counties.

Of note, and in an interesting twist of fate, I officially appointed Rob Gleason to the Pennsylvania Turnpike Commission. Rob was the loyal opposition, a leader of the Republican Party in my home area, and my opponent for the 35th district Senate seat way back in 1980. The time had come to acknowledge that Rob was an effective businessman and prominent community leader, and I appreciated both things. What I didn't appreciate was his constant partisanship that would blossom into a long tenure as chair of the State Republican Party. I was not expecting any support (either in 1993 or when I would run for governor in the following year), and I did not get any!

One of the craftier members of my staff suggested that I simply "misplace" the appointment document for a week or two. I did not feel the need to play any games, though; I certainly had enough other things on my plate.

By mid-week, the word was out that leaders in both the House and the Senate were ready to wrap things up for an extended summer and fall outside of the glare of Harrisburg. This was fine with me since I had more than enough to do without having to referee the Senate proceedings. It was also true that two special elections were now scheduled—one for July 13 and another for November 2—that could alter the makeup of the Senate and disrupt what I believed had been a productive flow of progressive legislation. We were now safely through the budget process, but if the legislature would reconvene after July 13 (with an expected win by the R candidate) and before November 2, they would recapture control and drive an entirely different agenda. Better to send them home and revisit all remaining legislative priorities when there was a full complement in November.

This, of course, did not sit well with the Republicans and the normally routine adjournment resolution became the flashpoint:

The Senate Journal of June 23, 1993, notes that Senator Lincoln offered a resolution *"that when the Senate adjourns this week it will reconvene on Monday, November 22, 1993 unless sooner recalled by the President . . ."*

Senator Jubelirer, ever suspicious of Democrats and always prepared, had his amendment to the adjournment resolution ready: *"When the Senate adjourns this week it will reconvene on Monday, August 2, 1993 unless sooner recalled by the President Pro Tempore of the Senate . . ."*

The short amendment would accomplish three things for the Republicans: it would tip the balance of control in that chamber to 25-24 following the election in Bucks County, it would give the Republicans three months to undo or alter what the Democratic majorities had accomplished in their brief shining moment, and it specifically precluded the president (me) from recalling the Senate. The latter was just a procedural slap at my prerogatives. Just a typical paper cut that my GOP friends liked to apply from time to time.

Before we got to some serious policy debates at hand, the adjournment battle was engaged:

> Senator Jubelirer: *". . . Mr. President, we believe it is appropriate that the Senate do indeed have the opportunity to swear in a new senator, and that is the reason for the August 2 date. . . . There is no justification, Mr. President, for staying out of session until Thanksgiving. The move can only be described as power politics and selfish politics, which rises above good government. Leaving now means putting off for many months . . . an overhaul of our welfare system; meaningful tax cuts for jobs . . . local tax reform, education reform . . . and the list could go on and on . . .*
>
> *"If your fingernail grip of power is the motivation, then, frankly, I think that is showing disdain for the people of Pennsylvania, the sort of insult that has already been handed to the people of Bucks County, and now to the people of Philadelphia County in the second senatorial district . . ."*

This was not the first time that the good senator from Blair took direct shots at the presiding officer—me. It was grating to me that I was procedurally barred from engaging in debate from the chair. This was one of many occasions that I had to hold in check my normal instinct to jump into the fray.

Senator Lincoln was up to the task.

Senator Lincoln: *"Last year at the same time . . . the Republican-controlled Senate adjourned until Monday, November 9 . . . they had been in session . . . 43 Session days, and had enacted a grand total of 23 bills. In the same period of time this year, from January through June 30, which is not even here yet . . . we have been in session 39 days, and we have enacted 62 bills as a majority party. . . . We have accomplished some major things that had not even been dealt with by the Republican majority in previous sessions—workmen's compensation . . . a good budget with no tax increases . . .*

"In fact, [in 1992] there were 85 bills passed in November after the Democrats took majority control . . . between now and the November 22 return date there will be active committee meetings. There will be hearings by committees. We will set up a nice legislative agenda for late fall . . ."

The political fangs started to come out a bit when Jubelirer persisted in his argument that the Democrats were skipping town to keep their slim majority as long as possible. While there was some truth to this, Lincoln was not about to let the hypocrisy of their position go unchallenged:

Senator Lincoln: *"The reason we left on July 1 last year and did not come back until November 9 was because the gentleman from Montgomery, Senator Pecora, had switched parties and had given every indication that he was going to join the Democratic caucus at some point in time in the fall. It was a deliberate effort on the part of the Republican Party to protect their majority . . ."*

At this point in the proceedings, and at the mention of the Pecora name—still salt in the wounds of the Republicans—a strange, steady thumping started from somewhere on the Senate floor. It didn't take long to identify the source.

Senator Ed Holl, a curmudgeon who had more idiosyncrasies than Elmer Fudd, was rhythmically kicking his desk in an effort to drown out the speaker or to just give sound to his petulance. Some senators on the Democratic side were offended; I was amused.

Ed Holl was eccentric. He was a talented painter and a musician. He was known to imbibe and practice his trumpet into the wee hours in the Capitol building. The eerie sound gave rise to legends about moaning ghosts, but we all knew who was doing the haunting. Being 35 years younger than Ed, I learned that he expected some deference. Every time that Senator Ed Holl entered or exited the Senate chamber, I stood respectfully and bowed from the waist. He returned the gesture with his own gentleman's bow and the routine secured a friendship between the two of us.

If Ed wanted to make some noise, I didn't care.

On the question of agreeing to the Jubelirer adjournment amendment, the vote was 24-24. Less than a majority of senators having voted "aye," the amendment failed.

This got us finally to the original Lincoln adjournment resolution. The vote was, predictably, 24-24. This time, I was able to exercise the prerogative of the chair and voted "aye."

By a vote of 25-24, the senators would spend their summer and early fall away from Harrisburg. As indignant as Senator Jubelirer was, I knew that I had just handed him a new target—me. From this date throughout the summer, I would be on the receiving end of an endless series of letters, calls, and press stunts, demanding that I "bring the Senate back." It got to a point that, in addition to the official activities and communications, my staff advised me what the Jubelirer attack du jour was. At one point, I responded to one such missive with a six word letter: "Enough already. Have a nice summer."

Having spent way too much time on the procedural adjournment resolution, the Senate now hunkered down to deliver the balance of the Democrats' agenda for 1993. They had planned to chip away at a dozen different items and work straight through until the mission was accomplished. The journal notes that the session ended at 11:59 p.m. This, of course, does not account for the freezing of the clock to allow for the session to drift well past the start of a new day. While we were technically still working on the June 23 calendar, the session did not officially end until after noon on June 24!

The "all-nighter" included final actions on some landmark initiatives.

During this two-day session "day," the Senate:

- Provided for opening the Senate proceedings for public broadcasting
- Reenacted the Health Care Cost Containment Council
- Passed the Key 93 proposal to refinance the entire Pennsylvania park system
- Extended the life of the Pennsylvania Conservation Corps
- Passed a landmark telecommunications reform bill
- Passed a series of administrative bills related to the budget
- Passed all of the special "non-preferred" bills required for hospital and university funding (this occurred just around 2:00 a.m. on June 24)
- Enacted a new capital budget bill authorizing $300 million in new projects
- Passed stringent new requirements on "deadbeat dads" who were in arrears on child support

Before we concluded the session, the Republicans had two more political cards to play. It was about 2:30 a.m. and the minority whip, Senator Joe Loeper from Delaware County, rose to offer a resolution to establish a date certain for the oath of office to be administered to the senator elected in the 10th district. The election was to be held on July 13, and Loeper and his colleagues wanted to force the swearing in before the reconvening date so that their party could wrest the majority back from the Democrats by a vote of 25-24.

I made it clear that such a resolution required unanimous consent to be considered at that point. Senator Lincoln, right on cue, raised an objection, and I quickly gavelled down the motion as being out of order.

While we dispatched the matter quickly, the Rs had established yet another talking point: Singel and the Ds killed yet another effort to install the new senator. I could detect another lawsuit being drafted.

The other ploy was to oppose a procedural motion to table a bill that had to do with corporate taxes. Senator Peterson led the charge to force a negative vote on SB 1190 that would have been a tough one for Ds to explain to their business constituents. There was also the possibility that it would result in a tie vote and force yet one more tough decision for me as the presiding officer. Senator Peterson was a particularly partisan member with a speaking style that I found to be abrasive. As was his habit, he plunged into his arguments for the bill before we had dealt with the motion at hand. I ruled him out of order.

118

Senator Brightbill, a clever Republican from Lebanon County, jumped into the fray with the intent of interrogating Senator Peterson, thereby getting the substance of his arguments on the record. Even in the wee hours of the morning, I found myself needing to be on my toes.

The President: *"The interrogation is out of order. . . . The chair, with all due respect, indicates that the debate is limited to the substance of the motion itself, which is strictly on whether to take the bill over, and the chair will not allow you to interrogate Senator Peterson so that he can display his amendment. We are not at that stage and we do not intend to get to that stage. Therefore, the gentleman's interrogation and the direction he was charting is out of order."*

Senator Loeper: *"Mr. President, did the chair just indicate or pre-suppose what the vote of this motion may be?"*

The President: *"The chair indicated that he presupposed what the interrogation was going to be."*

But the vote, by design, was 24-24. My "aye" vote killed further consideration of the bill for the moment and placed yet another arrow in the Republican quiver.

Senator Jubelirer fired one more shot across the bow with some prepared remarks on the Loeper effort to speed up the swearing in of their newest senator. I would see those remarks again in several of the letters and news releases issued by the loyal opposition in the coming months.

The sun's rays were now coming into the chamber. We had pulled an all-nighter and folks were wearing out from the political sparring of the last 24 hours. Thankfully, one kinder, gentler soul took to the floor to provide some much-needed human perspective. It was Senator J. Doyle Corman of State College, who injected some humanity back into the proceedings:

Senator Corman: *". . . I would like to say that this extended evening of June 23 has been a very interesting evening. It marks the 36th anniversary of the marriage of my wife and I, and also in the process of the evening, I became a grandfather for the seventh time, with a grandson named after me, Matthew Doyle Erlichman. So it was certainly a very interesting and productive evening in many different ways."*

Senator Lincoln: *". . . I think a lot of things happened here yesterday that may not be remembered . . . although I think it was a very productive day . . . I think that the experience of a grandchild and a wedding anniversary probably make the day one that Senator Corman will remember a lot longer than for what we did here . . . and I just wanted to offer my congratulations."*

And my own special order of business:

The President: *"The chair wishes to announce that in the Senate chamber today we have three very special guests. First, I have my daughter, Allyson Jean Singel, who is with us; and my niece whose name is Amy Dominguez; and my wife, Jackie Singel, is here."*

Some might consider these types of exchanges to be non-essential—especially in light of the brawling that had just occurred on weightier matters. I, on the other hand, thoroughly enjoyed them. It bolstered my belief that elected officials need not be excessively ideological or partisan. There was nothing wrong with just being friends.

And finally, some kind remarks from Senator Vincent Fumo of Philadelphia. Vince and I didn't always agree on issues or tactics, so it was particularly rewarding to hear him take the microphone:

Senator Fumo: *"Mr. President, I would like to thank the chair for doing such an excellent job during these last few trying days. They were long hours, at times heated, and I think the chair conducted himself admirably in keeping the Senate in order and calm and getting as much work done as we did."*

A little past noon on June 24, wrapping up the session that began twenty-four hours earlier, there was one final piece of business for the Senate before it would return on November 22. Naturally, even the adjournment resolution was a political statement. The Democrats voted "aye" and the Republicans voted "no." The final vote of the session was a tie-breaking "aye" vote from me that sent everybody home.

Most of the legislators were heading to vacations or at least some downtime with their families. My own schedule was just heating up.

The Navy Ships Parts Control Center in Mechanicsburg was on the target list of the federal Base Closure and Realignment

Commissions, and Governor Casey had come under fire for what the locals considered a weak effort to save the facility. I walked into that fire and spent much of the afternoon with the officers and staff. I was presented with a petition with 55,000 names on it.

The base realignment presented a number of economic and political complications—the kind of issues that present tough choices for governors or acting governors. The SPCC meant about $1 billion annually to central Pennsylvania, but so did the military supply functions in the City of Philadelphia. The feds were basically telling us to choose one base or the other and consolidate functions in one location. No matter what was decided, thousands of jobs were going to be cut somewhere. In the end, the Philadelphia facilities, the SPCC in Mechanicsburg, and the Letterkenny Army Depot all escaped major cuts. This was due to a powerful congressional delegation that worked together to protect Pennsylvania jobs.

Like most public appearances throughout those summer months, I faced a gaggle of reporters, microphones, and cameras. While the topic du jour was always covered, the pundits were more interested in looking for signs of stress in the interim government. I assured them that things were fine and that, in fact, Casey's staff and my own had gelled nicely into an effective group of professionals intent on moving forward together. Despite wading through legislative challenges, facing tough issues like potential base closings, and juggling numerous responsibilities at once, some of the crustier wags were not buying the "Kumbaya" spin. They insisted that there were rifts between Singel staffers and Casey loyalists. This simply wasn't true—at least not yet.

Good friends from Penn State, Dr. John Brighton, Government Affairs Director Dave Schuckers, and Dean of the Liberal Arts College Dr. Susan Welch stopped by later that day to discuss the Penn State Future Committee Report. My favorite topic was the future, and it was good to know that Penn State was focused in the same way.

After a late afternoon videotaping with the Senate information studio, I was able to get home for some much needed rest.

Ten days into the Singel interregnum, pundits were beginning to assess the transition. While most assessments were complimentary to me, it was clear that the respectful decorum concerning the situation was beginning drip away.

David Buffington, who published a political notebook known as the *Pennsylvania Report* had this to say:

"Singel has carefully avoided looking like a latter-day Al Haig, but he has not run away from his responsibilities. As 'acting governor,' Singel has signed a few non-controversial bills and attracted media attention to his ongoing 'issues offensive.' Plus, he's used a newfound pulpit to derail plans for a legislative pay raise . . . that's a perfect position for a gubernatorial candidate."

He couldn't resist some ghoulish speculation:

"If Casey remains disabled . . . for Mark Singel, this would be the equivalent of biblical purgatory. . . . For example, could Singel advance his local property tax reform legislation? In theory, yes. However, Casey has voiced opposition to the Singel plan, and from his hospital bed, Casey could instruct his staff to torpedo the plan . . .

"If Casey dies. . . . While this is the most tragic scenario, it is also the simplest. If Casey dies before the end of his term, Mark Singel becomes Governor Singel. After he sacks every Casey loyalist in the front office, Singel then begins his campaign for reelection in 1994. As the incumbent governor, he could raise a ton of money and probably fend off any Democratic primary challenge."

Whew, I thought, he doesn't pull any punches. My staff thought the part about sacking the Casey loyalists was funny; I just thought it was completely inappropriate. At that moment I was getting nothing but unconditional support from the front office, and even in the most extreme case, I would have insisted on keeping most or all of them.

Editorial distractions notwithstanding, there was much more business to complete.

I also approved another tax exempt bond approval for higher education. In this case it was for a $16 million project at the Philadelphia College of Textiles and Sciences.

I also signed the re-authorization of the Health Care Cost Containment Council, part of our ongoing efforts to rein in costs while we tiptoed toward real health care reform.

There was the continuing parade of proclamations like "Ice Cream Month" and greetings to what I was told was a huge reunion of the Cabbagestalk family. Really.

There were, of course, weightier matters to attend to and, occasionally, correspondence of historical significance occurred.

I was pleased, for example, to honor the Honorable Genevieve Blatt upon her retirement from public service. Genevieve was the first woman elected to a statewide office—treasurer. She served for 55 years as a judge and a candidate for various offices and blazed a trail for countless women and men who followed in her footsteps.

Here is a footnote that only true political nerds could appreciate. On June 30, it was necessary for me to correct time itself. Questions had been raised about the passage of a bill establishing an advisory commission to the department of health. The substance of the bill was not a problem; the timing was.

In a letter to the Senate (since I was the presiding officer, I was literally writing to myself) I wrote:

Apparently, when the Senate Journal is printed it will reflect that this bill (SB 1018) and eight others were signed by the presiding officer of the Senate on the session day of June 23, 1993, while the House Journal will reflect that these bills were not passed finally by the House of Representatives until Thursday, June 24, 1993. It therefore might be argued that Article III, Section 8 was violated since the two journals will imply that the House had not yet finally passed these bills when the presiding officer of the Senate signed each of them.

As the president officer of the Senate, I know from personal knowledge that such is not the case. Although the Senate had not yet adjourned its Wednesday calendar of scheduled activity nor convened a Thursday calendar, I in fact signed the bills following their passage by the House.

In other words, we were still operating on the Senate's Wednesday calendar when the House passed the bills on a Thursday. In the real world, I signed the bills on a Thursday; in the surreal world of the Senate clock, it was still Wednesday. The letter was to admit to this bit of legislative time travel to make sure that the new statutes could not be challenged someday.

On Wednesday, June 30, the day started with Budget Secretary Mike Hershock and me reviewing capital projects that had been authorized by the general assembly. He came with a list of "shovel ready" projects, and I had a few favorites myself. Together we identified $300 million worth of investments that we set in motion for construction all over the state.

That was just the beginning of a landmark day for me and for the state. In addition to the wave of public enterprise just approved, I traveled to Bethlehem to join Hank Barnette, president of the Bethlehem Steel Corporation, for the formal signing of a new contract between the company and the USWA. The ceremony secured thousands of private jobs at various locations throughout the state.

In a separate meeting that was not open to the press, labor and company leaders sat with me to discuss the situation in my hometown. Johnstown had been the birthplace of the steel industry in the late 1800s and early 1900s. It had a proud tradition of immersing its community into good, family-sustaining jobs in steel mills, garment factories, and coal mines. The work was tough but the hardy stock of largely immigrant populations was used to hard work.

After three generations in the mills, workers were facing the effects of foreign competition and cheap labor rates overseas. Some of the steel mills just couldn't compete and had already closed.

There was some interest from investors who thought major portions of the industry could be resuscitated. Today, we talked about an offer that had been made by Ispat, an Indian company, but it was rejected by the local union. We also received word that a new group of investors from Wall Street had an interest. We exchanged information, and I committed the state to full participation with whatever investor emerged. This set the tone for a deal that would happen late in the year.

It happens that I arrived in New York later that day to pitch Pennsylvania to some big money interests. Ken Jarin, a prominent Philadelphia lawyer with Wall Street connections, took me to visit key officials at Merrill Lynch, Goldman Sachs, and Lehman Brothers. I had the sense that they were assessing whether the state was secure with its interim governor. I must have passed the test because our bond rating never faltered, and some important bond issues came to fruition soon after those discussions.

Governor Casey called at the end of June. His voice was remarkably strong and he was upbeat. The conversation was personal and pleasant. I wanted to convey that we were all proud of his courageous battle for life, and he made it clear that he was pleased with my performance so far. He said he had "complete trust" in my judgment and left the conversation with a hearty "carry on." Just what the doctor ordered—for both of us.

At this point, even the press started developing a comfort level with the situation. So much so that at least one article took on a whimsical tone. Bob Zausner of the *Philadelphia Inquirer* wrote:

"An unusual thing happened earlier this week when Lt. Gov. Mark S. Singel held a news conference. Reporters showed up."

He went on to recount an incident after a speech at a Pittsburgh hotel—before I had become acting governor:

"He (Singel) rushed from a hotel and told his driver, 'Quick, to the airport.'

"The driver stepped on the gas and sped away from the curb in an instant. There was only one problem—he forgot Singel. The driver realized his mistake and returned for the laughing lieutenant governor after circling the block.

"But that hasn't happened recently.

"'The difference between lieutenant governor and acting governor is that you're not left at the curb,' said Singel."

While we were all adjusting to new routines in Pennsylvania, *Jurassic Park* was setting box office records; a Yale professor opened a package from the Unabomber and lost sight in one eye, hearing in one ear, and part of his right hand; and the United States launched a missile attack against the Iraqi Secret Service in retaliation for a thwarted assassination attempt against former President George H.W. Bush.

JULY

Just before the Independence Day holiday, we announced a major jobs initiative for Pittsburgh. At the announcement we also sent a signal that the state was running smoothly. So far, so good.

On Monday, July 5, I spent my morning at the PA Association for the Blind. I was recording some newspaper articles and other items on tape to be distributed to the blind community. This was the latest in a long string of volunteer events that was arranged for me by my staff. The idea was to do more than talk about public service; to actually roll my sleeves up once in a while. I had volunteered at soup kitchens, homeless shelters, blood drives, and other activities all over the state. I was only mildly interested in Operation Real World when my team concocted it, but I must say it broadened my perspectives quite a bit. I actually enjoyed the activities but, lately, found less and less time for them.

The state's chief information officer, Dick Walsh, met me at the office with General Counsel Dick Spiegelman and Legislative Counsel Dave Barasch. The topic was the recently passed legislation deregulating the telecommunications industry. This was a landmark bill that would bring us into the brave new world of cellular phones and something called the Internet. I had supported the legislation and agreed to sign it, making Pennsylvania a leader in this telecommunications revolution.

One more important item on the schedule that day: the bachelor party for my trusted aide, Joe Powers. Joe was already in his late thirties and had finally settled on the perfect mate. It was only fair that his close buddies toasted him at one of the Harrisburg haunts.

We launched a bill signing tour for SB 52, the Key 93 bill that would refinance the commonwealth's parks and environmental assets. It was a $100 million bond issue that had bipartisan support. In fact, the first event occurred in Ridley Park in the district of Senator Joe Loeper (R-Delaware County), a key author of the bill. I may have taken more than my share of arrows on the Senate floor,

126

but Joe was rarely one of the archers. He and I had a strong friend-ship then and now.

The bill was a giant step forward in preserving our natural re-sources, but it had a catch. It contained a requirement for a public referendum. Having been burned on a similar process relating to property tax reform, I was taking no chances with this one. We scheduled a series of events in some of Pennsylvania's most pris-tine areas to urge people to approve the Key 93 referendum. I was able to take the lead on a truly good cause, and it didn't hurt to hit all of the media markets on the adventure.

In Philadelphia later that day, I talked about the bill and a host of other topics on WPVI's *Issues and Answers* program. I also dropped by a key supporter's downtown office for a reality check on state politics.

Bill Batoff was one of the most interesting characters on the Philadelphia scene. Extremely well connected, he was able to shake the contribution trees of both Democrats and Republicans. He en-joyed politics at all levels and insisted on a personal relationship with his candidates before throwing himself into their cause. He was quirky and a little bit of a hypochondriac, but he was without question one of the most sincere and loyal supporters I have ever known. Governor Casey had introduced me to Bill back in the 1986 campaign. I liked him from that point on.

Today's encounter was a little different. Bill said that there was something different about me, and I knew what he was talking about. It had been less than a month, but I felt the weight and the exhilaration of actually being the governor. Bill sensed that and had some thoughtful observations about how to handle the weeks ahead and a possible campaign of my own.

And he had one request—a title. Bill wanted to know that he would continue to be one of the key go-to guys in my campaign, a role that he had played for Casey over the years.

It was premature to be making any campaign announcements I told him, but that didn't stop us from coming up with the proper term of endearment. After kicking around several possibilities, I suggested an odd but appropriate soubriquet: the viceroy! From that day on, I addressed him publicly and privately as the viceroy, and we both loved it.

My political world experienced a tremor the next day.

Jim Cunningham flew in with several binders of opposition re-search—on me. We had agreed earlier that we would spend some money to do whatever digging was necessary to expose any weaknesses that could arise in a gubernatorial campaign. From 9:00 a.m. to 1:00 p.m. on that July 7, Jackie and I sat through an ordeal that included bad votes, dumb statements, financial details, negative press clips, and just plain nasty rumors that the research team had uncovered. The material was presented like it was coming from my worst enemy or a rabid opponent. It made us both squirm.

Still, there was nothing criminal in those binders, and after we caught our collective breath, we decided that we could face whatever the opposition could throw at us. While we were still months away from any announcements, the private decision to run for governor was made.

Cunningham also laid out the fund-raising plan. His team was already scouring through lists of my family, friends, contacts, associates, lobbyists, and organizations in order to construct targets for an aggressive fund-raising effort that would begin on August 1. On that date, he warned that I would have to be obsessive about dialing for dollars in the call room. He was going to, in his words, strap me on that bronco and make me ride until my saddle was worn through.

I was thinking about the intense schedule that I was already keeping and assuming that this was just the pep talk that he gave to all his clients. I was wrong. By the end of the year, I logged more hours in that saddle than I can count.

Joe Powers and Joyce McCullough were married on July 10, 1993. Jackie and I were honored to attend the festivities and to unwind with a happy couple on a pleasant afternoon. We didn't get too many of those days.

The second week in July began with a continuation of the campaign for Key 93. I would be signing HB 52 three more times in an effort to bring voters on board. Presque Isle State Park, on the shores of Lake Erie, was a beautiful and appropriate location for the pitch. Local folks have said that Erie has two seasons: Winter and the Fourth of July. Well, this particular summer day was gorgeous and the event was well received.

There was something else noteworthy about this trip. Terry Way, the governor's official photographer, was on board; and he would accompany me on flights and in cars for many such events in the coming weeks. This was not just my staff looking for ways to build my public persona; it was also a new requirement by the fourth estate to actually chronicle my activities. It seems that my pronouncements actually mattered—a different reality for me. On a more lugubrious note, I remember hanging out with the press during the presidential campaign of 1992. On a tarmac at the Wilkes-Barre/Scranton airport I wondered why so many photographers and videographers caught every word and gesture of the candidate and continued filming as the plane sped down the runway, went wheels up, and disappeared from sight. A grizzled cameraman told me the truth: "We're all waiting for the 'death shot.'"

It seems that plane crashes and assassination attempts make great footage.

Terry Way was not looking for a Pulitzer Prize. In fact, we had a close friendship and some interesting shared memories. Here's one story:

In August of 1988, a delegation of Pennsylvania office holders and political leaders convened in Atlanta for the Democratic National Convention. This was Michael Dukakis vs. George H.W. Bush, and we were all touting the Massachusetts Miracle and the Dukakis candidacy. Governor Casey had a prominent speaking spot in prime time, and the Pennsylvania delegation was ready to root for their first term governor.

One enterprising operative took it upon himself to stack the Pennsylvania section of the Staples Center with folks by way of some authentic looking fake credentials. There was clearly something amiss when the seats, the aisles, and a chunk of the balcony had enough "delegates" in them for *two* states. The credentials forger forgot two things:

First, there were holographic markings on the real credentials that would clearly show the difference between fakes and the genuine article if the ushers took a close look. Secondly, it was a federal crime to make or use such fake credentials.

Terry Way was one of the recipients of the phony passes, along with about 20 others who were promptly rounded up by the Secret Service and held in a detention room under the grandstands. I got wind of the fact that several county commissioners, state representatives, and wives were about to be charged and whisked away to some Atlanta magistrate, and so I hurried down to the holding room. While Governor Casey was talking about Democratic values and the Massachusetts Miracle, I was trying to keep Terry and some pretty prominent Pennsylvanians out of jail.

Fortunately, the Georgia State Police and the Secret Service looked gently upon our political exuberance. We agreed to send the trespassers back to their hotels and consider the matter closed.

Now, in July of 1993, I often reminded Terry that I saved him from his "life of crime." Or I just chanted "Free Terry Way" at every opportunity. He was a great photographer and an even better sport.

The Presque Isle event continued the drumbeat for voter approval of our environmental funding program. I also took some time to connect with a local prominent banker who served on the Penn State board with me. Ted Junker of PNC bank was a solid, active Erie citizen who took his obligations to his customers, his employer, and his community seriously. He also had a very active sense of civic involvement, and I was honored to consider him a friend. The problem was that he was a staunch Republican, and I knew that it would always be a tough sell to get his vote! (I never did.) It really didn't matter, though. It was enough for me to know that we could be candid and friendly with each other. I sought to have that kind of relationship with a number of my Republican associates.

The trip also featured visits to Mercyhurst College and the Lord Corporation as well as a late lunch with State Representative Linda Bebko-Jones—LBJ to her many friends.

A key Democratic player in Erie at that time was Attorney Don Wright. He had arranged a meeting with some possible contributors. I knew that my status had risen dramatically when I found out that the meeting was to take place on a yacht. We cruised Lake Erie for an hour in what was a very pleasant intermission from my official responsibilities.

It seems that trade associations and key stakeholders in Pennsylvania needed affirmation that their interests were safe with the interim administration. I knew these folks previously so I thought it was strange that the chemistry of the meetings was noticeably different. Larry Light from the PA Medical Society stopped by the next day with some concerns about the department of health; Matt Steck, representing the architects, needed to make sure I showed up at a design competition event. Bill Titelman of the PA Bar Association needed to gauge my feelings on several issues. Ed Keller from AFSCME needed to report to state workers that I was still "a friend." Even my erstwhile golfing buddy, Bill Greenlee, presented a new client to me with a deference that I found unusual.

On Wednesday, we were back on the state plane to Pittsburgh.

An event at a vocational rehabilitation center was a backdrop for the release of statewide retraining funding. I had planned to visit with the governor at Presbyterian Hospital, but he was just not ready for visitors.

We went on to the Babst Calland law firm where two very close friends, Ron Frank and Ted Wesolowski (the latter an old fraternity brother of mine), introduced me to their colleagues. While we talked only policy, they were likely aware that the visit would be followed up with a fund-raising request at a more appropriate time.

The Education Commission for the States was holding its national convention in Pittsburgh, and I had the honor of making the introductory remarks as the host governor.

"A good week," I remarked on the plane ride home. Then the state trooper with me reminded me that it was only Wednesday.

Following a day that saw me back at the Board of Pardons and signing off on more official transactions, we embarked on another cross-state adventure that included remarks in Pittsburgh, a mock bill signing in Somerset County, a PennDOT highway dedication in the Poconos, an editorial board meeting with the *Pocono Record*, and dinner with some potential supporters at a wonderful Italian restaurant called Peppes in East Stroudsburg.

My wife and children met me at Shawnee-on-Delaware, a beautiful resort at the Delaware Water Gap, to get set for a family outing. We attended the Pocono 500 as the guests of the chamber of commerce, and I actually had the privilege of calling out "Gentlemen, start your engines!" to 50 race car drivers and 100,000 fans.

On the way back from the Poconos, I arrived in time to give a luncheon speech to the PA Pharmaceutical Association. When we all got back to Indiantown Gap, we hosted a Sunday reception for Jackie's alma mater, Albright College.

While we were mixing some truly interesting and enjoyable events with the official schedule, the reality is that actual downtime was non-existent.

The next week I was back at the desk and amid another batch of paperwork. While most required only a signature from me, the documents all mattered deeply to individuals and organizations. I took that responsibility seriously and made sure that I was comfortable with the pronouncements that went out under my name.

On Tuesday, I spoke with the PA Commission for Women and then met a host of legislators and key Pennsylvania business leaders for the signing of SB 1, the workers' compensation reform bill. Labor was still grousing a bit about some of the cost reductions, but the business community and most observers knew that the changes would make it considerably easier to do business in Pennsylvania.

In a little media dust up, I was criticized for sending the state plane to deliver Senator Mellow to the ceremony in the rotunda of the Capitol. Since Mellow was the coauthor of the bill along with Senator Roger Madigan of Williamsport, I felt that the significance of their presence outweighed the cost. I insisted that both of them— and a host of other key actors—witness the landmark occasion.

Just before signing the bill, I noted that the requirements in the bill would not only hold down any immediate premium increases but that I was expecting to see some reductions in companies' workers' compensation policies. The experts expected between $200 and $350 million in cost savings, and I believed that we had ushered in an era of rational labor/management policy making. I also noted that we expected the insurance industry to do its part by keeping rates low. We would soon revisit that issue.

The next day and the balance of the week were dedicated to some Philadelphia commitments.

After a breakfast at the Pyramid Club with some heavy hitters and a visit to the Scott Paper Company, I arrived at the Franklin Institute to announce the restructuring of the State Planning Commission. My idea was to reshape it both in membership and in structure to highlight issues that would have an impact on Pennsylvania's future. And what better way to roll out the idea than under the watchful eyes of Ben Franklin, Pennsylvania's original futurist. This was an opportunity to feature some of the efforts that I had started or participated in as lieutenant governor and to pencil myself in as a key player. The Pennsylvania Futures Council was really an outgrowth of the Future Focus groups that I had established in all parts of the state. This would make that orientation and my participation official state policy.

The idea was to make sure that, upon Governor Casey's return, I would not go back to cutting ribbons and attending funerals. It may have been a bit bold to issue an executive order that seemed little self-serving, but I felt strongly that I could and should continue to shape policy in some fashion, whether it was in the final year of being lieutenant governor or working with the new Futures Council as governor in my own right.

There was some mumbling from the staff in the front office about the executive order, and we were not at all certain that it would continue when Governor Casey returned.

Two important meetings that followed were with John Elliott, the dashing senior partner of Elliott, Vanaskie & Riley. John was a close friend and counselor to Governor Casey, and he was gracious to and supportive of me during this unusual time. He was a great example of a Casey loyalist who was not afraid to give full-throated support to my acting governorship. He understood completely that I was exercising the powers of the governor while trying not to antagonize the man.

I also stopped by to visit Ralph Roberts, the head of a large and growing communications firm called Comcast. He, too, was the epitome of style and competence. It was a pleasure being in his company.

It was only fitting that I would end the week with a swing through the opposite side of the state.

Southwest PA was a bastion of Democrats who hearkened back to the days of Franklin Roosevelt. These were blue collar folks who believed strongly that government was on their side. They had not yet been seduced by the Reagan era spin that government was inherently bad and that, somehow, by securing the wealth of the rich, benefits would trickle down to them. It would take a few more elections and the constant pounding on right wing drums to turn southwest PA from blue to red.

In 1993, though, strong Democratic majorities at the county level meant that commissioners and party chairs called the political shots. It was important to maintain friendships with them. Commissioner Frank Mascara in Washington County, Commissioner Fred Lebder in Fayette County, and Commissioner Ted Simon in Westmoreland County were solid supporters and close friends. I could not have felt more welcome in their offices than if had I been in my own living room. After some courthouse walk-throughs and two interviews at local newspapers, I found myself at the *Greensburg Tribune Review* for a visit from their editorial board.

Did I say visit? With the *Greensburg Tribune Review*, it always was more of a grilling. Part of the reason for the rightward drift that was already in progress in southwestern PA was because this newspaper was unabashed in its right-wing editorializing, and readers were fed a constant diet of anti-Democratic screeds.

Too harsh? Consider my first encounter with the *Trib*. It was in October of 1980, and I was running for the 35th Senate district. A small portion of that district spilled into Westmoreland County, and it was necessary for me to present myself to their editors and writers. In a wide-ranging interview we covered everything from education funding to local sewage ordinances. They were also pressing me on the big ticket race that year: Ronald Reagan versus President Jimmy Carter. Of course I supported my party's president, but my philosophies then and now were moderate with a compulsion to find progress even on the thorniest issues. While I was no "supply-sider," I was not for excessive taxes or wasteful spending in the public sector. I left the session feeling like I acquitted myself well.

Days later, the *Tribune Review* gave my opponent a ringing endorsement. In fact, it made a point of tossing in some verbiage that was sure to find its way into campaign ads. One of the suggestions made was that I had "socialistic tendencies."

It was so over the top that I called the editor on it. Paul Heyworth had been fair to me prior to and during the editorial board meeting.

"What happened?" I asked him.

"Well, let me put it this way," said Paul. "The good news is that the vote on the endorsement actually was 5 to 1 for you. The bad news is that Dick Scaife was the one no vote."

Richard Scaife was the publisher and an absolute Republican stalwart both locally and nationally. There was no way that his paper was going to support a 26-year-old Democrat! Lesson learned.

Anyway, this editorial board meeting, 13 years later, was further evidence of how my world had changed. There was no political agenda, there was no luring me into questions to betray my alleged Marxist inclinations. There was, instead, a genuine concern for Governor Casey's health and a legitimate interest in the course we were setting in his absence. It was good stuff—and a redemption of sorts.

The next day, I completed my swing of county fiefdoms with a visit to the Butler County commissioners.

Before leaving the Pittsburgh area, though, I was able to spend a little time with Art Rooney, a key leader of his own law firm and the son of the legendary Dan Rooney, owner of the Pittsburgh Steelers. Art was a class act and someone who would have succeeded in the political arena if he had chosen that course. Art, in fact, had been approached in 1991 by Governor Casey about filling the seat of former US Senator John Heinz. He would have been an outstanding senator.

I also met with the colorful and vibrant Lefty Palm. Lefty had worked his way up to the state presidency of the United Steelworkers of America. He had been in my corner from my first campaign, and I had come to think of him as family. Lefty had asked for a meeting to discuss the pending sale of a Johnstown steel facility. The steelworkers had already rejected the terms offered by an Asian company and were wondering if it was worth waiting for a better offer. Andy Greenberg, our secretary of commerce, had come in for the meeting. He brought along Joy Pooler, one of the state's best economic development experts, and the four of us discussed the high stakes involved: Rejecting the offer was already putting thousands of steelworkers at risk of unemployment. Accepting it would have put those workers in a substantially weaker financial position—anathema to a proud union whose purpose was to seek more, not less, for their workers.

We left the meeting agreeing to search for a better deal from a new investor. It was the best we could do at that moment, but I had a feeling it was not the last development we would have on the matter.

Weekends were always crammed with official and personal events. This one was no exception.

We were on a Saturday road trip to Hazelton for breakfast with key legislators from Luzerne County. I was also there to welcome a friend of mine from the great state of Virginia to a Korean War veterans' event. L. Douglas Wilder, the governor of Virginia, had been invited by a friend to keynote the event. My role was to introduce him.

Wilder and I had become close during our time as lieutenant governors. We, in fact, joined in some press activities and diversions at the otherwise staid National Conference of Lieutenant Governors. I recall with fondness riding through the streets of Des Moines at one such conference with a trolley full of lieutenant governors chanting: "We're number two! We're number two!" Anyway, it was great to see him again. A few years earlier I had watched with pride as he was elected as Virginia's first African American governor.

I got home in time to host the local chapter of the Penn State Alumni Association at my residence at Indiantown Gap. Always an enjoyable group.

Sunday was equally enjoyable. We took the kids to the small chapel on the base for what they called "cookie Mass." The Army priest always had a plate of cookies for children who behaved during the service.

Jackie and I then hopped back in the car for a fund-raising visit at the home of Richard A. Sand. Richard was the principal in his own law firm and lived just outside of Philadelphia. He was also a renaissance man who wrote mystery novels, collected autographed memorabilia, and mastered Tae Kwan Do. I found him to be engaging, intelligent, and strongly supportive of me. I could depend on Richard to organize events, cajole contributions from heavy hitters, and give me candid feedback on issues and tactics. He was so effective in all of these tasks that he won the sobriquet "the general." He would remain a key operative for years to come.

In the hottest week of the summer, our office was focused, oddly, on snow.

That is, the federal government had come through with their reimbursements for recovery from the January blizzard. I had played a role in declaring the emergency six months prior to that, and it was rewarding to actually dispense some checks to municipalities throughout the state.

Things were heating up a bit on the political front, too.

This marked the first week that we began a regimen of phone calls from the campaign office. Jim Cunningham and his team had successfully pulled together 26 binders (one for each letter of the alphabet) of potential contributors based on previous campaigns, assorted lists, and personal contacts. It fell to L.A. Harris and a young associate by the name of Jeff Hewitt to hog-tie me and keep me locked into dial-for-dollars mode for as long as they could. Given the other demands on my time, we started with what I thought was an ambitious three hours per day on this chore. I would soon find out that it required much more time than that.

We plunged into what became known as the "No Liars" system of fund-raising. It worked like this:

Jeff would pull out a target sheet from the A binder. The target—say Mr. John Adams—would be listed with all pertinent information: business address, home address, office phone, cell phone, fax number, and the suggested amount that I was to request. My pitch was simple, but the wording was important.

After 30 seconds or so of the "Why I'm running for governor" rationale, I plunged right into:

"May I count on you to contribute $1,000?" If that encountered resistance, I could fall back to:

"May I count on you to try to contribute $1,000?" If there was any hesitancy, I could lower the amount or ask:

"May I count on you to raise $ 1,000?" Thereby giving the target the "out" of reaching out to others for the amount. If that was not successful, there was one more level to the ask:

"May I count on you to *try* to raise $1,000?"

After securing a commitment to one of those requests, the staff took my handwritten letter that repeated exactly what had been agreed to and faxed it to the target with my gratitude. The same letter was dropped in the mail serving as a friendly nudge in the next few days.

If we did not receive a check within 10 days, a second letter went out.

Note that we did not have access to the internet or to an efficient e-mail system in 1993. The fax machine was the quickest way to get messages out.

Anyway, it did not take long to ascertain whether the monetary commitment was real. We either got a check or, after the third or fourth contact, the target sheet was placed in a "call later" binder. We were not about to let anybody off the hook!

Our target was to achieve 40 commitments in a day. This meant an average of five per hour in a full eight hour day. We had to place about 30 calls per hour to successfully reach five.

The campaign staff was determined to strap me into the call room; the official staff tried to cooperate but had to drag me back when duty called. The tug-of-war for my time had begun.

I was able to break away from the call room for the summer ritual of the Big 33 Game. This was a football game that pitted the best high school athletes in Pennsylvania against the always formidable Ohio team. Many of these athletes went on to successful college and pro careers, and it was a welcome break in the heat of political and official activities.

Another event was the annual picnic at Montage Mountain for State Senator Bob Mellow. Few events were as well organized or as well attended as this one. Bob positioned himself at the entrance to a huge park just outside of Scranton and welcomed about 1,500 paid guests to a good old-fashioned picnic. The event included great food, free flowing beer, and oldies music from one of my favorite bands, the Poets. Mellow and I were known to take the stage for an occasional rendition of "Teenager in Love" or "Unchained Melody." Great fun.

There were, of course official events. A visit to Williamsport meeting with local editors; an interview with Kit Seelye of the

Philadelphia Inquirer on current issues (Kit was an excellent writer who went on to the *New York Times*), and a presentation to the US Steelworkers of America, among others.

No rest for the weary, though. I was back in the call room for most of the week; our mission was to get $250,000 in commitments and at least some cash flow at the outset of the campaign effort. By the end of the week, we had surpassed $350,000 in pledges.

Mark Singel, 1962

Mark Singel, 1964

Mark (far left) as a page to PA State Rep. John Murtha, 1970

High School graduation photos, 1971

Legislative intern in
Harrisburg, 1973

Congresswoman Helen Meyner and President Jimmy Carter, 1977

The famous Sen. Bob Mellow summer picnic at Montage, 1983

Going to vote in Johnstown, PA, 1986

Archbishop Stephen Kocisko, Bishop Michael Edward Bullock
inauguration, 1987

Lt. Gov. Mark Singel, right, takes a break during the governor's tour of the Pennsylvania State Farm Show to share a chocolate milk shake with his son Jonathan, 9.

Casey, Singel share spotlight at opening of 78th Farm Show

Lt. Gov. Elect Mark Singel retrieving M&Ms in the Governor's office, 1987

On the campaign trail with Jackie

Phoenixville Democratic Committee Clambake, August 1987

Groundbreaking for the Harrisburg Hilton, 1988

Family at Indiantown Gap, 1988

With Lt. Gov. Derek Hodge, St. John, U.S.V.I.

Governor's residence, 1988

The Pennsylvania State University Board of Trustees, May 1988

Bill signing for expanding volunteer fire services programs with
Casey and Joe LaFleur

Capital for a Day, November 1988

Singel Chairing the PA Emergency Management Council

Capital for a day in Johnstown

Mark and Jackie, 1989

With David McCollugh at the Centennial of the Johnstown Flood, 1989

Original Senate staff: Joe Powers, Veronica Varga, Patti Heckman,
Greg Youra, Jean Brannon

Day after election, November 1990

Act 63 Telecommunications bill signing

Mark, Jonathan, Allyson, Christopher, and Jackie, 1990

Mark with Mayor Ted Kollek in Jerusalem, 1991

Singels and Caseys, 1991

With Sen. Bob Jubelirer at the Raystown Hydroelectric Project, 1992

On the trail with Bill Clinton and Al Gore, 1992

With Bill Clinton, 1992

With U.S. Senator Ted Kennedy

With Joe LaFleur announcing Emergency Management Actions

With friendly adversaries: Billy Meehan - Philadelphia Republican
Chair, Andy Lewis - Rep. County Leader, and Fred Anton - PA
Manufacturers Association, October 1992

With Billy Joel and Jackie

Mayor Ed Rendell at 1992 U.S. Senate Announcement, 1992

Crosby, Stills, and Singel!

With Jim McNulty WARM Radio in Scranton

With Roberto Clemente's son, 1992

Family members with presidential candidate Bill Clinton, 1992

Coal agreement signing in Warsaw, Poland, 1993

Lt. governors at the White House, March 1993

Bill signing with Sen. Mike Dawida and Rep. Greg Fait

Official photo, 1993

With Secretary Andy Greenberg (Dept.of Commerce and Economic
Development) in London, April 1993

Bill signing with Secretary Don Carroll (Education), Secretary Karen
Miller (Dept. of Community Affairs), and Secretary Art Davis (Dept.
of Environmental Resources)

With Jonathan, Allyson, and Christopher at the Pocono Raceway, June 1993

With Chairman of Bethlehem Steel Curtis "Hank" Barnette and President,
USWA – PA Chapter

Bill signing in Scranton with St. Senator Bob Mellow and Lackawanna County Commissioner Ray Alberigi

Inpromptu press conference between events (Trooper Bob Schott), June 1993

Bill signing, July 1993

Typical press swarm in Pittsburgh, June 1993

Acting Govenor, June 1993

Lt. Gov. Singel with Jackie and supporters: U.S. Reps Bob Borski,
John Murtha, Paul Kanjorski, and Richard Gephardt

Big 33 pose, July 1993

With DER Secretary Art Davis and Mayor Sophie Masloff in Pittsburgh,
July 1993

With President Clinton and State Senator Ed Zemprelli, 1993

Signing the Telecommunications Reform Bill - Act 63, July 1993

With the graduating class of the PA State Police

Bill signing with Secretary Art Davis (DER) and State Rep. Bill Lloyd
(Somerset County)

Acting governor with young supporters of "Key 93"

With Gov. Roy Roemer (CO) at National Education Summit in Pittsburgh,
July 1993

At Cameron Run State Park supporting Key 93, July 1993

Workers' Comp signing with Secretary Tom Foley (Dept. of Labor & Industry), Cindy Maleski (Commissioner of Insurance), Pat Beaty (Governor's Legislative Councel), Walt Carmo (Governor's Legislative Liaison), July 1993

Reports on visit to Casey at UPMC

Workers' Comp. - Seated (L-R): Sen. Roger Madigan, Sen. Mellow, Mark Singel, Rep. Ivan Itkin. Standing (L-R): Tom Foley (Labor & Industry), Cindy Maleski (Insurance), Sen. Barry Stout, Sen. Ray Musto, Rep. Mike Veon, Pat Beaty

At Presque Isle with Rep. Connie Maine of Crawford County and Rep. Bernie Dombrowski

With D.A. Lynne Abraham on the streets in Philadelphia, August 1993

With Johnny Cash

With Arnie Palmer

COMMONWEALTH OF PENNSYLVANIA

Date August 18, 1993

Pay to the order of — Allegheny County $ 272,307.00

Emergency Access
Snow Plowing

Mark S. Singel, Lt. (Acting) Governor

With Comm. Tom Foerster (Allegheny County), August 1993

With Governor Mike Dukakis in Gettysburg

At Ebensburg Cogneration plant news conference (presenting copy of
PA Energy policy for time capsule), August 1993

With Governor Evan Bayh at National Governors' Conference in Tulsa, OK,
August 1993

Signing Act 52 Environmental Preservation with Sen. Joe Loeper at
Ridley State Park

With Mayor Ed Rendell and V.P. Al Gore at U.S. Constitution Center,
September 1993

Chairing the Governor's Economic Development Partnership Board,
September 1993

First electric vehicle in Harrisburg, PA, September 1993

With Hall-of-famer Jack Ham, September 1993

Bringing home the bacon - the largest Pennvest grant/loan delivered to Mayor Pfuhl of Johnstown

With Joe Paterno

With childhood neighbor Louise Cavanaugh in Johnstown, 1994

With Gen. Barry McCaffery and Gen. William Lynch at Scotland School
for Veteran's children, 1994

USA Flight debriefing in Pittsburgh, 1994

Addressing the crowd with Bill Clinton and Ed Rendell, Philadelphia
City Hall, October 1994

With Hillary Clinton at the 1996 Convention

With Vice President Al and Tipper Gore, 1996

Post election, 1994

AUGUST

The following Monday, after a morning of phone calls, I had my usual meeting with Jim Brown and a string of rapid-fire meetings with folks interested in health care, energy, and education issues. I found myself getting better at focusing on their issues and asking them politely to keep on point. I didn't want to appear rude, but I simply needed to allocate time properly.

We had some unfinished business with the insurance industry as well.

Despite dramatic changes in safety requirements and other cost savings contained in the recently enacted workers' compensation reform bill, the first filing from an insurer to the public utility included a request for a 10% increase in their rates! I thought this was outrageous and said so at a well-publicized press conference. In my view, we had a deal that, in exchange for passage of the landmark bill, the industry would reduce their premiums by 10% or, at least, hold their rate request at 0%.

The Philadelphia Inquirer quoted me accurately:

"Two months ago, we struck a bargain. It's now up to the insurance companies across Pennsylvania to hold up their end of the deal."

It seemed to have the desired effect, and we avoided dramatic increases in premiums for the first time in years.

Tuesday, August 3 was mostly official business that involved 12 separate events in nine locations. Here is a glimpse at what we crammed into one day:

6:30   AM Depart Lt. Gov. Residence (Lt. Gov., PSP)
6:45   Arrive Indiantown Gap Airstrip, Depart 84PA (Lt. Gov., ERIC, Joe Cullen (Will Fly from Capitol City), PSP)
7:15   Arrive Washington National Airport, Signature Flight Services 703-549-8340 PSP – Arrange pick up

8:00	Arrive Capitol, House Dining Room, Washington, DC Breakfast with Congressman Tim Holden Use main entrance and ask for directions to dining room
8:45	Depart Capitol (Lt. Gov., PSP)
9:00	Arrive Governor's Washington Office, 444 N. Capitol Street NW, #700, Washington DC, Interview w/ Henry Stouffer – Pittsburgh Post Gazette 202-662-7075
9:30	Depart Gov. Office (Lt. Gov., PSP)
10:00	Arrive 2322 Rayburn Office Building, Press Event w/ Congressman Sharpe, Gov. Bayh, Gov. Boirnovich, RE: Interstate Trash Dumping, Contact: Earl Gohl
10:45	Arrive Old Executive Office Bldg., Room 115, Meeting with Joan Baggett (Political Director of the White House) PSP – Use Northwest Gate on W. Executive Avenue
11:15	Depart White House (Lt. Gov., Joe Cullen, PSP)
12:00	Arrive Washington National Airport, Depart 84 PA (Lt. Gov., Joe Cullen, PSP)
12:35	Arrive Philadelphia International Airport, Atlantic Aviation 215-492-2970 FYI – ERIC & Joe Cullen to return to Hbg.
1:00	Arrive Springfield Inn, 417 E. Baltimore Pike, Springfield, 215-543-9751 Lunch with Delaware Co. Labor Leaders Contact: Randy Canale 215-328-6286 PAT
2:00	Depart Springfield Inn (Lt. Gov., PSP)
2:30	Arrive SAB Engineering & Construction Inc., 464 S. Old Middletown Road, Media 215-565-3327, Meeting with Ashok Kheny PAT
3:15	Depart SAB Engineering (Lt. Gov., PSP)
3:30	Arrive Cohen, Shapiro Law Firm, PSFS Building, 12 S. 12th Street, Philadelphia, 922-1300, Contact: Andy Hillman, PAC Committee Meeting PAT/ELEANOR
4:30	Arrive State Office Building, 1400 Spring Garden Street, Phil., Interview w/ Moo Yu (Korean Newspaper), Contact: Marwin Kreidie ELEANOR
5:30	Depart State Office Building (Lt. Gov., PSP)
5:45	Arrive Teamsters Local 115, 2833 Cottman Avenue, Phil. 215-335-4600, Meeting with John Morris ELEANOR
7:00	Arrive Dilworth Inn, Old Wilmington Pike, West Chester 215-399-1390, FOMS Bill Lincke DIANE/PAT
8:30	Depart Dilworth Inn (Lt. Gov., PSP)

9:15	Arrive 6800 Block of Sprague Street, Mount Airy, Flashlight walk w/ Thelma Gaskins (Spague Street Neighbors) National Night Out Event ELEANOR
10:00	Arrive Andora Shopping Center, Cathedral Road (Just east of Ridge Ave) Andora Townwatch Unit, National Night Out ELEANOR
10:30	Depart Philadelphia (Lt. Gov., PSP)
11:00	Arrive Holiday Inn King of Prussia, 260 Goddard Blvd. King of Prussia, 215-265-7500 Rate: $69.00, Lt. Gov. & Trooper Conf. 68208405, R.O.N.

The reason for ending up at King of Prussia was so that I could attend the next day's funeral for the father of my assistant, John Lord. His father had been a prominent judge in Delaware County, and I admired him and his son very much.

This was followed by a trek back to Harrisburg and, of course, more time on the telephone. We were pounding away at our daily money goals, and the early responses were positive. By now I had gotten the pitch to 30-45 seconds, and I confidently took on the challenge to hit or exceed the five-commitments-per-hour goal. It was also becoming clear that the generally positive response I was getting in the media was helping with the fund-raising.

One headline in the *Altoona Mirror* was "Surprising Singel Making Points – Understudy prepping for his own run." In the body of the story was this sentence:

"Casey spokesman Vince Carocci praised the acting governor for handling the added pressure with grace and sensitivity, putting off his own political aspirations for the sake of smooth operations."

And this from Harrisburg's most quoted pundit, Dr. Terry Madonna of Millersville University:

"I think that most people think that he took over under very difficult circumstances and handled the job."

The *Pittsburgh Post Gazette* had its own take on the situation:

"Pee Wee's Big Adventure – Dennis B. Roddy watches as Mark Singel hones his act as governor."

Indeed, Dennis Roddy, a gifted and somewhat sardonic writer, had taken pen in hand and said:

"There have been bills to sign: workers' compensation reform on which Casey's will was previously known; a telecommunications act on which Casey had taken no stand. Into the mix of routine proclamations, Singel has tossed an occasional item with his own unique signature, such as an order to revive the old state planning commission under a new name. . . . Ready he was. After six years of searching for ways to matter to the state's electors, fate conferred on Singel the role of acting governor—a chance to try out the levers of power that imbues the post of lieutenant governor with a previously unimagined gravity."

And, in an odd column in the *Reading Eagle*, John Forester Jr. wrote:

"There has been some speculation this week that Gov. Robert P. Casey will resign, possibly as early as today, and turn the keys to the governor's mansion over to Lt. Gov. Mark S. Singel. . . . Of course, no one in Harrisburg officialdom would confirm the rumors."

What it meant was that my phone calls—even those that involved money—were now being returned. It is true that we were careful to keep the campaign activities under the radar screen, but the donors were following the news and it was having a beneficial effect.

Sometimes the schedule reflected appearances that were equal parts official and political. The Sheet Metal Workers in Pittsburgh had been big supporters of mine. It was a good time to reach out to them and solidify our friendship at their convention. I then was able to sneak in a fund-raising event at the Rivers Club with an old high school friend, Michael Zamagias. Michael was a self-made millionaire who was not afraid to take on bold development projects. His support was meaningful to me, and we kept in touch in the political and private worlds.

Lou and Dennis Astorino, the founders of a prestigious architectural firm in Pittsburgh, took me on a tour of their firm. They were very proud to display renderings of the new housing facility that they were building in Vatican City for the College of Cardinals. The firm had won a bid over a number of other concerns, and their mission was to construct something that was functional in the same surroundings that Michelangelo and da Vinci had adorned with their own artistry. I would often point to that endeavor as the kind of excellence to which Pennsylvanians should aspire.

From that uplifting event to the realities of the streets of Wilkinsburg. The mayor and community leaders were not focused on art; they just wanted to survive. Figuring out meaningful solutions to crime and drug use was just as much a part of my life as fund-raising and schmoozing.

The day ended with an address to the Allegheny County Medical Society and the short plane trip home.

Once again, there would be no day off because the campaign team had complained loudly about falling behind in call time. While weekend solicitations were a little less effective, we did some marathon planning over beers and burgers and moved the cause forward a bit.

I had already agreed to intensive call room time for the early part of the week of August 9.

This did not stop a stream of official interruptions. There were daily folders full of papers to sign and decisions to be made on extraditions, commendations, and fiscal matters. These were all carefully logged and distributed to the right agencies. During the summer, for example, there was an ongoing exchange with the White House and several federal agencies about policies and programs that affected Pennsylvania. Most of these were the culmination of truly outstanding research and writing from both the Casey and Singel staffs.

But it was important to fulfill the campaign requirements as well—particularly since I was about to embark on another adventure.

I had scheduled some much needed downtime with my sister, Joyce Dominguez, and her husband, Joe, in Denver. It turned out the president and the pope picked that exact time to join me! Actually, President Clinton had invited a number of governors to be on hand to greet the pope when he landed at Stapleton Airport. So, there I was, in a holding room with two of the most power leaders on the planet. Governor Roy Roemer of Colorado was cagey enough to throw his own party related to all of the international media attention and his own reelection plans.

Joyce and Joe joined Jackie and me for some serious VIP treatment at the Roemer event. I must say it was a gratifying moment when President Clinton, in his usual boisterous style, greeted me at the event:

"How's it goin', Mark?"

We talked for a while about Casey's health, the state of Pennsylvania politics, and a topic near and dear to him—the pending North American Free Trade Agreement (NAFTA) legislation. We agreed to continue that conversation at a later date. For now, he was the Schmoozer in Chief, and my sister and her husband loved it.

The Colorado trip resulted in one of my favorite news stories of the year. Here's what appeared in the Philadelphia Inquirer the next day:

It's a tough job, but . . . Singel gets to rub shoulders; with a pope and a president

By Robert Zausner
INQUIRER HARRISBURG BUREAU

HARRISBURG — in May, highlights on the schedule of Lt. Gov. Mark S. Singel included posing for pictures with Cindy Judd Hill, Ms. Pennsylvania Senior America 1993, attending a conference on recycling trash and joining Hempfield High School students at a seminar on government.

But now, holding the power of governor—and title of acting governor—while Gov. Casey recuperates from transplant surgery, Singel finds himself in the company of kings.

Well, not exactly kings. The Pope and the President.

Today, Singel will be in Denver when Pope John Paul II arrives for his U.S. visit and is greeted in a ceremony at Stapleton Airport by President Clinton, who invited governors to the event.

Not only that, but Singel also is invited to a VIP reception after the arrival, an event that may be attended by only about 50 people. That's elbow-rubbing distance from the Pope and the President.

The planned get-together happened sort of by coincidence. Since Singel was planning to attend the summer meeting of the National Governors' Association in Tulsa on Saturday, Aug. 21, he decided to head out west a few days early and stop in Denver.

But not to see the Pope or the President. He wanted to visit his sister, Joyce. It was not until after he had made his plans that Singel found out about the Pope and the President.

"We must have the same travel agent. It was uncanny timing my plane gets in at 11:30, the President lands at 1:30 and the Pope at 2:30," he said. "All l have to do is hang out at the airport for a while and meet some pretty important people."

Singel also plans to attend a fund-raising event for Colorado Gov. Roy Romer on Friday night in Denver.

And guess who the main speaker will be? Clinton.

In fact, since taking over temporarily for Casey, Singel said he had met with the President, as well as Hillary Rodham Clinton, on several occasions.

"I don't pretend that we're on a first-name basis," Singel said, then he thought a second and corrected himself. "Well, yes we are. He calls me Mark."

He did, however, note, "It's not like we're in the same bowling league or anything, but we have spent some time together."

Singel, though obviously enjoying his time in the limelight, did not want to comment on whether he thought it might benefit his expected candidacy for governor next year.

"I think it would be unseemly for me to comment on my own political fortunes. I'm just doing my job," he said.

He also said he planned to pay for his side trip to Denver out of his own pocket, even though he could probably get away with expensing a meet with the top government and religious brass.

After he leaves Denver, Singel will travel to Tulsa to attend the Governors' conference. There he's likely to see a familiar face as the main speaker at Monday's opening plenary session President Clinton.

Or Bill, to Mark Singel.

In fact, the next leg of the journey the following week was the National Governors' Association meeting in Tulsa, Oklahoma. I had spoken directly with the governor to get his thoughts on the conference. He thought it was a good idea for me to represent Pennsylvania, and he was especially interested in the current discussions about innovations in education. I told him that I would attend and gather whatever intelligence I could from his colleagues.

My name card had the longest title, "Acting Governor and Lt. Governor Mark S. Singel," but the governors greeted me as one of their own, and the entire conference staff treated us warmly. In addition to education, there seemed to be a focus on the things I was grappling with in Pennsylvania. I participated on panels relating to reinventing government, education, and health care.

The receptions and dinners were elaborate, and Jackie and I were able to reacquaint with leaders we had known on a different rung of the political ladder. Mel Carnahan of Missouri, Evan Bayh of Indiana, George Ryan of Illinois, Doug Wilder of Virginia, and others had been lieutenant governors. They all welcomed me to the big leagues even though mine was a temporary assignment.

I was comfortable in their company. It reassured me that the complications of this unusual year, the relentless fund-raising, and the occasional sniping from various camps might all be worth it someday.

By Tuesday, after my whirlwind with family, presidents, popes, and governors, I was back to the reality of the call room. The fundraising was interspersed with so many appearances and official functions that I was grateful that the legislature was off for the summer. I didn't have the added responsibility of refereeing the usual Senate donnybrook.

This week it was the PA Building and Construction Trades Convention in Hershey, a health care summit in the governor's reception room, some meetings with the federal department of energy on emergency planning (we had survived record snowstorms in the winter and were now in a record heat wave), and an array of financial matters with Budget Secretary Hershock. I still hadn't gotten used to moving millions and millions of dollars around with the stroke of a pen!

I also continued the pendulum-like swing between Pittsburgh and Philadelphia.

Commissioner Tom Foerster, the larger-than-life leader of Allegheny County, was sponsoring his annual Free Senior Citizens' Picnic. An event with huge media and political benefits, it was Tom's baby, and I was pleased to get invited to it. It didn't hurt that I brought an oversized check for several million dollars to defray some county costs related to the blizzard back in January.

On the eastern side, District Attorney Lynne Abraham asked me to walk north Philadelphia with her. While the staged press event focused on drug enforcement and gun policies, the street scenes were very real. Used heroin syringes and bullet casings were everywhere. Noises from boarded up tenements conjured up images of the wasted lives inside. There were whole blocks of poverty that seemed beyond recovery. I appreciated the dose of reality and made a public and personal commitment to help in some way.

That event was still in my mind when I met with David Boldt and the editorial board of the *Philadelphia Inquirer*. They were not looking for any breaking news. They were just interested in the "state of the state." I was grateful that I could let my guard down a bit and just give an honest assessment of how things were going.

Health care reform seemed to be the pressing topic the following week.

To say that the issue and the proposed solutions were complex would be a gross understatement. I had participated in at least two sessions conducted by First Lady Hillary Clinton herself, and today was a debriefing with four different cabinet secretaries on the subject: Secretary of Health Alan Noonan, Secretary of Education Don Carroll, Secretary of Welfare Karen Snider, and Commissioner Cindy Maleski (insurance). All of them were gifted administrators and leaders, but none of us had a clue as to how to proceed with a Pennsylvania version of health care reform. For now, we were all committed to some kind of program that would insure as many

Pennsylvanians as possible. That was the Clinton administration's goal as well, but it was clear that they were running into insurmountable hurdles at that moment. It was going to take much more research and thoughtful discussion.

This was also a good week to take advantage of a summer lull. Many of the Philadelphians were observing their annual summer ritual "down the shore." The legislature was not in session, and I was free to advance my own cause a bit.

This involved a ratcheting up of the cash calls and some interviews with potential campaign personnel.

Eric Schnurer arranged a meeting with Dane Strother of Strother Duffy—a big league campaign management and media firm out of Washington, DC.

Bill Batoff wanted me to meet Bob Schrum and David Doak, who were campaign operatives at the top of their game, and they made a strong pitch to run the Singel for Governor effort.

In the end, I went with Carl Struble and Tom Oppel of Struble Totten Communications. These guys showed me some very appealing ads, and I was impressed with their commitment to being hands on. The quality and the management of the media campaign that resulted was outstanding. I never regretted that decision.

Another tip of the hat to "General" Richard Sand and his law partner, Jonathan Saidel: I thoroughly appreciated the pleasant evening they arranged at a Philadelphia Phillies game and reception. It was a beautiful summer night among a lot of friends. Incidentally, we raised a tidy sum for the cause!

So, in the doldrums of a very hot summer, I had already put the pieces of a gubernatorial campaign into place and was well on my way to posting a big campaign fund number by the end of the year.

John Forester of the *Reading Eagle* was sniffing around the Capitol for rumors about Casey's impending resignation. He had already editorialized about the governor's slower-than-expected return and the forces that were building both for and against his reassuming power. It had gotten to the point that both Jim Brown and Eric Schnurer suggested that I hit the rumors head on.

In an interview in my office on the last Monday in August, I told him in no uncertain terms that the governor would be back. How did I know this? Because I, more than most, understood Casey's determination. The thing that kept him alive in June and kept him focused in August was the idea of his mission to take his seat back.

Was I offended or surprised by that? In no way.

Was it politically acceptable to me? It didn't matter. Casey was coming back; that was that.

When would the governor return? That, I really didn't know. My impression from our limited discussions was that his body was recovering from the equivalent of a train wreck. It was remarkable that he was functional at all. It did not seem unreasonable to me that it would take months for him to feel ready to return.

I think I was able to help put all the conspiratorial and political speculation to rest. But there were some lingering concerns that would begin to surface soon.

The press stories that week included a cautionary video that I sent out on the heat wave, an announcement of $3 million in funds for dislocated workers in Erie, and a new program for low interest loans to homeowners through the PA Housing Finance Agency.

A series of documents relating to various bond issues and other legal requirements was executed with the help of Casey's front line team: Jim Brown, Mike Hershock, and Pat Beaty. I was reminded just how effective and professional they had been throughout this strange interlude; any animosity or sniping from the Casey camp certainly wasn't coming from those three.

Department of General Services Secretary Dave Janetta joined me in a visit to crusty old Representative Camille "Bud" George's district to announce funding for a new prison in Clearfield County.

As we headed into the Labor Day weekend, I found myself with some duties that I can only describe as delightful. One such event was Saturday's Penn State football game against the Iowa Hawkeyes. Jackie and I had been attending games since we were college students, and this game was truly memorable.

Local radio and TV stations caught me coming and going to the press box. The Penn State radio network did a pregame interview with me and, believe it or not, we talked about football! I was escorted to the 50-yard line at the beginning of the game for the coin toss.

This was Penn State's first game in the Big 10 Conference. Iowa Governor Arne Carlson and I initiated the competition for the governor's trophy to be awarded annually to the victor of the PSU-Iowa game. It was especially gratifying to return to the field after the game to award the trophy to the mighty Nittany Lions.

On the way back to Harrisburg, we made a stop at Mike Aumiller's residence in Selinsgrove. Mike was a top staffer in the Pennsylvania Senate. He and his wife, Kathy, were friends long before and long after my stint as acting governor. Mike was celebrating his

40th birthday, and we joked that I would catch up to him when I reached that same age on September 12.

With all of the travel, call time, public exposure, and decisions that weighed heavily on me, there were rewarding moments like this for which I was truly grateful. We were working hard, and in my mind, governing well, and we were making some memories along the way.

PART THREE — THE MEANTIME

This is what the LORD says: "When seventy years are completed for Babylon, I will come to you and fulfill my good promise to bring you back to this place."

—Jeremiah 29:10

SEPTEMBER

On this Labor Day, Bill Peduto had arranged a schedule packed with Pittsburgh area activities.

First up, the traditional Labor Day parade. In Pittsburgh, this is a pretty big deal. Every aspiring politician wants the coveted invitation to walk alongside the union leaders who can help them with volunteers and financial resources. Your labor standing is directly related to your position in the parade. The banner that is carried directly behind the fleet of motorcycles at the very beginning of the parade proclaims: Pittsburgh Central Labor Council. Its president and other officers wave to the people alongside of their current champion. On this date, that champion happened to be me.

In fact, the relationship I had with labor across the state was more personal than political since my family worked in the steel mills, coal mines, and garment factories in Johnstown. The workingman's wages that my grandparents, uncles, and others received were earned in tough conditions over many years. It was natural for me to gravitate toward folks like George Becker of the Steelworkers Union, Rich Trumka of the UNWA, and John Wright of the Plumbers and Pipefitters.

One quick story about my labor friends. On the eve of the election in 1986, candidates Bob Casey and Mark Singel ended up in Scranton together. We were making our final pitch in Casey's hometown to a bank of television cameras on the local airport tarmac. Earlier in the campaign, in a rousing speech to union members in Philadelphia, I promised that, no matter what, I would make my own last appearance at their union hall.

I found myself sheepishly asking Bob Casey if I could borrow the rented plane for one last jaunt to Philadelphia. When I told him that it was to fulfill an obligation to a powerful union group he understood and sent me on my way.

I arrived at the union hall (which will remain nameless) to a rousing election eve rally. Beer was flowing, and hundreds of labor volunteers were already celebrating what they hoped would be a

Casey/Singel victory. As I was escorted into the hall, I couldn't help but notice thousands of political signs—the kind that hang on telephone poles—stacked from floor to ceiling. I also noticed that they weren't ours!

"You know," I said to my host, "you guys shouldn't be stealing the other guys' signs."

To which he replied in blunt Philadelphia labor-ese:

"Hey, we left the fucking poles up!"

Grabbing opponents' signs was, at best, inappropriate. But it was impressive to watch hundreds of activists whipped into action for causes they believed in. When labor leaders were able to focus that activism behind a candidate or a cause, (within ethical and legal boundaries, of course!) the results could be dramatic. I benefited from that surge of activism at various times in my career. I was grateful to have labor on my side.

In 1993, the grand old man of labor in Pittsburgh was Paul Stackhouse. He could be tough as nails in a negotiation, but he was a gentle man who liked me and most people. Bruno Delana, the western PA AFSCME leader looked on me as a nephew, and I often called him "Uncle Bruno."

Stackhouse and Bruno walked me down Fifth Avenue in Pittsburgh that day.

Later, I spoke at a huge rally of working families at a park northwest of Pittsburgh and could not have been treated better.

The Pittsburgh swing drifted into Tuesday; I had been booked as the guest speaker for the 75th annual National Convention of the American Legion. This was followed by a short river cruise with another veterans group aboard the *Gateway Clipper*.

I topped off a truly enjoyable visit with union friends and veterans with the pleasant assignment of announcing a $52 million PA lottery winner at the Pittsburgh State Office building.

I knew that I would face more hours in the campaign call room in the very near future, but the Pittsburgh swing and the hope of continuing to have those kinds of days in the future seemed to make the fund-raising less onerous.

Indeed, we were ramping up fund-raising, and the notation "207 State Street—Telephone Time" started appearing on my schedule on a regular basis.

A string of meetings in my state office included cabinet officials, PEMA briefings, and some sensitive administrative discussions with the front office. Jim Brown, Jack Tighe, and Dick Spigelman were the "palace guard" for Governor Casey, and it was important that we were all on the same page.

Recent media speculation about the governor's intentions was rampant:

Would he return? Should he return? Was he healthy? Was Singel overstepping? Were we focusing on next year's budget? Were we planning for the legislature's return?

All of these and a variety of other sensitive items had begun to make these meetings a little more tense.

To make matters worse, there was growing editorial comment—including public opinion polls—that Casey should resign. While I was scrupulously careful about avoiding any such talk, the Casey team was aware of it, and they were not pleased. I was determined to manage all of the consternation and some egos without a public spectacle. The fact that there was so little discord reported between the Casey and Singel camps during this period shows that we were successful.

I even managed some personal time. My daughter, Allyson, received her first scholastic award from the local school board and I actually caught one of Jon's soccer games.

I also celebrated my 40th birthday on that Saturday night.

Turning 40 is a milestone in most peoples' lives. For me it was a revelation.

Family, politicians, staff, contributors, and some neighbors and friends filled the lieutenant governor's residence. Many brought presents (against strict instructions to the contrary), and most brought agendas. The family and friends had always been supportive and a pleasure to welcome. But who were all of these other people?

Yes, I knew them all, but many of them had never attended any political or personal function of mine before. They were there specifically to further their own cause or just to be seen.

It was clear to me that the next phase of my life, whether or not Casey returned, would be similar to this evening. It was like being onstage. I enjoyed performing, but I was painfully aware that the applause and the adulation of the crowd would disappear the moment someone with a better song or a stronger voice came along.

It had been a long three months, and I had methodically worked through endless discussions, news conferences, Senate sessions, staff meetings, and other official proceedings. What I needed right then was a little detachment.

I stepped outside into the pleasant evening to strum a few chords on my guitar.

The person who found me on the porch was my brother, David, who was also in no hurry to return to the buzz of conversations and clinking glassware inside.

David Singel had worked his way through his own political maelstrom. He often talked about the politics of academia in a way that struck me as being similar to electoral politics. He had undergraduate degrees in music and chemistry with a PhD from the University of Chicago. He taught at Harvard and did post-doctoral work at the University of The Hague. He had found a niche at the Montana State University heading their department of chemistry.

"You know, in the scheme of things, we really don't matter much," he said. "You might continue as governor, you might get elected governor, but there are things that you just can't control. There will always be hangers-on; there will always be enemies running you down."

"I get it," I said. "But there will also be destiny. Being in the right time and place to do some good. Like some chemistry breakthrough. Maybe we're both hanging in there to actually make a difference."

"Hey, it's possible," David said. "Israel and the PLO are about to sign a peace agreement. Anything can happen."

A moment of clarity was followed by a ritual of sorts—we sang a few tunes together. He is a choral music scholar and I am more of a Van Morrison man. I think we settled on Neil Young and spent some time back in our teens.

The two of us shared a room as boys. We couldn't help but be affected by each other's quirks and personalities. We were close in the awkward way that cats and dogs interact under the same roof—they have enough affection to tolerate their differences.

One of the things that we shared were intimations about our individual existences and our respective places on the planet. We were arrogant enough to think that we could matter someday; realistic enough to know that it would be a complicated journey.

Here's another odd revelation. I had a recurring dream that I was headed for an early death. In fact, at that birthday milestone, it was almost imminent.

In the dream, I was in a small airplane. I am sure that it was the twin engine Navajo that was maintained and operated by PennDOT.

While the pilots told me that it handled "like a brick" I preferred it to the larger King Air that carried ten or twelve more passengers. I always regarded the larger plane as the governor's; the Navajo was better suited to my needs.

Anyway, the dream was vivid. I was in my normal back right seat reading through some papers when a pilot announced, in a practiced, calm voice, that something was wrong. His job was to reassure, but I had already been through too many emergency situations not to detect the concern in his voice. We were going down.

Oddly, I wasn't sure where I was heading but I knew two things: I was on official business as the governor of Pennsylvania and that I was forty-three years old. That's right: I felt that I had been blessed (or cursed?) with the knowledge that I would die in the first term of the Singel administration.

This knowledge was never far from my mind. I believe that it was one of the reasons that I pursued my own political goals in such a hurry. It may have been unseemly to some that I was ambitious enough to reach for the next political rung unabashedly. I felt like I didn't have a choice.

This insight also helped clarify things for me in political and personal settings. While I was convinced that my time was limited, I was equally convinced that I had to follow the course I was on. In debates or other public settings I had a slightly crisper perspective knowing that I would have limited chances to make my points.

Most politicians have a phobia about looking past the next election. The idea is that the presumption of winning would jinx the outcome. I never let on to staff or family the reasons why, but I simply could not avoid contemplating the things that needed to be done in my compressed period of time. While the workload was heavy now, in would be more intense in the few years I felt I had left.

I understood completely what Governor Casey was feeling in terms of his own mortality. I really did hope and pray for his return so that I could focus on my remaining tasks at hand.

"Nice party," said Jim Brown when we met the following week.

"Did you know that Jack and Jackie Kennedy got married the day you were born?"

Indeed, I did know that.

"Did you know that President Kennedy died when he was forty-three?" I asked.

I could tell that he thought the factoid was a little odd.

In the world outside of Harrisburg, there was a momentous development. September 13, 1993, marked the announcement of the Oslo Accords, an Israeli-Palestinian peace agreement that followed extensive efforts by President Clinton and the Norwegian government. These kinds of developments gave context to the relatively trivial pursuits that occupied us at the state level.

Approaching forty-three and facing new challenges daily, I was certainly not about to dawdle. In fact, there had been some new rumors circulating about the governor's return, and that meant that the campaign team was winning the tug-of-war for my time. They wanted to exploit the "acting governor" title as much as possible.

The days ahead consisted of a continuous stream of campaign events, phone calls, and media events, interrupted occasionally by the realities of being the acting governor.

We started in Philadelphia at the Stradley Ronon law firm. Breakfast with smart, wealthy lawyers was always a good way to jump-start the week—especially if they were willing to write checks. The official functions included remarks at the Pennsylvania Technology Conference and presiding over the PA Economic Development Partnership Board. After a brief stop back in Harrisburg (courtesy of the Navajo shuttle) to tape a segment for the upcoming PA Firemen's convention, we were off to Scranton to visit another prestigious man of the law.

Bob Munley was the president of the PA Bar Association and a respected community and statewide figure. More important to me, he was one of those die-hard Casey confidants who also happened to believe in Mark Singel. Bob Munley and his entire family of lawyers and professionals welcomed me warmly and supported me without hesitation. In fact, in private moments, Bob and others like him shared some consternation about Casey's actions with me.

Where was Bob Casey?

Was he just not going to return?

Why wouldn't he just resign and let me jump-start the campaign as governor?

For those who knew Bob Casey well, those kinds of questions were clearly rhetorical. We all knew that sheer stubbornness would motivate Casey to fulfill what he believed was his calling.

Still, there was a growing list of supporters who believed that the governor had already made his point. He had survived a medical event of historical proportions. His impact on Pennsylvania history was clear. His major initiatives like PennVest, the Economic Development Partnership, and support for education would place him on a short list of outstanding PA leaders. But there was something else happening here—something related to Governor Casey's own perspectives about next political rungs, and it might just be that I was in the way. I really did not have the time to speculate on the governor's mindset, however. There were places to be and money to raise.

That trajectory was helped by some strong editorial support I was receiving at that time:

In an editorial entitled "Singel answers the call," the *Scranton Tribune* said:

"It must be noted as well that Acting Gov. Mark Singel has done a commendable job in Casey's absence, under difficult political circumstances. . . . He must be credited with being on top of the issues and knowing the political turf well enough to help fashion several compromises.

"He also faced the extremely difficult task of trying to honor Casey's agenda while following his own instincts—a tightwire act that he has performed quite well."

There was even some national attention from *USA Today*:

"Politicians in both parties say he's handled the awkward transitional period as acting governor with aplomb and benefited from the spotlight."

The next day I was whisked to the Laurel Valley Golf Club for an outing that reconnected me with key leaders from home. Sam Catanese, a CPA and the principal in his own firm and a great friend from my high school days, was the organizer. Somehow, I walked off with the medalist honors with the best score. I know that Sam is a better accountant than that!

The campaign team, of course, could not allow a pleasant day of golf to be our only activity. They parked me in the offices of another great friend to, what else?—make phone calls. We had gotten into the pattern of having at least one aide accompany me with a call book always at the ready. George Zamias, a successful developer, was more than happy to allow us to commandeer his phones.

I went to school with George's sons and got to know the whole family well. George had a great thirst for life and wasn't afraid to show his affections loudly. He was endearingly known as "the mad Greek" by the campaign team; I thought of the whole Zamias clan as my own extended family.

The rest of the week I bounced like a ping pong ball between official functions and campaign fund-raising events. Official events included some serious matters of state including the first review of revenue estimates for the current and coming fiscal years. Mike Hershock brought Deputy Secretary of Revenue Eileen McNulty along for the briefing. She, like Mike, had command over every facet of state spending and could tell exactly what the numbers meant. It was the beginning of what would be a first for Pennsylvania—we would construct two separate budgets. More on that later.

The campaign events ranged from County Democratic Committee keynotes to cocktail parties and dinners arranged by early supporters. These occurred in Huntingdon, Clinton, Jefferson, and Centre Counties. I never got too far away from Philadelphia, though.

The big event there was the celebration of the anniversary of the signing of the US Constitution. It was always a thrill for me to be at Independence Hall, especially with history buffs and true guardians of the most remarkable document in the history of government.

I also managed to indulge a more recently acquired taste: Philadelphia Eagles football. While Jackie and I remained die-hard Steelers fans, it was hard not to enjoy a game at Veterans' Stadium when we were treated like VIPs courtesy of our good friend Rick Welsh and his employer, Corestates Bank. The campaign gremlins, of course, insisted on two radio interviews and a private post-game event to make sure that I didn't take a whole Sunday off!

The annual Gridiron Show, like its national counterpart, the Press Association Dinner in Washington, is designed to allow politicos and pundits to poke fun at each other. I had been attending these events since I arrived in Harrisburg, and they were always light-hearted.

The unwritten rule was that the barbs and responses were confidential—not for the next day's newspapers. This allowed an uncharacteristic amount of candor and resulted in some unforgettable moments.

I remember laughing out loud to a stand-up routine delivered by the fastidiously reserved Dick Thornburgh. Philadelphia politicians were easy targets, and anybody who had some embarrassing moment during the year could expect it to be highlighted with abandon.

We set new standards for comic relief in the Casey/Singel era. While Bob Casey was indisposed in September of 1993, we had teamed up in previous years to do some funny stuff together. The very fact that Casey participated was remarkable given his own buttoned-down image. On these occasions he was determined to show his humorous side, and I was not above egging him on. In one skit, he showed that he could, literally, let his hair down. We had taped a parody of the popular *Saturday Night Live* skit "Wayne's World," with Casey as the long-haired Wayne and yours truly as his spacey sidekick, Garth.

The top ten list of "Babes of Harrisburg" was revealed with Casey's wife, Ellen, featured as "babe-a-licious" and "Babe ra ham Lincoln." At the appropriate time, Casey was encouraged to emphasize his own affections by giving the notorious "schwing" gesture with his hips. The normally dead-serious Bob Casey was hilarious when he attempted the move.

In fact, he was not a big fan of *SNL* and had no idea what the "schwing" meant. What was really funny was watching his son, Bob Jr., explain it to him at the dinner. I saw the governor turn bright red, and the edict went out the next day to confiscate all copies of the tapes. I, of course, purloined one and still smile when I view it.

This year's Gridiron Show had a decidedly more somber tone to it. The press did not feel comfortable jabbing Casey as he continued to recover from his surgery. Nor were they as acerbic toward me. We had a taped a segment that consisted of a few lame jokes and friendly shots at political adversaries, but it was nowhere near the raucous event it had been in the past.

I do remember getting in a shot at the ever-irascible Bob Jubelirer. I was talking about my visit to the National Governors' Association in Oklahoma and referred to Will Rogers:

"You know that Will Rogers is like the patron saint in Oklahoma. He's the guy who said, 'I never met a man I didn't like.' Will Rogers never met Bob Jubelirer!"

Bob was still on the warpath about the legislature's long absence from Harrisburg. His campaign focused directly on me and was now spilling out into the world of Republican activists. The Republican State Committee had issued buttons with the phrase "Where's Mark?" to emphasize the point. The Young Republicans, who staffed the Republican State Committee and represented the "next generation" of its leadership, carried milk cartons with my image, as in, have you seen this missing child?

Joe Serwach covered the antics for the *Harrisburg Patriot News*:

"Republicans mostly praise Casey, who can't seek reelection. But if they're ready to throw some barbs, they name Singel, Casey's lieutenant governor and designated stand-in . . . Robert Jubelirer has drawn the contrast the most starkly, referring to Casey as 'the real governor' . . . Attorney General Ernie Preate Jr., a near certain GOP gubernatorial candidate, called on Republicans to 'Send a message to Lt. Gov. Mark Singel, *acting* governor, President of the Senate and Lord and aspiring king!'"

I found it comical since I had spent the summer working in every corner of Pennsylvania. Not only was I visible, but I had probably been in their individual hometowns.

My own troops were loyal, though. I got a "Fortune's Up" the next week in the Harrisburg newspaper: "the acting governor's backers were all over the place at last weekend's Democratic State Committee meeting, wearing stickers saying 'I'm with Mark' and 'Every Singel vote counts.'"

Even the reporters and editors understood that Bob Jubelirer's professed indignation was completely self-serving. Convening before the November election date would mean a one-vote majority in the Senate and allow them to run roughshod over the progress that we had made in this strange interlude of governance. Worse, it would give majority power to all committee chairmen, and who knows what direction they would take?

I do not deny that holding the opposition at bay was political. But I submit that politics, in this, case, enabled us to proceed with good policy. And, yes, it also freed me to pursue my aggressive campaign schedule, which was already in full swing.

Still, there was a limit to the tolerance that both parties and the public had for the acting governor interregnum. Here is what we were starting to see in the press:

Kit Seelye wrote in the *Philadelphia Inquirer.*

"Few would argue that even if he (Singel) hasn't achieved star status he, he has skillfully parlayed his opportunity as acting governor to enormous political advantage. . . . While Singel said he and his senior staff consult with Casey's senior staff on governmental matters, he is more than an acting governor. . . . The newfound assertiveness hasn't gone unnoticed by the Casey team, which remains largely intact in the governor's suite of offices down the hall. 'The tension level is rising,' said one Capitol insider."

While the press speculated on front office politics, they were often unaware that there were always matters of importance looming.

At that moment, for example, President Clinton was personally lobbying key congressional delegations to support his North American Free Trade Agreements initiative. I had heard from several PA congressman who were getting pressure from labor to oppose the measure and others who were hearing arguments from agricultural groups to support it. It was one of those times when a governor's judgment regarding the impact of the bill on the state would matter.

I convened an extraordinary meeting in my office with Andy Greenberg (commerce), Boyd Wolff (agriculture), and Tom Foley (labor & industry) to explore all of the aspects of the proposed trade agreement and its impact on Pennsylvania. Boyd was strongly for it, based on the increased potential for the sale of PA agricultural products in Mexico and Canada. Tom was strongly opposed based on the anti-competitive posture in which it would place PA workers. Andy saw both sides of the argument but came down opposed, arguing that the short-term damage to steel and other heavy industry in the state would be devastating.

I agreed with the president that we were headed toward a global economy and that international trade agreements made sense. But not now; not for Pennsylvania. Having seen the Industrial Revolution turn into a rust belt right in front of my eyes in Johnstown, I could not support NAFTA.

Sure enough the president was on the phone later that day:

"Maaark," he said in that unmistakable Arkansas drawl. "I need your help on NAFTA."

We talked for a while, and he made his arguments. We also had some time to compare notes on recent political goings-on in the state. As always, I was impressed by the accuracy and the breadth of his information. I was committed to this man's reelection and wanted to maintain the friendship. He was surprised when I said:

"Sorry, Mr. President, I can't help you."

I gave him my reasons and told him that I was confident that the entire delegation would oppose the bill. He would have to get his votes from the states that would benefit like Texas, Oklahoma, and California.

Without missing a beat he said:

"Ah understand. That's what I thought you would say. Give my best to Jackie."

Remarkable, I thought. The president thought I might be malleable—even though he conceded that NAFTA might not work for Pennsylvania. When I stood my ground, he wasn't offended in the least. In fact, I seemed to score points with him.

I gave my guys some cover and, indeed, the delegation, with the exception of four Republicans, voted "no."

Another item of international interest was planning the commemoration of the 50th anniversary of D-Day and the eventual liberation of Paris in 1944. Pennsylvania's 28th Infantry Division led the column of American troops that marched down the Champs Elysees. It fell to me to approach the French government to allow a return visit of the 28th Division band and an honor platoon to participate in the 50th anniversary celebration of the liberation of Paris scheduled for August 24, 1994. That letter to His excellency Jacques Ambreani, the ambassador of France to the US, read, in part:

"Pennsylvania and the people of France have had a close relationship from the days of Benjamin Franklin, the first American ambassador to your country. . . . There have been many high points in that relationship. One that we Pennsylvanians treasure is the honor accorded by your government to our own 28th Infantry Division to lead the American forces down the Champs Elysees in August of 1944. That was a thrilling event for our troops everywhere, and a reenactment would be equally powerful."

The request was granted, and 150 servicemen and women would visit Paris the next year.

I was in Washington the next day discussing Pennsylvania's groundbreaking work in alternative power to the National Electric Transportation Coalition. Brian Castelli, an old friend and energy expert, along with Jan Freeman of the Pennsylvania Energy Office accompanied me. These two, along with a forward-thinking crew of idealists produced concepts and policies that were twenty years ahead of their time. The direction we had charted for Pennsylvania included electric cars; renewable sources like wind, solar, and water; and an emphasis on clean coal technologies. The idea was to take full advantage of the state's resources in an environmentally sound way. We were leading the nation in those efforts.

There was another direction that we had charted as well—a full deployment of natural gas. Cleaner, cheaper, and safer than petroleum-based products, I was convinced that natural gas was the immediate future for Pennsylvania. In fact, mine was the first vehicle in the state to run on compressed natural gas. We also installed natural gas in several bus and truck fleets to demonstrate its potential. This was twenty years before anybody was talking about something called the Marcellus and Utica Shale formations.

On September 21, 1993, I was able to do something truly extraordinary.

While the sniping from the Senate Republicans continued and while I was juggling the numerous responsibilities of being acting governor and lieutenant governor, I remained chairman of the Board of Pardons and chaired its monthly meetings. Today was unusual in that I was about to complete a task that the board had undertaken earlier. I was about to sign a commutation for a prisoner serving a life sentence for murder.

The case of Eddie Ryder was unique in that after twenty years in prison, there were lingering questions about his guilt. He was in Holmesburg Prison in 1973 on a petty theft conviction when a disturbance broke out that involved the killing of a Samuel Molten by Black Muslim inmates. Molten was killed in his cell by four inmates who were reacting to some form of disrespect that Molten had displayed. The four drew life sentences but two of them later said that Eddie Ryder was not involved. In the twenty years that followed, notables from Philadelphia like *Daily News* columnist Chuck Stone and Sheriff John Green came to Ryder's defense. Even former Mayor Frank Rizzo weighed in on Ryder's behalf.

In prison, Ryder earned his high school diploma, took a number of college courses, and taught himself to play jazz trumpet. Temple University thought so highly of his musical talents that they dedicated their renowned Philly Fest to him.

Eddie Ryder had lost hope when Casey stepped aside as governor. He thought he would have to wait until Casey returned to take up the 5-0 recommendation of the Board of Pardons. When it became clear that Casey's absence would drift well into the fall, I decided that certain things couldn't be put off—including letting Eddie Ryder play the trumpet as a free man. When Ryder heard the news of his commutation he said: "There's no doubt in my mind I'm going to be successful, because I know how now."

Here's what the *Philadelphia Inquirer* said in an editorial:

"While the Governor was hospitalized, Ryder languished in jail, where he's been trying to prove his innocence for twenty years. But in time, Mr. Casey's disability actually paved the way for Ryder's parole.

"Lt. Gov. Mark Singel had voted as a member of the pardons board to free Ryder in March. Standing in for Mr. Casey, Mr. Singel commuted Ryder's life sentence last week in what was a wise and humane use of his powers as acting governor."

On the other end of justice, I also signed the death warrant for Frederic Jacob Jermyn. He had been sentenced in 1986 for the murder of his own 81-year-old mother and had been on death row ever since.

Putting your name on a piece of paper that could end a man's life is not an easy thing to do. I made it clear that I was in no rush to sign death warrants but would fulfill my responsibilities under Pennsylvania law.

The official warrant to Joe Lehman, the secretary of corrections, read, in part:

"Now, therefore, this is to command, authorize, and require you, the said secretary of corrections or your successor in office, to cause the sentence of said Court of Common Pleas to be executed upon said Frederic J. Jermyn within the week beginning the sixth day of December, A.D. one thousand nine hundred and ninety-three, in the manner prescribed by the Act of the General Assembly (lethal injection) . . ."

It wasn't long for yet further legal challenges to complicate this case. In one odd twist, Frederic Jermyn was interviewed and used the peculiar defense that he couldn't be executed because the acting governor had died recently from complications related to syphilis. While I was alive and well, it became clear that Mr. Jermyn might have been less than stable. The courts intervened to stay the execution based on his questionable mental health. I felt a sense of relief under the circumstances.

Incredibly, I was sued by an aggressive district attorney from Northampton County for that compassion. D.A. John Morganelli felt that we should accelerate the signing of death warrants for the 166 other inmates facing a death sentence. Fortunately the courts agreed with me that, in matters of life and death, justice needed to be meted out with due deliberation and great care.

For the duration of the week, when I was not in the call room I was on the road at fund-raising events. My entire campaign team recited incessantly: If it wasn't money or media, it didn't matter.

Montgomery McCracken law firm and the viceroy, Bill Batoff, helped to shake some more dollars from the Philadelphia tree. Sam Becker, an old college buddy, lined up his law partners and brought them on board.

In Pittsburgh, architect Lou Astorino gathered his colleagues for a luncheon at the Duquesne Club. He had, in fact, landed the contract to construct new living quarters for the Cardinals in Vatican City. His task was not simple: He had to plan for an edifice amid the works of da Vinci and Michelangelo—on a budget. It was a story that I would use in future speeches.

After one or two other events, I found myself playing host to US Senator Lloyd Bentsen, who was in Pittsburgh to tour a manufacturing facility.

We wrapped the week up in Pittsburgh at the annual meeting of the Newspaper Publishers Association. All politicians feel that they are misunderstood by the media occasionally. Worse, many believe that they are targeted or deliberately abused. Nixon's famous exit speech comes to mind: "You won't have Nixon to kick around anymore!" Anyway, this event was a good exchange of viewpoints and I appreciated the candid conversation.

I had no animus toward the media. They had been more than fair with me during my years in the state Senate and lieutenant governor's office. I tried to be as open and as candid as I could in return. This was, of course, an unusual time. I was realistic about the tone changing when I was no longer acting governor and seeking the position on my own terms. For now, despite an occasional editorial slap, the relationship with the press was pleasant.

Things remained quiet enough on the legislative front for me to rack up extensive call time the last week in September.

We were now well into the full list of potential donors and making call backs to some. All of this had to be done as quietly as possible for several reasons. First, it would be unseemly for the acting governor to appear to be preoccupied with political fund-raising. Second, we wanted to hold our financial cards close to the vest. This way, we could catch potential opponents off guard when we announced a formidable balance at the end of the year.

Things were going according to plan and were helped considerably by pundits who were writing regularly about the coming gubernatorial campaign. The consensus seemed to be that the Singel stewardship of the Pennsylvania government was effective, but most cast doubt on whether we could raise the money necessary for prime time. We hoped to add a strong cash balance number to that projection of competence when the time was right.

There were, of course, commitments to keep, and I was grateful for the break in fund-raising to tend to those fires.

A trip to Erie featured a grant to the Lake Erie College of Osteopathic Medicine and a live appearance on WJET-TV. We also raised some money for the Friends of Mark Singel at an evening fund-raiser at the Erie Club.

Back at my post in Harrisburg, we went through an extensive exercise in the Emergency Operations Center relating to the Limerick Nuclear Power Plant. This involved observers from the Nuclear Regulatory Commission and every agency of state government. I took these exercises very seriously having faced enough live situations to know that someone had to make the right calls under duress. Joe LaFleur was always on hand during exercises and real events, and I was always impressed by his grace under pressure.

By week's end, I was in full campaign mode having commandeered the governor's board room at the Harrisburg Hilton to host a VIP reception for the state Democratic committee. There was a strong and growing sense of support among the party faithful, and I was grateful for it.

The weekend was, typically, busy with official and political functions. A Saturday evening fund-raiser in Montgomery County drifted into a full day on Sunday in Philadelphia. I spent the morning with the Mid City B'nai B'rith Lodge as their honoree and speaker. B'Nai B'rith translates to "Children of the Covenant," and the organization's dedication to the Jewish faith dates back to the relationship between Abraham and God Himself. I always found the elders of the Jewish community to be thoughtful and engaged. It was an honor to spend time with them. From there, I trekked up to State College for the Center County Democratic Fall Dinner.

Sometime during that trip it dawned on me that I had been on this seven-day-a-week schedule for many months. I did my best to tend to family events, and I reserved most Saturday mornings for kids' activities. But it was during these long road trips that I realized that my wife's recent complaint was a legitimate one: I was definitely not holding up my end of the parenting bargain. I am not sure that I will ever be able to make that up to her.

OCTOBER

The first week of October seemed to arrive under a cloud as world events were casting a shadow on our daily activities.

Boris Yeltsin declared a state of emergency in Moscow and, in fact, had troops loyal to him to occupy the Russian parliament. At the Battle of Mogadishu, Somalia, eighteen US soldiers died in an attempt to capture the warlord Farrah Aidid. A thousand Somalis died in the fighting. In China, the government successfully tested a nuclear weapon at Lop Nor.

It was not unusual to take note of world events to determine what, if any, impact they might have on the Commonwealth. But this was more than just an academic exercise. Pennsylvania has always played a key role in the deployment of troops from the 28th infantry division housed at Fort Indiantown Gap. When hot spots erupted in foreign countries, we tended to go into a slightly higher state of preparedness.

The more mundane activities of the week included a presentation to an urban development seminar at Carnegie Mellon University, a luncheon briefing with the PA Newspaper Publishers Association, and the usual load of proclamations and administrative functions.

On the fund-raising side of things, there were two events in southwest PA and an unusual foray into Ohio to meet with some movers and shakers from the Youngstown area. By the weekend I found myself at the home of Dr. and Mrs. Vic Greco of Hazelton. Dr. Greco was the president of the PA Medical Society and a highly respected community leader. He was also a terrific guy with a keen sense of humor. Victor, his wife, and their son, Tom, became close friends of mine as well as reliable supporters.

What was a little unusual was the mid-week trek to Washington, DC. I had been asked by US Representative John Murtha, the "dean" of the PA congressional delegation, to come down for a face-to-face visit with the Democratic members. Murtha and I were close associates and friends. My first political stirrings centered on his campaigns for the General Assembly and Congress, and I knew I

217

could rely on him for unvarnished opinions and advice. In fact, I counted on it.

The meeting occurred in the "hideaway" office that Murtha had commandeered in the Capitol building. I knew all the House members but was not coming with any agenda. It turns out that the meeting was to reassure Murtha and his colleagues that the state was in good hands. I brought them up to speed on the legislative initiatives we had taken, our position with regard to several federal initiatives—like NAFTA—and my own perspectives on the state of Pennsylvania's economy.

However, the meeting was more important than I thought. Murtha, through unknown sources, had been convinced that Casey was not returning to office, and he had arranged the meeting to reassure his colleagues that I was up to the task. This was important to them not only because each of their districts were impacted by actions we were taking at the state level, but they needed to make a judgment as to whether I was worthy of their support in the coming gubernatorial election. That, of course, depended on whether I was going to run strongly enough to help them with their own reelections.

The meeting must have gone well because Murtha whispered to me as he walked me to my car: "Ya done good, kid."

Back at the office, I had on my desk the annual proclamation naming October 12 as Columbus Day. One thing you learn quickly in a state as ethnically diverse as Pennsylvania: even mundane commemorations like these could spark hostilities. Sure enough, the very next document was naming October 9 as Leif Erickson day. Amusingly, they were presented to me with some curiously similar introductory language:

"On Columbus Day, we commemorate the bold, visionary hero Christopher Columbus . . ."
"Leif Erikson Day is a day set aside to commemorate the bold, visionary navigator . . .

Just covering the bases . . .

With state offices closed on Monday for Columbus Day, we visited Ursinus College for a town meeting that was produced by a media consultant by the name of Jay Silber. This was the first of two "Q&A" sessions with a live audience that were uploaded to satellites that fed both network and cable television stations. I made some introductory remarks then roamed the set, fielding questions.

It was recorded live with no editing, and there was certainly some risk involved. The truth, however, is that the audience had been preselected and we were confident that they would not be hostile.

Stations across the state picked up parts of the discussion—especially when I said something that was news to them. For example, I was able to share with the studio audience and with stations statewide what bills had just been signed and what funds were being released. I enjoyed the format and chuckled when Jay reminded me of what one pundit had written years before: "Singel is like a game show host." Maybe I was!

The campaign team had lined up a travel day for Tuesday, which started in Philadelphia, touched down in California (PA, that is), and ended up back in Harrisburg. The events included a big donor breakfast at the Four Seasons, a presentation to the Penn State Club of Philadelphia, a law firm reception, and a reception at the home of Judy Ansill, the chairman of the board of trustees of California University of Pennsylvania in southwestern PA.

I was back at my post to unveil the first electric vehicle prototype manufactured by General Motors to be introduced to Pennsylvania. We had high expectations for the development of electric vehicles given the cost and volatility of the fossil fuel supply. The General Motors "Impact" car was heading in the right direction but was expensive. The industry needed to get the cost of the battery technology under control and we were determined to establish a network of electric recharging sites across the state for consumer convenience. A number of key players from the legislature and industry were on hand to launch what I thought would be a revolution. With the state's full support we were encouraging a shift to low-emission vehicles like electric and CNG trucks and cars. Pennsylvania was already a leader in alternative energies, and it is a source of great regret to me that we abandoned that focus in subsequent years. It was only with the emergence of the Marcellus and Utica Shale gas opportunities that we regained our footing in this area. We could have been there 20 years earlier!

This also was an important week for Johnstown and for the steel industry.

My hometown had been pummeled by the loss of steel jobs. Bethlehem Steel and US Steel had closed their operations, and what remained of this proud industrial community were a few specialty mills and acres of abandoned sites. Lefty Palm, the colorful leader of the USWA in Pittsburgh never gave up on the industry. Nor did the state's Department of Economic Development and Community

Affairs. Secretary Andy Greenberg of DCED and Lefty introduced me to two young venture capitalists at the State Office Building in Pittsburgh. They were ready to make an offer on several of the abandoned properties in Johnstown and put several thousand steelworkers back on the job. Tom Campbell and Ken Brotman of Veritas Capital laid out their plans and were looking for concessions from labor and incentives from the state.

I remember asking them: "What do you know about steelmaking?"

"Not a damn thing," was the startling reply. "But we know a lot about making money."

That set the tone for a frank discussion that put us on a path to an agreement. I was hopeful that the deal could be made before the end of the calendar year. That became the target.

On October 15, 1993, Nelson Mandela and South African President F. W. de Klerk were awarded the Nobel Peace Prize. Browning wrote that "a man's reach should exceed his grasp." My journey seemed so much less important than folks who could triumph over apartheid against impossible odds. These kinds of events reminded me of my limited grasp but encouraged me to extend my reach.

In that spirit, Thursday and Friday were "diversity days," according to one of my creative staffers. I chaired the Pennsylvania Heritage Affairs Council and had a genuine interest in understanding the nuances of the state's many cultural and ethnic groups. For some reason, statewide and national groups were holding conferences in different parts of Pennsylvania, and it was a chance to reach out to some new constituencies.

We started with the annual Latinos in PA Conference. Lillian Escobar Haskins, the governor's representative on the Latino Advisory Committee, along with my staff, did some artful writing that included some Spanish paragraphs, which I bungled badly at the event. Still, the effort was noted by the organization—and nobody booed.

The Association of Baptists was kicking off its world evangelism crusade in Harrisburg that Friday as well. This wasn't my usual audience. Here I was, a Catholic Democrat amid a strongly Republican, arch-conservative crowd. I didn't speak Spanish there, but I'm sure my address still sounded a little foreign to them.

I was actually more at ease at the Annual POPEC dinner in Philadelphia. The Pride of Philadelphia Election Committee was the political arm of the well-organized gay community in the city. Mark Segal, publisher of the *Philadelphia Gay News*, was a leader there. We got together occasionally, and he couldn't resist filling me in on officials who had not yet emerged from the closet. I enjoyed his company and his political savvy. At one point in my career—long before the broadening of perspectives on gays and gay marriage occurred—he offered the full support of the gay community for my candidacy. I was pleased to receive the endorsement, albeit leery of conservative backlash.

"Don't worry, cuz," Mark said. "You don't have to ride on any gay pride floats!"

Anyway, the POPEC dinner was a showcase of talent and achievers in the Philadelphia area who did not suffer fools or bigots lightly. Governor Ed Rendell and a number of local politicians had already established their bona fides with them, and I was pleased with the reception I received.

I was also in my element at the Greek Catholic Union's annual banquet in western PA. It was a lot easier for me to speak some Old Slavonic from the Divine Liturgy than it was to speak Spanish to the Latino audience. I was at home with the good folks who baked holupkis and pierogis—those folks who built their churches by hand and celebrated St. John Chrysostom as enthusiastically as St. Patrick's Day.

Ethnic pride, sexual orientations, racial differences, and religious diversity—these were all tiles in a mosaic that I thoroughly appreciated. I truly felt that my own background and the tolerance that was taught in our household during my formative years allowed me to throw myself into the masterpiece of diversity that was Pennsylvania. I enjoyed plunging into the history and culture of every group like a singer dropping his mic and body surfing into the audience. One of the few pieces of advice that I give to aspiring politicians is to shake every hand, read every face, and enjoy every moment.

Speaking of enjoyment, I can't say enough about the kindnesses I received from my alma mater, Penn State. Michigan was playing at Penn State that weekend, and we were guests of Dave Schuckers of the PSU Government Relations office in the press box. This was always a great time, and the Singels were always treated like family. In fact, Dave's colleague, Frank Forni, and Frank's wife, Vickie, had done something extra special this trip. After the legislators and alumni had left the post-game cocktail party we followed Frank and Vickie to their residence where they had a full Italian dinner waiting for us. What's more, they invited my parents to join us.

For one delightful evening we all decompressed from our respective responsibilities. We talked about Kerry Collins, Ki Jana Carter, and Kyle Brady. We ate good food and drank good wine with great friends. This, despite a stinging loss to the Wolverines: PSU – 13; Michigan – 21.

By the way, even with the loss, Penn State was in the middle of a great season that would end with a victory at the Citrus Bowl: PSU – 31; Tenn. – 13. Penn State would finish the season with a 10-2 record, ranked No. 8 in the country.

The following Monday began a nose-to-the-grindstone week for fund-raising. The campaign team virtually tied me to the chair in the call center. I extricated myself for the monthly Board of Pardons meeting and a few hours of administrative duties.

There was also a dust-up caused by a dozen or so Ku Klux Klansmen who had staged a rally spewing their white supremacy nonsense on the Capitol steps. I was proud of the fact that even this extreme exercise of the first amendment was handled discreetly and professionally by the Capitol Police and by the good people of Harrisburg who stayed away from the rally in droves!

I spoke at the counter-rally. This was a vigil two days later that featured local clergy and a new group called Greater Harrisburg United, which went on to sponsor other events to counter hate group activity. Another learning moment for me: Sometimes silence is unacceptable.

We had now arrived at a time on the campaign clock when even the non-call room hours had fund-raising overtones. I snuck in a Pittsburgh press conference on the environment followed immediately by a reception at a law firm of an old college friend. I stepped out for a few minutes to attend the birthday celebration of John Baughman of the PSEA. Jackie and I had a pleasant dinner with Alice and Richard Angino at their beautiful Blue Mountain estate. Richard was a prominent attorney in Harrisburg. He and his wife built a beautiful mountain estate that featured a replica of Monet's garden at Giverny, Italian sculptures, and Japanese bonsai trees. Social events at the Anginos' were always elegant and educational.

I got Saturday off for good behavior and spent it at a hay ride for the kids and some classmates, which we hosted at the lieutenant governor's home.

Sunday found me back in my hometown at the annual Cambria County Democratic Committee Dinner.

Even though this was an "off" election year—that is, no presidential, gubernatorial, or legislative offices were at stake—the political machinery always cranked into gear in late October. This meant that I needed to do some cheerleading in organizational bastions like Philadelphia, Scranton, and Pittsburgh.

I was always happy to accommodate Bob Brady, the chairman of the Philadelphia City Committee. He was a solid union guy who loved his city, state, and country. He had a keen understanding of human nature and was able to cajole votes or bludgeon opponents as the circumstances warranted. Philadelphia was a big, burly bastion of political battles. It took someone like Bob, who worked as a dockworker and longshoreman, to fully understand and epitomize the hardworking, blue-collar mentality that permeated Democratic politics at the time. I observed him emceeing the boisterous Philadelphia Committee Dinner and keeping speakers—elected officials and wannabees—on strict time constraints. I saw him intervene between feuding ward leaders and dole out patronage jobs from his perch in Center City. I also saw a deeply compassionate side to him when he attended funerals and family functions for many of his committee persons. If there ever was a politician who knew exactly where he came from, what he stood for, and how to get things done, it was Bob Brady.

The long and short of it was that I was being held up for an excessive amount of money by one particular faction of Philadelphia party leaders—against the directives of the chairman. When I appealed to Bob Brady for assistance he was, as always, ready to help.

"Come with me," he said.

And we headed off to a meeting of the aforementioned politicos.

"Tell them what they want to hear," he whispered as we walked into the room.

The meeting got real very quickly.

"We want the same amount of money that you promised the chairman." (For get-out-the-vote activities, this was, and is, commonly known as "street money.")

I said something to the effect of "I appreciate and expect your help on election day." I said, "I will work closely with the chairman to see that all of your needs are met."

On the way back to Brady's office he said, "Nice job."

"What are you talking about," I said. "There is no way that I can fork over the kind of money they want."

He intimated that they knew that but only needed to hear me speak. Bob Brady went on to be a powerful congressman, and I am pleased that we remain close friends.

Anyway, today was his show, and I made a few remarks at the Democratic Committee of Philadelphia's fall event. Similarly, I touched down in Scranton for the Lackawanna County Dinner and Pittsburgh for several private meetings with some movers and shakers.

One of the official meetings in Pittsburgh was vitally important to a thousand workers in adjoining Armstrong County. It involved mushrooms.

For weeks, my staff and I were looking for ways for the Moonlight Mushroom farms to stay in business. This was the largest employer in the county and their closure would have meant massive layoffs and millions of dollars lost. Management was looking for major concessions; the union, in this case the steelworkers, was willing to talk but was not giving much ground. After several conferences it was time to lay some cards on the table.

The president and CEO of Moonlight Mushrooms made a special trip to see me and some labor leaders in a last-ditch effort to save the operation. The *Valley News Dispatch* reported it this way:

"Some 11th-hour bargaining Monday between Moonlight officials and the United Steelworkers of America has resulted in an amended contract proposal from the company and a new vote by the union . . . it also includes an idea from Acting Gov. Mark Singel that eventually would give employees 15 percent ownership of the mushroom mine."

The article went on to say that:

"Sylvan Foods Holdings, Inc., Moonlight's parent company, said it will close the mine, Armstrong County's largest employer, if the concessions are not accepted."

Given the thousand jobs at stake, even the *Pittsburgh Post Gazette* weighed in:

"Singel's plan included deal sweeteners for both sides: To the company, unspecified state assistance; to workers, a contract shorter than the one the company wants. The state assistance could be grants or loan packages in addition to the possible forgiveness of some company fines owed to the Department of Environmental Resources."

In fact, we were offering $300,000 from the state in the first year of the contract to be followed by additional support later. I had strong bipartisan support from County Commissioner Jim Scahill and the local state representative, Joe Steighner, throughout the negotiations. Still, it was up to the rank and file union members to accept or reject the contract.

The workers had rejected previous offers. In October the vote was 618-169 against. In early November the vote was 516-264. On the final offer, nearly a thousand workers lost their jobs by a vote of 378-357.

At the same time, the negotiations on the steel mills in Johnstown were ongoing, and we were able to forge an agreement with Amtrak to revive some rail lines to Philadelphia—a big deal for commuters and for the economy of central PA.

The lesson about economic development is to be persistent. Even though it is a one-step-forward, two-steps-back proposition, and even though you don't win every battle, it is critical to continue to take those steps forward.

On a lighter, more enjoyable note, I attended a meet-and-greet followed by a live performance by none other than Johnny Cash. This was courtesy of my friend and supporter Commissioner Ted Simon of Westmoreland County. Ted had some association with Cash and was kind enough to squire me backstage to meet the Man in Black. A scrapbook night for me!

The heavy travel schedule and call time meant that a number of previously scheduled items had to be addressed in rapid-fire order. Friday's schedule featured a 7:30 radio show at WHP; a meeting with community activists on LIHEAP (Low Income Heating Assistance Program) as they faced another winter; a PA Business Roundtable luncheon speech on the state of PA's economy; and an evening call-in to the *Phil Musick Radio Talk Show* in Pittsburgh.

NOVEMBER

Election week and most pols are in their districts. This meant a quiet start to the week with the exception of a medical event. Jackie had come down with an infection and required emergency gall bladder surgery. I was able to stay close to Harrisburg and did what I could to provide some comfort to her.

She recovered fully, but there was some related press coverage that befuddles me to this day. Shortly after she returned home and I was back at my post, I found myself discussing some issues of the day with a few reporters.

Out of the blue, a reporter from the *Allentown Morning Call* called out an odd question: "What can you tell us about flowers?"

I had no idea what he was talking about. For some reason, my mind raced to the infamous incident in 1992 in which Governor Bill Clinton denied involvement with a woman named Gennifer Flowers. Did this have something to do with her? With Bill Clinton who was now president? How was I tied in with any of that?

"Your office expense filing lists flowers sent to your wife, Jackie. It was an inappropriate use of state funds," the reporter alleged.

In fact, I had sent flowers when Jackie was in the hospital. And technically, it should have come out of my personal account; not the office account.

My first reaction was:

"My wife just got out of surgery. *Please* report that I sent flowers to my own wife!"

Then I had to admit that my office had simply used the wrong checking account for the transaction.

Certainly it was not an earth-shaking issue. I am still bemused that the newspaper went ahead with a story on such a minor matter.

On election day itself, Commonwealth Media Services had lined up a series of taped and live interviews. I had discovered that the governor (or acting governor) always got prime billing, and I appeared on most of the television stations in the state—without leaving my desk!

Governors are not nearly as newsworthy as presidents, of course. But it happens that my own travels intersected with President Clinton on November 3, 1993. I started the day with a posh morning fund-raiser at the Philadelphia Four Seasons, arranged by Ken Jarin. Then it was off to Pittsburgh to welcome the president, who was coming to Allegheny and Beaver County events at the request of Congressman Ron Klink.

At the Pittsburgh airport I joined Allegheny Commissioners Tom Foerster and Pete Flaherty, Senator Bill Lincoln, and Beaver County Commissioner Jim Albert in a welcoming party.

The president and I got a few moments alone, and he gave me some grief about not supporting NAFTA. He was convinced that he could find the votes elsewhere, though, and I was relieved that there was no damage to our relationship.

I joined the president and his entourage for one or two stops then had to split off to return home for a dinner speech I had scheduled long before. I believe it was with a statewide group of housing officials. I scored some serious points with the group when I told them I had to leave the president to attend their event.

While the state was assessing the week's election results, it was back to business for us. This included presiding over the State Planning Board Meeting, a meeting with the Judicial Conduct Board, and a rare appearance at the governor's mansion to give the opening remarks for the Commission on Children and Families.

At the State Planning Board Meeting, I signed an executive order that I thought would have positive impacts for Pennsylvania for years to come. The Pennsylvania Futures Council was created to do the thing that governments fail to do all too often: think ahead. The "whereases" of the order noted that:

"Whereas, state government increasingly must undertake long-range strategic and innovative planning if the commonwealth is to remain a leader in the next century; and

"Whereas, the Commonwealth has an opportunity to promote economic development, including the improvement of the industrial base while protecting the environment and saving energy, through prudent application of sound economic development and sustainable development concepts;

"Now, therefore, I, Mark S. Singel, Lieutenant Governor, Acting Governor of the Commonwealth of Pennsylvania, by virtue of the authority vested in me by the Constitution of the Commonwealth of Pennsylvania and other laws, do hereby designate the State

Planning Board, as part of its duties, to serve as Pennsylvania's Futures Council reporting directly to the Lieutenant Governor."

Some of the purposes outlined in the order included:

"Identify areas of existing and potential advanced technology business growth . . .
"Identify public and private initiatives that promote sustainable development . . .
"Undertake a further examination of issues that will affect the Commonwealth's long-term economic strength and future . . ."

The order went on to direct all commonwealth agencies under the governor's jurisdiction to cooperate with and assist the Futures Council in fulfilling its responsibilities.

If nothing else, I thought, I had elevated the position of lieutenant governor to play an important role in planning Pennsylvania's future. That, of course, depended on what credence Governor Casey would give the executive order once he returned. I would soon learn yet another lesson about the evanescence of power. The Futures Council eventually suffered death by neglect from the governor and his staff, who simply moved on to other priorities.

Saturday and Sunday saw me sling-shotting from Harrisburg to yet another fund-raiser in Philadelphia to a black tie event in Pittsburgh and back home again.

I was on the ground on the second Monday in November but still facing a hectic schedule.

Several representatives were in town to discuss some district concerns. My good friend, Mary Del Brady, an executive at the Allegheny Health Care System, brought her boss, Sherif Abdelhak, to talk health care reform, and the entire campaign team (then a total of five people) came to dinner to assess our current status and to discuss next steps.

Off to Pittsburgh on Wednesday for an environmental forum speech sponsored by Babst Calland law firm. Of course, we found a friendly office from which to make calls before and after the event. Jeff Craig, a talented and successful investment banker, offered us his office in the Mellon Bank Building. I had known Jeff since my campaign for State Senator in 1980. He and his wife, Melissa, were fun, savvy people who took a genuine interest in Jackie and me. We enjoyed their company and still consider them good friends.

On Friday, November 12, I visited with Governor Casey at his residence in Harrisburg. He had been recovering there since early September. We had had several conference calls, and I was keeping in touch through key staffers throughout the summer, but this was the first time the governor asked for a face-to-face meeting at his residence. He looked thin but healthy and sipped on hot water in his private library. I was expecting a critique of my performance or at least some discussion about items he might have seen in the press or heard from aides.

Instead, the conversation was more social than substantive. I got the impression that he wanted to demonstrate that he was almost at full strength and that he was coming back soon—as if I needed convincing.

We did discuss the upcoming session just a bit, and I told him I expected the Senate to be raucous following the election of William Stinson to the 2nd district seat in Philadelphia. He was aware of the reports of fraud and election violations on the part of both Democrats and Republicans and said something like "That's Philadelphia for you." I also told him that we were standing our ground and taking a lot of abuse for the long hiatus, as we had not been in session since June. The governor understood completely the precarious nature of the Senate majority. "[The Republicans] will reorganize the second they can," Casey said.

I think he understood the pressure I was under as the tie-breaking vote in the Senate. I did not get the sense that he understood the array of other appearances, decisions, appointments, and duties that I had fulfilled on his behalf to that point.

He did note that we were getting close to the point where a budget needed to be developed for the coming fiscal year. I had some definite ideas about the direction I wanted to go with the state's spending and revenue plans. The governor was not enthusiastic about me putting my imprint on them. We agreed to discuss that particular subject further at a later date.

The meeting was cordial but a bit stiff. I just chalked that up to him not functioning at 100% quite yet, nor did he seem up to the buttoned-down demeanor that was his trademark. I really had no reason to suspect that animosity was building on his end.

I felt the brunt of it at an event later in the evening.

At a $500-per-plate reception in Philadelphia for the "Real Bob Casey Committee" the governor took in $300,000 to bolster his own campaign coffers. As to the reason for the fund-raiser, Vince Carocci, Casey's press secretary, simply said:

"He intends to be a player next year."

Some insiders were concerned that Casey was tapping into resources even though he could not run again. Others wondered how he could attend events like this and one in Washington a few nights before if he was not ready to return to office.

The Casey team was kind enough to invite Jackie and me to the party and we certainly knew it was a fund-raising event for his own campaign account. Still, it was customary at these kinds of affairs for the governor to at least mention that his understudy was on hand—particularly since I was still functioning as acting governor. However, we felt about as welcome as wedding crashers. Here is how John Baer of the *Philadelphia Daily News* described it:

"One source said the Singels 'stormed out' after Casey's address.

"The snub [by Casey] was so evident it was described by one long-time Casey loyalist as 'ungracious.'

"Another source, a Casey contributor, said it was 'clearly intended to show there'll be no support for Mark' from Casey."

It was not true that Jackie and I stormed out. It *was* true that we had been sent a message.

It was hard for me to understand that Casey could be anything but grateful for the slings and arrows I had taken for him—not just in the past six months but over the course of the last seven years. There was something odd about this new iciness that went beyond policy disagreements. It was as though he wanted me to fail in order to burnish his own legacy of success.

Every governor since Shapp had endorsed his lieutenant governor as his replacement. Even Dick Thornburgh, who had some serious disagreements with Lieutenant Governor Bill Scranton, got on board and played by those rules.

I was looking at some uncharted waters here. It was becoming clear that I would be launching my own craft alone.

Monday began the last week with no Senate session, and my staff had planned a road trip of sorts to tie up some loose political and official ends. I spent some time in Philadelphia with the Sheet Metal Workers and the American Jewish Congress.

In Hershey, I participated in a session with Pennsylvania farmers that included a debate between me and the likely Republican for governor, Ernie Preate.

We touched down at the Latrobe Airport and at a private residence in Pittston for two fund-raisers.

The official events ran the gamut of topics including: entertaining a delegation from Australia; a tour of the Hollidaysburg Veterans Home; speaking at the Pottsville Chamber of Commerce; and visiting the Ford Electronics plant outside of Philadelphia. The Ford facility had just won an award from *Industry Week* as one of America's best plants.

I was continuing the effort to secure the steel industry in Johnstown and took a moment to visit with leaders at a similar plant in Steelton. They understood the importance of labor/management cooperation to assure their own viability and offered to help in other steel locations in the state.

Every year on the anniversary of the assassination of John F. Kennedy, I find myself thinking about his short administration and his long-lasting effect on America and the world. I had used so many of Kennedy's quotations and witticisms in speeches that I felt, somehow, connected to the concept of Camelot. At least I felt that I should aspire to the style of the man who once said that his role was "to exercise power along the lines of excellence."

When the Senate returned to session on November 22, the Democratic leaders had Kennedy on their minds as well. We exchanged Kennedy stories at their pre-session luncheon. Senator Bill Lincoln was going to make some formal remarks on the floor, and we were all hoping that the shadow of this thirtieth anniversary would afford some dignity and somberness to the Senate session that was about to convene.

The Republicans evidently didn't get that memo.

After a five month hiatus, the boys were back in town—and they were feisty.

The Senate convened at 2:00 p.m., and the Reverend Paul D. Gehris, who served as the Senate chaplain when there was no guest to offer the invocation, said this in his prayer: "Empower these, Your servants, to rise above any temptation to pettiness and self-serving and keep the high ground of integrity, magnanimity, in the service of this commonwealth."

"Good luck with that," I thought.

The fact is that there was a reservoir full of rancor ready to burst over the dam in the Pennsylvania Senate. The Republicans were still smarting from the lengthy adjournment and itching to add David Heckler of Bucks County to the roll call.

231

He had won his special election on July 13 and had been performing district duties since that time. He was not, however, formally sworn in—which required an officer of the Senate to preside over the taking of the oath in Senate session.

On the other hand, a new senator by the name of William Stinson from Philadelphia had been elected on November 8. The Democratic leadership wasted no time in swearing in Stinson during a four-minute session on November 18. President Pro Tem Robert Mellow convened the session and presided over the event. The secretary of state certified that Stinson had won a narrow victory over Bruce S. Marks by a vote of 20,518 to 20,057.

Thus, the session of November 22 was opened with Stinson officially on the roll but Heckler still in a kind of political limbo.

After the prayer and the approval of the previous journal, the first order of business is always communications from the governor. In this case, those missives came from the acting governor and included notification that I had signed fifteen bills into law, including a Capital Budget Bill authorizing $650 million new projects for the commonwealth. There were also dozens of appointments made to university boards of trustees, state boards and commissions, and district justice and judge vacancies throughout the state.

What was on the minds of the Senate Republicans, though, was the makeup of the Senate.

The Republicans had a valid point. David Heckler had been elected in July. William Stinson was elected in November. We were on an extended recess and neither could be sworn in until either the president of the Senate (me) or the president pro tempore of the Senate (Senator Mellow) convened the Senate.

Bob Mellow wasn't taking any chances. If there was a remote chance of upending the leadership of the Senate, and possibly disrupting the legislative priorities of Governor Casey and the Democratic team, he wanted to nip it in the bud. He had quietly convened the Senate one week earlier to swear in Stinson (but not Heckler), thus assuring that the opening votes, at least, would go in his favor. Until Heckler was sworn in by the Senate, the Democrats had a 25-24 vote majority.

It was an extremely brief session with just a handful of Democrats in attendance. While Mellow was on solid constitutional grounds, the maneuver infuriated the Republicans. Heckler, who had been waiting four months to be seated, was livid.

I learned about this quiet "swearing in" session after the fact. Looking back on it, there really was no need for it. The fact is that we could have sworn in both Senators at the same time. That would have taken the Senate to a tie of 25-25, mine being the deciding vote on procedural questions. What this means is that the majority (25 Democrats plus my tie-breaking vote) could determine which bills would be considered and what procedures would be in place for the remaining days of the session. We could also prevent a Republican takeover if we would just keep our parliamentary wits about us.

I had stood my ground over the last five months, and I was not about to waver now that the battle was back in the Senate arena. Still, I fully understood the Republicans' frustration.

They were in full battle mode. Armed with the crafty and capable Republican Counsel Steve MacNett, they proceeded to fling every possible parliamentary maneuver into the proceedings in hopes of catching me in a mistake or, even better, trapping me into a ruling or two that they could use to haunt me in a future election. I, on the other hand, had the advantage of the majority and believed that I could get through whatever maze they wanted to create for me.

The Republicans had spent the summer and fall bemoaning the fact that the Senate had not convened, but it was less about governing and more about control.

Senator Jubelirer began the debate by challenging my ruling that Senator Stinson could vote on his own suitability to vote as a senator. The opening salvo showed exactly where Bob was going:

Senator Jubelirer: *"Mr. President and members of the Senate, members of a free press and independent press, for five months this Senate has been in recess because some 24 Democrats, with the assistance of a tie-breaking vote supplied by the president of the Senate, Lieutenant Governor Singel . . ."*

At this point, Senator Lincoln, the Democratic leader, jumped in to assure that we remained focused on the issue at hand. It was a valiant effort, but I knew it was not going to stop Jubelirer and his team from administering a few lumps to me.

Constitutional arguments, points of order, challenges to the rulings of the chair, parliamentary inquiries, moves to cut off debate, and a previous question motion finally brought us to the first roll call. Oddly, the distractions and political warfare delayed the swearing in of Senator-elect Heckler—which would have been in order before any vote was taken. That reality sank in when the first vote was an unusual 25-2. Senator Jubelirer and Senator Bell, to their credit, hung in there, maintaining the not-so-loyal opposition's position and representing the only two votes from their party. It seemed that the other 22 Republicans were either just confused or annoyed by the proceedings and sat it out.

After five roll call votes on various challenges to the chair and hours of legislative jousting, we finally got to the actual swearing in of David Heckler. That, of course, was not the end of the bickering.

Senator Williams, a Philadelphia Democrat, couldn't help but refer to an earlier, unofficial swearing-in of Senator Heckler as a "rump" proceeding. (This term refers to unofficial proceedings conducted by the minority. While the Republicans had their own "swearing in" of Heckler earlier, it had no standing since the Senate had not been formally convened.) Senator Peterson, a particularly volatile Republican, took the term literally and cast his own aspersions in terminology far worse than "rump." A moment of calm broke out when those remarks were expunged from the record.

It was only the beginning of the verbal volleyball, though.

Senator Jubelirer was at the microphone asking for a special order of business to address the issue of the qualifications of Senator Stinson to serve as a senator.

I was disturbed that this matter had become personal and that William Stinson, a humble, decent man who just wanted to serve, was being sliced and diced in the official record and in front of the state press.

Having already spent too much time establishing the credentials of both new senators, I ruled the request out of order. That didn't stop the discussion:

Senator Fumo (D): *"The mere fact of the matter is, Mr. President, that William Stinson won an election in Philadelphia fair and square. The other fact of the matter, Mr. President . . . is that there will be another election in this district in November of 1994, and the Republicans, through the help of the* Philadelphia Inquirer *and some others, have been able to put a wonderful spin on this so as to kick off their campaign—"*
Senator Jubelirer (R): *"Point of order, Mr. President, I believe the gentleman is out of order."*
Senator Fumo: *"Oh, shut up. . . . So they can kick off their campaign for 1994—"*
The President (Singel): *"Will the gentleman yield? The gentleman will make his point."*

Senator Jubelirer: *"Mr. President, we have listened to the pontification, but I believe he is out of order. I believe I asked the chair to rule on the Constitution which states the election and qualification of a member. That is all I am asking."*

The President: *"The gentleman has made his point. . . . The chair has said that it finds the gentleman, Senator Jubelirer's point to be out of order at this point."*

Senator Fumo: *"Mr. President, point of personal privilege."*

The President: *"The gentleman will state his point of personal privilege."*

Senator Fumo: *"Mr. President, I would ask that the chair admonish the minority leader for making references to my remarks as being pontification. They are personal insults to me, and I would ask for an apology or an admonishment."*

The President: *"The chair is somewhat confused, to be quite frank about it. The term 'pontification' is not necessarily a major pejorative denigration."* (I was allowing myself to begin having a little fun with all of this wordplay.) *"The chair . . . suggests to all members that perhaps we are getting a bit far afield and a bit too sensitive to comments that are being made on both sides. The chair would proceed to conduct the business of the day."*

Nice try, Mark.

There were still a dozen or so points of order and a final effort by the minority to reconsider the constitutional point of order that had allowed William Stinson to remain a senator.

The President: *"Let the record show that it* [the point of order] *was defeated. The constitutional point of order went down, just so we are all clear."*

Senator Jubelirer: *"That is two in a row that MacNett missed."*

This was a remarkable admission. Steve MacNett was the most knowledgeable legislative counsel in Harrisburg. Most considered him the 51st senator, and I had come to like and respect him. The fact that the Senate Ds and I had held our ground and exercised the slimmest of majorities adroitly enough to outmaneuver Steve was high praise.

Senator Jubelirer went on to add hundreds of pages of newspaper articles into the record, all of which raised issues about election practices in the Stinson race.

Senators Fumo and Mellow responded in kind with instances of fraud reported on the Marks side. At some point in the proceedings, Mayor Rendell was quoted as saying that both sides made mistakes.

The debate continued in the "Petitions and Remonstrances" section of the agenda with both sides firing shots from their podiums and perspectives. Someone made reference to a colleague needing a psychiatrist; another got personal about somebody's divorce attorney. Most stayed focused on the politics, which was bare-knuckle enough.

The Senate adjourned having passed over any substantive legislative items on the calendar. On this, the thirtieth anniversary of the assassination of President John F. Kennedy, the Senate of Pennsylvania was certainly not asking what it could do for its country. They were cravenly jockeying for political position.

Back in the sandbox the next day, the Senate Republicans were not quite done with tarnishing the newest senator. The first bill on the calendar would have named a bridge on the Allegheny River. It turned out to be the cause of another free-for-all.

Senator Jubelirer once again questioned Senator Stinson's right to be on the roll call. He asked to insert yet more editorial fodder into the record and, when the Democrats objected, he simply read the entire article. Senator Fumo decided two could play that game, and he read a favorable editorial from the *Philadelphia Daily News*. This is where it got comical.

One of the issues that incensed the Republicans was a report that Stinson workers had dramatically increased the number of absentee votes for their candidate by reaching out to the Latino community with "la nueva forma de votar." John Baer, the ever-cynical reporter from the *Daily News* was not buying the notion of widespread fraud in that community. He wrote:

"Last night, Marks returned a phone call after his press conference and again invited me to come to his headquarters where he would produce evidence of—I'm not making this up—hundreds of illegal absentee voters.

"I accused him of inventing 'la nueva forma de cow pie.'"

Fumo had to make sure that the point was made clearly. "In other words," he intoned on the floor, "bullshit!"

Here's what happened next:

236

The President (Singel): *"Before Senator Jubelirer makes the objection, let the chair make it for you. The epithet is not acceptable language for the floor of the Senate."*
Senator Fumo: *"Mr. President, I was merely interpreting the writer's remarks."*
The President: *"The chair understands and is familiar with the phrase."*
Senator Fumo: *"Could I call it cow manure?"*
The President: *"'Cow manure' is somehow acceptable."*

What ensued was a constitutional point of order challenged by a point of order based on the fact that it was redundant compared to what had transpired the day before. This was followed by points of personal privilege and at least two other parliamentary challenges. Each one required a ruling from me, which was followed by an appeal of that ruling. What the Republicans thought they were doing was building a case against my heavy-handedness for future political use. What they were really doing was tarnishing William Stinson relentlessly and running into the brick wall of a majority exercising its will—even if it hung by the thread of my tie-breaking vote.

I was mindful of being the adult in the room and not letting even personal attacks get in the way of rational rulings and fairness for all of the speakers. That is, until one or two of the loyal opposition accused me of squelching the discussion.

The President (Singel): *"The chair thanks the gentleman, and from the chair's perspective, I do not appreciate and do not agree with the characterization that anybody is trying to gag anybody. I think the gentleman's comments are somewhat theatrical. I have striven to listen to all points of view on the various points of order. I have rendered the decisions based on my best judgment, given the presentations, and I have given much more leeway than normally would be expected in the circumstances . . . a continuation of the debate on Senator Stinson's qualifications could very well be construed as being dilatory. I am willing to deal with that today."*

That seemed to assuage things a bit and, after two hours of political jousting, the most we could accomplish that day was to rename a bridge in Pennsylvania.

But Senator Lincoln was finally able to pay homage to John F. Kennedy in comments delivered under the "Petitions and Remonstrances" portion of the day's agenda.

The fisticuffs in the Senate were frustrating and somewhat diversionary. I had other things that had to be addressed and wanted to make the best use of whatever time I had left with the pen in my hand.

One such item was the possible creation of a new window manufacturing plant in Indiana County. Senator Pat Stapleton brought a dozen local officials and key business leaders to my office to see how the state could fill in some financial gaps in their start-up plan. At stake were 200 jobs in a local economy that needed the boost. We made a substantial commitment to the potential owner and helped launch a new enterprise—a much better ending than the Moonlight Mushroom saga.

A final function for the week was welcoming the Ukrainian ambassador to Pennsylvania. It was a pleasant official duty to perform before heading back to Johnstown for Thanksgiving with my own family, my parents, and several brothers and sisters.

That weekend several of us spent some time with the homeless at the Wood Street Commons in Pittsburgh. Ladling out soup to the needy was a powerful reminder of just how fortunate my life had been to that point. I had a dedicated wife, three terrific children, a strong extended family and, for the moment at least, a key role in shaping Pennsylvania's future. I was blessed and, after some downtime and reflection, ready to get back into the fray.

Pittsburgh was becoming a satellite office for the embryonic gubernatorial campaign. Specifically, Jeff Craig was more than generous in allowing us to use desks and phones in his office in the Mellon Bank building, and we were back at it on the last Monday in November. It was important to retreat to a non-state site when I was making fund-raising calls or conducting any type of political business. Before the end of this week, we would have logged twenty to thirty hours in the Steel City.

Between fund-raising calls, I was able to meet with key supporters like John Connelly, who owned the Gateway Clipper fleet and the Station Square Sheraton; and Ish McLaughlin of the Dick Construction Corporation.

I also had some other responsibilities to attend to including a couple of television interviews, a presentation to the Pittsburgh

Founders Council, and hosting a reception at the William Penn Hotel for the Democratic State Committee. All seemed solid on the western side of the state, and I was determined to keep my contacts warm and close.

Cancer and crime were also on the agenda that week.

The Lehigh Valley Hospital System was dedicating its Morgan Cancer Center, and Judge Max Davidson of Allentown had invited me to participate. I was pleased to lend some state support to the cause. The center remains one of the largest and most effective cancer research and treatment facilities on the East Coast.

On crime, we were unveiling an aggressive anti-crime effort including controversial legislation to ban assault weapons. The first in a series of events was at the Camp Hill prison. We had just completed rebuilding the prison following extensive damage caused by two nights of rioting that had occurred in 1988. It was a good backdrop for the anti-crime message.

The crime campaign would stretch into the following week and provided support for at least one specific action. The Pittsburgh City Council passed an ordinance banning assault weapons in the city. This was a bold gesture in the face of hunters and sportsmen who were being pressured by the NRA into opposing the initiative.

We took the same message to Philadelphia the following week and drew strong support from an equally courageous district attorney, Lynne Abraham, and a no-nonsense police chief by the name of Richard Neal. Abraham surprised everyone by pulling a shoulder-holstered mini-Uzi from under her coat—demonstrating how easy these weapons were to conceal. Neal spoke passionately about the three officers and forty-six victims who had been gunned down in the previous fifteen months. The trait that I admire most in leaders is courage. Once in a while you meet elected officials who care more about doing the right thing more than their own reelections. Taking on powerful interests and standing by your principles come with the job—if you are doing your job right. The Pittsburgh City Council, the Philadelphia DA, the police commissioner, and a handful of state legislators earned high marks from me for courage during this anti-crime effort.

DECEMBER

We plugged away at assault weapons at the State Police Training Academy. I actually did some practice firing and was amazed at how easy it was to squeeze off so many potentially deadly rounds in a few seconds. It still disturbs me that we as a nation cannot seem to face the reality of deadly weapons in criminals' hands. The carnage that we have seen on our streets and in elementary school classrooms should be enough to cause outrage. Instead, otherwise decent citizens and lawmakers buy into half-baked arguments invoking the second amendment to justify their positions on the proliferation of guns.

The fact is that I expended some political capital on this issue to help alter entrenched opinions. I don't know if it helped, but I can tell my children and grandchildren that I tried to protect them.

At least one newspaper, the *Pittsburgh Post Gazette*, understood and said so in an editorial:

December 7, 1993
Singel's shot – On guns, the acting governor chooses right over might

Acting Gov. Mark Singel has taken a gutsy stand against assault-style weapons.

With the House of Representatives considering a bill to prevent local governments from banning them, Mr. Singel has declared that he would veto such legislation. That means if legislators want to pursue their NRA-inspired gambit to limit municipal powers, the acting governor will make it more difficult for them by requiring the two-thirds' vote needed to override a veto.

Mr. Singel, of course, didn't have to take the political risk. As a candidate next year for the Democratic nomination for governor, he could have kept a low profile—vetoing the bill at the last minute or signing it into law after what politicians typically call 'much thought and consideration.'

Instead, he said: 'There is no rational reason for the legality of these weapons. They are meant to do damage to human beings. There is no sporting purpose for them.' That'll light up his phone lines.

The National Rifle Association—despite a strategy of stirring fear among sportsmen—lost to reason when Philadelphia last summer prohibited the possession of such weapons. It lost again last month when Pittsburgh City Council, led by President Jack Wagner, approved a similar ban.

Mr. Singel knows that 5 million Pennsylvanians are hunters. He also knows that letting local governments ban Uzis and M16s has nothing to do with them.

We wish the acting governor well in weathering the political threats that will come his way on this. It takes courage for an elected official to stand up to the NRA, but with the passage of the Brady bill and sensible gun laws in various states, it is something that's becoming more easy to do.

In the afternoon, I met with some key Pittsburgh leaders on the thorny issue of revenues for their regional assets development. Art Rooney II, grandson of the legendary founder of the Pittsburgh Steelers; Rick Stafford, professor and planner who had served in the Thornburgh administration; and Chuck Kolling, a gifted lobbyist with the Buchanan, Ingersoll, Rooney law firm, were making the case for a special sales tax in their region. I was more than willing to work with them just based on their strong reputations as community leaders.

From a morning fighting crime and an afternoon of solid policy discussion, I walked with some trepidation back into the arena of the Pennsylvania Senate.

The session opened with the usual amount of communications from the acting governor. It continued to amuse me that that I was writing official letters to myself. This batch of correspondence included nominations of judges, members of various state boards, and some other housekeeping.

Senator Williams brought an uplifting moment to the proceedings by introducing Shonda Schilling, the wife of Curt Schilling, a Phillies pitching standout in the recent World Series. She took to the podium and made some gracious comments to the chamber. She went on to give an extemporaneous presentation on Lou

Gehrig's disease and her involvement with the ALS association. Like a political pro, she advocated strongly for raising reimbursement rates for some ALS patients and even challenged government with a deadline:

"We are asking the Committee on Public Health and Welfare to require DPW to increase the reimbursement. . . . We hope that this can be accomplished before the Phillies bring the World Series back to Pennsylvania next year."

The rates were raised—in no small part because of Shonda Schilling's class act.

Equally well received was the Dairy Princess of Pennsylvania, Jennifer Grimes. Her cause was easing regulatory burdens on dairy farmers and recognizing that "the farm and the animal work together." She actually uttered (uddered?) the phrase: "A contented cow gives the most milk."

Enough of the pleasantries; Senator Jubelirer and his staff had the previous week off to devise more ways to harass Senator Stinson and the Democrats. The weapon of choice today was a resolution requiring that Stinson stand aside as a senator. When that drew the inevitable objection from the majority, Jubelirer raised the constitutional point of order—for the fourth time—that Stinson was ineligible to vote.

It fell to me, once again, to rule the motion out of order, which, of course, drew an appeal to the ruling of the chair. The appeal failed on the now typical vote of 25 to 25, but not without several comments placed on the record aligning me with the majority and the world of Philadelphia politics. Just more posturing for 1994.

The next matter was a business tax proposal that Democrats had espoused earlier in the year. The Republicans wanted to add additional business tax cuts to the package and were now ready to offer amendments. The Democrats reminded them that no R had voted for the bill six months earlier and they assumed that the Rs were still not prepared to vote for the shifts necessary to fund any business tax cuts. It did provide the Republicans with a stage for burnishing their pro-business credentials and for dredging up yet more parliamentary hoops for me and the D team to jump through. After two hours of debate and verbal volleyball, the bill reached the ultimate vote on final passage—and failed 25 to 25. (The rules preclude the Senate president from breaking a tie vote on final passage.) Ironically and unbeknownst to either party, I was planning my own business tax reduction plan for release later in the week.

This was going to make for some interesting moments when we returned next week!

Needless to say the Rs couldn't let the day's activities go without stuffing the record full of more press clips and political charges. In fact, the December 6, 1993, Senate Journal is unusual in that it contains the entire filing of a law suit to force a court decision on whether my recent rulings on Senate procedure vis-à-vis Stinson were legal and appropriate. It was not the first time that I had been sued. In fact, I believe that Jubelirer and his legal team set some kind of record by suing me eleven times over the course of my service as lieutenant governor and acting governor. It comes with the territory.

While the Stinson fracas continued on December 7, the legislative fight was welfare reform. Knowing that they were in 25-25 limbo, the Republicans felt that they could produce some hot-button items to force some difficult votes on the Ds. The side benefit, of course, is that every procedural move that I made would then be tucked away as evidence that I was mired in what Republican candidates loved to characterize as wasteful welfare spending.

Predictably, the debate devolved into motions and counter-motions and some amusing name calling. Senator Peterson, an R from Venango County, and Senator Lincoln, the majority leader, were both getting a bit red faced when Lincoln lost it. Senator Jubelirer was on his feet:

> Senator Jubelirer: *"I would request that the personal attack on the gentleman from Venango, Senator Peterson, be expunged from the record . . ."*
> The President (Singel): *"The chair thanks the gentleman and recognizes the gentleman from Fayette, Senator Lincoln."*
> Senator Lincoln: *"Mr. President, I would apologize for the reference to not having a brain."*
> (Whereupon, at this point remarks were expunged from the record by order of the Senate.)

Maybe the Senate had punched itself out for the week because the Wednesday session was routine.

No new accusations, no Stinson resolutions, no challenges to the chair. Just some wrap-up items and some positioning of nominations and legislation for the following week—which was expected to be the last week of meetings for the year. This, and the fact that many of the House and Senate leaders were already preparing for the annual Pennsylvania Society festivities in New York City meant that, for once, the proceedings were mercifully brief.

This is not to say that there was any downtime on the campaign side of things.

Thursday was full schmooze mode in Philadelphia under the direction of Viceroy Bill Batoff. His office in the heart of the city served as a kind of welcome center for donors who wanted to assess me and my candidacy. Most were positive and generous with their early contributions. The viceroy was especially good about drawing a clear line between political and official realities. If a donor seemed a little too demanding or if we were getting anywhere close to a suggested "return for their investment," Bill was ready with a little speech that went something like:

"You understand that there is no *quid pro quo*. We deeply appreciate your support of Mark's campaign for governor, and you know that he will be accessible to you. We are not in a position, however, to commit to any specific item or action."

Bill Batoff was famous for his personal quirks, but one thing I always admired was that he played it straight and never once crossed any ethical or legal lines.

Meanwhile, the acting governor's office was buzzing with activity relating to the upcoming New York events. The Pennsylvania Society Dinner was a time-honored tradition that began with a handful of rich Pennsylvania industrialists and their wives socializing and shopping in the New York holiday season. It soon became a must stop for politicians, strategists, industry leaders, and news reporters looking for some insights about current and upcoming political adventures. A predominantly Republican affair, the receptions and the back room meetings prior to and after the actual formal dinner could launch or derail political campaigns. Any and every serious candidate knew that they should see and be seen at the events.

Fred Anton, a rock-ribbed conservative Republican and the president of the Pennsylvania Manufacturers' Association, spent a fortune each year renting the staid Metropolitan Club to showcase his candidates and to offer a forum for elected officials. The sitting governor and US senators were always invited to make some remarks. While we didn't agree on much politically, I had come to appreciate Fred's candor and leadership abilities. He had a commitment to business and conservative values that was strong and genuine, and I admired that.

He was also fair. In the first Casey/Singel term, his annual seminar occurred on the heels of a difficult vote in the Senate concerning a "fair share" contribution for non-union state workers. The Republicans called it "Agency Shop" and viewed the measure as a way for unions to coerce funds from non-members. It happens that I had cast a tie-breaking vote that cleared the way for passage of the bill.

This became the focal point for several of the Republican speakers at the PMA seminar. Since I had not been offered the privilege of the podium, I sat in the front row watching speaker after speaker lay the blame for "rampant unionism" right on my shoulders. It was, of course, Bob Jubelirer, who actually pointed his finger in my direction and made sure the 400 or so captains of industry knew who the enemy was. While it was not possible to alter the program for a rebuttal from me, Fred Anton was clearly upset. He had never witnessed such a public dressing-down in his life he told me and he would absolutely make it up to me by having me state my own case at his next event. He made good on that promise and, to this day, I believe I was the only Democratic lieutenant governor to address the PMA seminar in the hallowed hall of the Metropolitan Club.

This year, things were a bit different. Casey was still limiting his public appearances. He would be at the dinner as an honored guest, but I had been invited to give the state of the state speech as acting governor.

My staff and I had worked hard on a blueprint for Pennsylvania. This was not just an academic exercise. By law, the governor was required to present an outline of the next year's budget to the legislative leaders by December 15. I fully intended to fulfill that responsibility with a plan that reflected my priorities.

What was causing heartburn in the Casey camp was that the governor was not ready to tackle all of the issues related to a full-blown budget presentation. In a private discussion at the governor's residence, he asked me to buy some time so that he could put his own budget forward when he was ready. After six months of steering the ship of state through some choppy waters, and knowing that I was already being viewed by many as the state's next potential leader, I was not about to tap dance in New York or in front of the legislative leaders. I had been careful to respect Casey's positions, and I passed up every opportunity to grandstand, but I was not going to appear hapless if I had the opportunity to lead with vision and clarity. That was just asking too much.

"I'm sorry," I told the governor. "But I intend to make my own budget presentation."

In all of our previous conversations, I had assumed the deferential role that would be expected of the second in command. This time, even Governor Casey knew that I had a point: I could not just tell the public that I would wait another two months for marching orders. As we wrapped up our conversation, I caught something in his voice that told me he accepted this reality. I detected something like respect for standing my ground. After all, I learned that from him.

The PMA seminar was the natural place to preview that package. These are the prepared remarks that served as the basis for the presentation to the leaders at the PA Society Dinner and to the leaders of the legislature:

ACTING GOVERNOR MARK S. SINGEL'S
REMARKS ON THE 1994-95 BUDGET

These are unusual times for Pennsylvania. We have nevertheless carried on with the usual duties of government.

We now know that Governor Casey will return to office in one week. I know you all join with me in welcoming that return. It is my anticipation that soon thereafter the governor will clarify the direction in which he intends to take the 1994- 95 state budget. I think it only proper to defer to Governor Casey the full explanation of his plans for the next fiscal year. But that does not discharge my duties to the people of this commonwealth or the leaders of our General Assembly.

Secretary Hershock will detail the state of the current year's budget and the preliminary forecasts of the macro-economic variables and major mandated programs for next year's budget. But Section 619 of the Administrative Code also mandates that the Governor "brief the legislative leadership on the issues he can foresee as being imminent in the budget for the next fiscal year." It requires that this briefing shall include, among other things, "major anticipated increases or decreases in programs." Because Governor Casey has not yet reassumed his authority, as of this date all of his duties are still devolved upon me, and thus Section 619 of the Administrative Code today applies to me. I am thus compelled by statute to present to you the issues that I foresee as imminent in the budget for the next fiscal year, including major program increases or decreases that I anticipate.

I believe that the foundation stones of the next budget must be these:

(1) Tax cuts to provide stimulus to protect, attract, and create jobs for more working Pennsylvanians.

(2) Reform of our welfare system to transform it into what welfare was intended to be—not a permanent hand-out, but a temporary hand up—by instituting both incentives and opportunities to work, to save, to attend school, and to establish stable families.

(3) An educational system second to none through stronger statewide financial support and stronger local responsibility and choice.

(4) Fiscal responsibility that ensures a balanced budget without the need for new net revenues either in the coming budget year or, as a result of actions we take this year, in future budget years as well.

In short, the principles that guide my thinking on next year's budget are in sync with the budget contemplated by Governor Casey. I therefore do not expect that the return of the baton to the governor, when it occurs, will be the least bit hampered by the work that I have put into the budget to date with Secretary Hershock.

I therefore also do not think there is any danger in my complying with my statutory duty to report to you today on what my thoughts are as of this date relative to the next budget. Nor do I expect anyone to hold Governor Casey to my thinking any more than he has expected me to adhere to his in discharging the duties of the governorship.

The ways that I am examining meeting the four challenges outlined above are as follows:

First and foremost, I would propose a sweeping tax-cut program to bring a new burst of job creation to Pennsylvania. One newspaper recently reported that our two major economic centers—Philadelphia and Pittsburgh—rank one-two in the nation for highest business tax burden, and that is in large part due to state taxes on business activity. We must reduce our corporate net income tax below 10%, but due to the massive size of such a tax cut—approximately $300 million—we must phase it in over a period of three years.

I would go further, moreover, and propose a similar reduction in the millage rate for the capital stock & franchise taxes, in order to spur the small businesses that generate the vast majority of new jobs. Many would also like to see restoration of the net operating loss tax credit; I would favor that, if we can replace

247

the lost revenue with revenues derived from a new incentive and disincentive policy, one that taxes social evils such as pollution instead of social goods like hard work and successful business endeavors. I am currently exploring the feasibility of such a revenue trade-off. We must make clear, however, that the ultimate goal of tax reductions is to help working Pennsylvanians; to that end, I am formulating proposals to raise the low-income exemption to the personal income tax, and to institute a state earned income tax credit to bring tax relief to working families.

Second, we need meaningful welfare reform. As I have been advocating all year, we must provide fair education, training, job placement, and support services—and, in turn, beneficiaries must produce a fair return: a fair day's work and a firm commitment to their family and social responsibilities.

I am advocating a bold new federal-state initiative to break the bonds of welfare dependency and promote work and savings among AFDC recipients through state waivers to the federal Aid to Families and Dependent Children (AFDC) program. While such a federal-state AFDC experiment must form the foundation of any welfare reform efforts, there are other important and needed initiatives that I am proposing to complement and enhance this initiative, to break the cycle of dependency and promote work over welfare. I am also calling for the use of new technology to make benefits more efficiently available to beneficiaries—and to cut down on welfare fraud.

Taken together, such a reform package could save Pennsylvania taxpayers tens of millions of dollars while providing welfare recipients with real opportunity. We must also show the people of Pennsylvania that we can make welfare cost-effective in the short-term; I would therefore propose a range of spending reductions or freezes on those components of our current welfare system that do not help move people off welfare into productive lives but simply maintain them on a stagnant system of handouts. I believe that we can achieve net welfare spending cuts in the neighborhood of at least $30 million.

Third, we must expand upon the initiatives of Governor Casey to bring equity to school finance. We must attempt educational finance reform within a broader framework of educational policy reform, however, that recognizes the importance of placing funding responsibility on larger units and returns educational responsibility to smaller units.

Pennsylvania must ensure that our children are prepared to meet the future—to live in the future, work in the future, compete in the future, and succeed in the future. To do that, we need a future-oriented education system, which must build on this new understanding: Results-oriented, flexible, individual-centered, and proper dispersal of responsibility and authority. In short, the education system of the 21st century must resemble the technologies of the 21st century, with centralized mass production giving way to individuality, inventiveness, change, and flexibility.

For too long, we've been doing it wrong. Parents, teachers, and local officials, not state bureaucrats, can best determine what particular educational program meets their needs in achieving those ends. School management and educational choices must be made by parents, teachers, and communities. Education financing, however, must be more broadly shared. State government must take more responsibility for—but assume less authority over—our children's educations. Our families, our local schools and communities must be given greater authority to ensure that our children really learn.

I am therefore examining a new distribution of educational funding responsibility. I believe that the state should assume the lion's share of the burden for funding teachers; this would largely equalize the state's support of each student's education across the commonwealth while relieving local school districts of this tremendous financial load. In return, the state should give local districts greater control over and financial responsibility for the remainder of the school's programs.

Last—but certainly not least—we must demonstrate fiscal responsibility. We cannot institute tax cuts of the magnitude that we're talking about without spending cuts as well. I do not think that we need an austerity budget or draconian measures—in fact I believe we ought to increase spending in various areas of social need, including treatment for and research into combating AIDS, funding for Low-Income Home Energy Assistance, additional help for shelters for families leaving abusive homes, and efforts to fight crime and assist victims. We must also enact a comprehensive health security program. But all of this will require that we cut elsewhere. I am currently examining ways to trim as much as $150 million in unneeded government spending from our state budget—the equivalent of a 1% across-the-board cut in government spending next year.

With these common objectives I have outlined, I believe that a consensus budget is and should be achievable this year, not only despite, but because of, the nearly even division in the legislature. While we may differ in the particulars, we all essentially share these same four basic goals. That is why I expect that partisanship will not stand in the way of enactment of a budget whose basic premises we all share.

I want to begin that process today by calling on you to help fulfill the statutory duties I have undertaken: Section 619 of the Administrative Code mandates that the governor not just brief, but also "exchange views with," the legislative leadership—and it mandates that you "inform the governor of financial matters which should be considered in the budget." Rather than turn what should be a consensus-building process into a war that may benefit one or another party or candidate but will not benefit the people of Pennsylvania one iota, I call upon all of you to join the process of budget formulation now, so that we can propose and enact a budget that achieves the shared goals I have elucidated.

I will therefore consult with the legislative leadership of both chambers and both parties after the first of the year, if I remain as acting governor; and if—as I fully expect—Governor Casey has returned to office by then, I expect all of us to work with him to make his vision a reality for all Pennsylvanians.

A story by the Associated Press caught most of the highlights: a reduction in business taxes, an increase in the tax exemption for the working poor, a transfer of education costs from local to state, and $150 million in state spending cuts. Budget Secretary Mike Hershock did his best to straddle between the Casey and Singel worlds by noting that there was "a lot of common ground" between the two of us on key items. The governor was not willing, however, to go as far on business tax cuts or on some of the program innovations as I was, and the press was on to us.

"Is this Governor Casey's budget?"

"The governor is saving his specifics for the February budget address," said Hershock.

"Is this a Singel budget, then?"

"This represents my vision for the future, but when the governor returns I will support whatever direction he takes," was my answer.

"Does the governor support this plan?" I honestly did not know the answer, so my response wasn't detailed.

"For the most part," I said. "But he plans to present his own version in February."

What I did know was that it was a hit in the business community. The folks in New York understood the balance I was seeking between a favorable business climate and compassionate government. But I knew that I was in for some cross examination by the loyal opposition when we got back to Harrisburg.

Governor Casey took his rightful place on the dais of the Penn sylvania Society Dinner. He received a warm ovation from the crowd, and every speaker spoke of his courage in facing his medical challenges and his determination to return to complete his job. The acting governor who was doing that job was at Table 83. *Of these no elegy.*

It was counterproductive, of course, to whine about political paper cuts. In fact, I just did not have the time to worry about how other players—possible opponents, pundits, even Governor Casey—were conducting their own business. I just knew that the time was coming when I would move on.

When I got back to Harrisburg, I ran into Art, the oracle, again. We never talked much about politics, and I certainly would not saddle him with my own political burdens. But in the course of our brief conversation, he came up with yet another gem:

"You wanna fly, you got to give up the shit that weighs you down."

"Is that from James Baldwin?" I asked.

"Toni Morrison," he said. "There you go."

The Senate reconvened on Monday and decided that it was time to end the Pennsylvania Crime Commission.

This group featured a number of prominent lawyers and jurists who were charged with making recommendations to address criminal activities in all of its forms in the state. They had focused on organized crime and issued reports that displayed pictures of purported crime bosses. About once a year the commission would identify a public figure or two who seemed a bit too cozy to this element. This amounted to little more than a yearbook of miscreants with little or no impact on actually reducing crime. After years of going through this annual exercise, the political leaders had had enough. The Senate voted to abolish the commission.

But the feature bout on the card for that afternoon was tax policy. Specifically business taxes. More specifically, my endorsement of a wide-ranging plan for business tax cuts and economic development. It seems that a few of the Republican leaders had been taking notes in New York. Senator Jubelirer and his ever-ready staff decided to press the issue by reinvigorating debate on a bill that had been tabled previously.

> Senator Jubelirer: *"Mr. President, because of newfound support, which certainly came from the chair, I move that we reconsider the vote by which Senate Bill No. 1190 was referred back to the Committee on Rules . . . so that the members know what it is, this is the bill that was referred to as the business tax cuts bill. . . . Recognizing your statement over the weekend, I thought perhaps it might be a good idea to at least let the members have an opportunity to bring that bill back in order to once again see if we can come to an agreement on the most important issue of business tax cuts. . . . It is a priority certainly for the Republican members of the body who have been trying now for almost two years to do this. It now appears to be a priority of the chair. . . . Boy, what a great Christmas gift it would be to Pennsylvania to be able to do some tax cuts . . ."*
>
> Senator Lincoln: *"Mr. President, we left this bill on the calendar through the months of May and June, every day waiting for the so-called amendments coming from the Republican side of the aisle. They never materialized . . . I think the acting governor's remarks in New York that I heard were that we are going to deal with this in a responsible manner after the budget is addressed tomorrow morning . . ."*

Once again, the Republicans were looking for a way to corner me into a "no" vote on reconsidering the tax cut bill. They could then construe that as a vote against tax cuts, and worse, presumably, against my own stated position. Bill Lincoln had it right, though; I was articulating a vision for the future that depended on sufficient revenues and on support from Governor Casey, who would be back at the helm soon.

The 24-24 vote on the motion gave me the rare opportunity to explain myself:

> The President: *"Prior to announcing the vote on this motion and prior to casting a vote in this matter, by way of brief explanation, the chair stands firmly in support of business tax reductions and has said so very publicly. Those tax reductions, however, are contingent on a number of assumptions about the economy*

and about a transfer of revenues that must occur in order for us to be able to afford them. For the past several weeks, I have been working with Secretary Mike Hershock, budget secretary, to craft the numbers necessary for the budget presentation that will be made tomorrow. I agree with Senator Lincoln that this is premature, given the fact that the business tax reductions have been proposed prospectively as part of the 1994-95 fiscal year budget. It would be only prudent for us to proceed carefully in assuring that the revenues exist for the business tax reductions. My belief is that they do, but they should be arrived at carefully in consultation with the General Assembly and developed over the course of the next several months for presentation as part of the fiscal year 1994-95 budget.

"That being the case, the chair can confidently and comfortably vote 'no' on this motion."

Senator Dick Tilghman, a bit of a curmudgeon and a stickler for the rules, didn't like the speech at all and said so:

Senator Tilghman: *"Mr. President, I was interested in your speech in the middle of a vote, and I do not think we are in petitions and remonstrances."*

It was irritating, to say the least, to sit in the presiding officer's chair day in and day out and listen to the histrionics of the senators. It was especially grating when the banter was directed at me—which had been the case many times over the past few months. I decided to set Senator Tilghman straight:

The President: *"The chair thanks the gentleman for his rather caustic comment but will correct the gentleman that when the chair is about to cast a vote, it is entitled to make an explanation. It is a part of the rules."*

Ah, that felt good but, of course, it would not be the last word. Senator Jubelirer was on his feet again in the free-for-all known as petitions and remonstrances, quoting again from my remarks in New York. This time, the rules precluded me jumping into the debate so, once again, it was Senator Lincoln who had my back:

Senator Lincoln: *"Mr. President, I see the chair is a little uncomfortable because the chair is a combative person and is being kind of hamstrung. But the only thing I want to say is that the gentleman from Blair, Senator Jubelirer, just paid you the biggest compliment I have ever seen . . . after listening to those six 'wannabes' in the Republican Party who want to be Governor . . . the only person whom he remembered was . . . the most responsible person who spoke the whole day at that PMA luncheon . . ."*

And this little snippet from Senator Mellow, who had just spoken to me at the dais:

Senator Mellow: *"I feel a little bit sorry for the chair, Mr. President, because . . . it is like you are up there in a boxing ring and you are trying to use a little footwork so you do not get hit with the punch, but both hands are tied behind your back and somebody is jabbing you in your face and you cannot respond, and I am telling you, that is a profile in courage. . . . I can assure Senator Jubelirer that the time will come again in the not too distant future where he will once again have the opportunity to vote, if he so chooses, to reduce business taxes."*

"Thank you, friends," I thought.

The tone improved even more on the last day of the session, December 14, 1993.

Senator Jubelirer: *"You will be pleased to know, Mr. President, that these remarks are not only going to be brief but I hope appropriate. I really just want to take a moment to wish my counterpart, the gentleman from Fayette, Senator Lincoln, and all my colleagues in the Senate, a very happy holiday season. These have been difficult days, and certainly the chair, Mr. President, especially knows that these have not been easy times for any of us. . . . Next year does not necessarily promise to be an easy year, but as I have always said, I hope that as I walk off this floor that the fellowship and the friendship that we make by just being in this business will continue . . . I wanted to wish everybody a safe and happy and healthy holiday."*
Senator Lincoln: *"Mr. President, I cannot think of a better way to end 1993 than echoing the sentiments of my good friend and colleague, the gentleman from Blair, Senator Bob Jubelirer, and join him in wishing the president of the Senate and all the employees and our colleagues a healthy and happy holiday ahead. I think*

that we need that holiday at this point in time . . . to renew our faith a little bit and to relax and be prepared to come back and face whatever the new year brings us."

The presentation of the budget to legislators was awkward. I was conducting the briefing alongside Budget Secretary Mike Hershock. The Republicans and Democrats knew where I stood on some of the business tax issues but were not quite sure if Casey was on board. What made it even more uncomfortable was the fact that we were doing the briefing in the governor's dining room. He was not at the residence at the time, but there were rumblings that he was not on board with my plan and was determined to make this one of my last official functions as acting governor. He wanted his seat back.

When we stepped into the hallway where the press had gathered for the post-presentation Q & A, they had clearly been tipped off.

There were very few substantive questions. They didn't ask about revenue projections or program cuts; they just wanted to know when the governor was coming back. Clearly, the governor's own folks had downplayed the event. They had sent the signal that the "real" budget would come from Casey in February. They had also deliberately, for the first time, blurred the lines of who was in charge.

There was some commentary about that in the press, and it was clear to me that the repositioning would occur soon. In fact, I forced the issue a bit with Jim Brown when we discussed the mixed signals coming from two front offices.

"Just have him send the letter," I said, "and I'll gladly step back into the lieutenant governor's office."

I knew it was coming so I got to the business of unfinished business. In the last week, I checked in once again with our folks at the Department of Community and Economic Development on the Johnstown steel discussions. They were proceeding nicely. I was still looking forward to some kind of joint announcement with the governor when we would step in together to help invigorate my hometown.

Next, I appointed my friend, Jim Maza, to chair the Trial Court Nominating Commission for Montgomery County. Jim had been a loyal friend over the years and had never asked for anything in return. The nominating commission made recommendations on vacant judicial posts in the county. For a prominent lawyer like Jim, this meant guaranteed access to all of his peers—especially those with the credentials and the inclination to seek judge status. It was a small favor that I was pleased to do for him.

Similarly, I felt the need to send a final message to Ed Rendell. He was always in my corner whether support from the governor wavered or not. He and I would go on to work together in future campaigns, and I was pleased to send along an official governor's proclamation congratulating him on his recent selection by the National Conference of Christians and Jews to receive the 1993 Brotherhood Award.

And, oddly, the final document I signed as acting governor was seeking clarification from Carol Browner, the administrator of the US Environmental Protection Agency on their enforcement policies relating to vehicle inspections. At the direction of EPA, and in compliance with the Clean Air Act Amendments of 1990, Pennsylvania had dutifully established a centralized inspection program and was now being told that other states were NOT facing such requirements. The feds changed their policies shortly thereafter and saved Pennsylvanians millions of dollars and countless hours by allow inspections at existing, decentralized stations.

I considered it a part of my job to give the governor as clean a desk as possible upon his return. Most observers noted that I had paved the way for a smooth transition for him.

Even the cankerous editors of the *Greensburg Tribune Review* said:

"Lt. Gov. Mark Singel has performed admirably during his tenure as acting governor. He could have been conducting his gubernatorial and ceremonial duties from Casey's offices; yet he did not. He could have exploited the governor's absence to pursue his own policy or political agendas; yet he did not."

One newspaper, the *Lebanon Daily News*, also noted the reality of the high wire that I was on:

"Mr. Singel, incidentally, deserves credit for steering the ship of state. Any student of state government or John Q. Citizen, for that matter, knows that it hasn't been smooth sailing for the lieutenant governor."

At the end of 1993, I considered the challenges that I had faced throughout the year. I believed then and I believe now that there are expectations of all of us. We may not be satisfied with our circumstances, and we may be thinking wistfully about better days to come. It is especially challenging to function "in the meantime" when a quickening of mind and spirit has occurred.

The letter from Bob Casey reclaiming his powers as governor was on my desk when I arrived on Tuesday, December 21, 1993.

To the General Assembly
Commonwealth of Pennsylvania
Pursuant to the Act of December 30, 1974 (P.L. 1072, No. 347), 71 P.S. Sections 784.1 -784.7, I hereby declare that I am no longer temporarily unable to discharge the powers and duties of the office of Governor, and that effective Tuesday, December 21, 1993 at 12:01 a.m., I shall resume the powers and duties of the office of governor.

Sincerely,
ROBERT P. CASEY
Governor

It was just after 8:00 a.m., and the letter noted that the transition had occurred at 12:01 a.m. that day. Just as I had experienced a palpable weight on my shoulders on June 14, I could now feel that weight dissipating. That was just the beginning of an emotional day.

Casey walked into the governor's reception room and said this to a room full of admirers and media:

"By the grace of God, a loving family, the skill of my doctors, and the support of our people, I am here today. I have come to believe that if you want something badly enough, and are willing to work hard to achieve it, nothing is impossible."

Later, Casey would write in his autobiography: "Standing up there as I spoke, I saw something I will never, ever forget. In the front row sat three of my colleagues in the trenches: Lieutenant Governor Mark Singel, who had been serving as acting governor; Senate Democratic Leader J. William Lincoln; and my long-time political foe, Senate Republican Leader Robert Jubelirer. They were weeping openly. If they were my own brothers they could not have been more happy for me. . . . At that moment, none of our differences through the years meant a thing. I had walked through the valley of death; I had come back; here were my friends to greet me; praise the Lord!"

He was right. The three of us blubbered like babies at the governor's miraculous recovery and at the poignancy of the moment.

The *Harrisburg Patriot News* carried a text of the governor's remarks that included this paragraph:

"I am personally very grateful to Lt. Gov. Mark Singel for his diligent and faithful service as acting governor during my absence. And our thanks as well to Jackie and the Singel family. They responded not just as public officials but as friends, and our family is grateful."

Casey also acknowledged that "there was no road map" for the journey that I had just been on.

Jackie and I sat in the reception room, truly moved and mindful of the ordeal that the governor and his family had been through. I was genuinely relieved to hand the reins back over to him. I was more than ready to accept the responsibilities of being governor in my own right, but the weight of following someone else's agenda as "acting" governor had been burdensome. Casey's return meant that I could now focus on the future as I envisioned it.

The governor's return showed me once again that there are things that transcend the routine in political life. He had resolved to do his job, and no medical challenge was going to deter him. And the most striking thing about Governor Casey was that his "job" was to fulfill a lifelong mission to help others.

When we first became political allies he told me the story about how he decided to make his run for governor in 1986. Having lost three gubernatorial elections and having established a comfortable law practice to raise his family, there was little incentive for him to return to the public arena.

It turns out that an incident in Philadelphia was what motivated him.

Heading to lunch with two colleagues from the prestigious Dillworth Paxson firm, Casey encountered a homeless man sleeping on a steam grate directly in front of one of the most prestigious restaurants in the city.

"Mark," I remember him saying, "if I could eat at the Palm, there is no way this man should be starving. As a state, we can do better than that."

Like Casey, I always believed that the purpose of politics is not to win campaigns—it is to do something of value with the office with which you are entrusted. And yes, those aspirations should include helping those who cannot help themselves. I like to think that I advanced that cause in the time that I held the pen in my hand.

One other declaration: I take a dim view of elected officials who equate leadership with riding the wave of popular opinion. The whole purpose of our form of representative democracy is to balance the "will of the people" with the informed governance of those who are in elected office. It may not be popular to stand up for the poor, the needy, the sick, the uneducated, the elderly, but it is important that we do so. It may be tempting to spew some "no new taxes" or other bumper sticker banality, but it is irresponsible. Those who wrote the Constitution said clearly that they wanted to "provide for the general welfare," to "establish justice," and, yes, to "form a more perfect union." This cannot be done on the cheap, and it cannot be done with weak politicians who are more concerned with their reelections than with the needs of those they purport to represent.

Casey understood this.

So did another figure who transformed America after he saved it from economic collapse. Franklin Roosevelt focused on all Americans when he launched the reforms of his "First 100 Days." Jobs programs, infrastructure investments, banking reforms, and, yes, Social Security itself were the results of an administration that understood its role and responsibilities. For his efforts, Roosevelt received a relentless stream of criticism from his opponents and the media. They called him a liberal; a socialist.

At the Democratic Convention of 1936, accepting his party's nomination for a second term, here is what Roosevelt said to those critics:

"Better the occasional faults of a government that lives in a spirit of charity than the consistent omissions of a government frozen in the ice of its own indifference."

I was definitely a Roosevelt and a Casey Democrat.

There were some lingering disagreements on policy and political items, of course, but in that moment none of that mattered. My role was to support the governor—whether it was truly reciprocated or not. I had done that faithfully for seven years, and I was not about to shirk that duty now. The *Patriot News* reported:

"Singel later stood beside Casey, saying he was emotionally moved by the governor's remarks. He called the Caseys 'one of the finest families' he has known and said he was pleased to relinquish power back to his boss.

"'Governor, I am delighted to take my place at your side,' he said. That's how we got elected in the first place. That's where I belong.'"

Two days later, I was jolted back to the reality of being second banana.

"Did you see the press clips?" asked Susan Woods, my press secretary.

There it was, in bold, 90-point typeface on the front of the *Johnstown Tribune Democrat*:

STEEL DEAL – 1,200 jobs returning to idled Bethlehem mills

There were comments from a Casey press release that read: "This agreement means not only the rebirth of the Johnstown plant but an investment in its modernization that will guarantee its competitiveness." He also noted that the state was committing $35 million to the deal.

Fortunately, we had gotten wind of the announcement and I managed to contact the local writers just in time to insert a comment into the article:

"For me, this is almost like a cap to my brief career as acting governor."

The newspaper also made sure that my early efforts were noted:

"Singel, while filling in for Casey during the governor's recuperation after transplant surgery, helped arrange the first meeting of Veritas and the USW on July 23 in Pittsburgh."

There was no effort to coordinate a release or a press event. The governor was clearly back at the helm, and his team was ready with a bucket of cold water to throw on any further expectations I may have had—even on items with which I have been intimately involved.

Still, I knew what my obligations were, and I was confident that I could complete the remaining items on my plate or transfer them to a rejuvenated governor and his staff. But the world had changed for me. My work during the past six and a half months had made some subtle and some far-reaching imprints on the commonwealth.

My staff, a tireless group of public servants who worked quietly and effectively in the shadow of both Bob Casey and Mark Singel, compiled a list of accomplishments that occurred during the interregnum.

LT. GOV. SINGEL. As Acting Governor of Pennsylvania:

- Stopped a legislative pay raise with his threat to veto any such measure during his tenure.
- Signed legislation to enact workers' compensation reform. Not only was he instrumental in facilitating final negotiations on the act, but he successfully jawboned the insurance industry into reducing their rates by 5 percent—a move that will save state employers $300 million per year.
- Promised to veto legislation that would prohibit local municipalities from banning semi-automatic weapons. Singel led the call for a statewide ban on these military style weapons, which received strong support from law enforcement officials across the state.
- Through extensive personal involvement in the negotiations, Singel helped to save 1,000 essential steel jobs in Johnstown by negotiating a deal with the Veritas Group and Bethlehem Steel.
- Proposed a crime package that would: create weapon-free school zones; provide grants to schools and communities to establish security programs to reduce school violence; give district attorneys access to the state police crime database for juveniles who have committed felony or firearm violations; and give district attorneys and the state attorney general the discretion to designate up to 25 percent of proceeds from drug forfeitures for community-based drug and crime fighting programs.
- Initiated contracts with National Westminster Bancorp, which ultimately located in the Scranton/Wilkes-Barre area, bringing 2,200 new jobs.
- Created the Pennsylvania Futures Council to identify ways to use advanced technology to make Pennsylvania's economy more competitive and its government more effective in the next century. The Futures Council executive order also became the legal vehicle for launching Singel's performance review of state government.
- Helped negotiate the bipartisan passage of HB 52, "Key 93" legislation, to save the state park system. He then actively campaigned for the passage of the referendum, which provides funding for improvements to the state's parks, forests, and recreation and historic sites.
- Other key legislative initiatives enacted under Singel:

- A tough new anti-crime bill, which includes a crackdown on stalking and carjacking.
- A landmark telecommunications law.
- Legislation authorizing partnerships among school districts, intermediate units, businesses, and colleges and universities to facilitate the use of distance learning in Pennsylvania.

• When the federal government initially rejected Pennsylvania's plan to provide comprehensive managed care to more than 620,000 medical assistance recipients in southeastern Pennsylvania, Singel personally lobbied the White House and directed the secretary of public welfare to craft a plan that would meet all federal concerns. Through Singel's efforts, Pennsylvania received federal approval to move forward with its health care reform plans for Medicaid clients in a six-county region beginning October of 1994.

• Signed the proclamation adding the judicial discipline amendment to the state constitution, selected and appointed the members to the Court of Judicial Discipline and Judicial Conduct Board, and formally convened the board's first meeting.

• Proposed a budget plan that would: significantly cut individual and business taxes to create jobs and opportunities for working families; save taxpayer money through welfare reforms that provide incentives and assistance to move off welfare and into productive jobs; restructure public education to increase local autonomy while boosting school equity; and trim unnecessary state spending by $150 million.

• Directed release of $3 million for the creation of an alternative fuels program in the Pennsylvania Energy Office that will help Pennsylvania meet its clean air goals; reduce its dependence on out-of-state gasoline; provide grants for the conversion of automobiles to natural gas, methanol, ethanol, or electricity; create natural gas fueling stations; and develop other alternative fuels technologies.

• Authorized $21.6 million for improvements to Camp Hill State Correctional Institution, enabling the prison to construct four new 128-cell housing units and renovate an existing building to create a new drug and alcohol treatment unit.

• Convened health care reform discussions between members of the executive branch and legislative leaders in both chambers and both parties, to begin building consensus on enactment of a Pennsylvania health security act in the coming year.

- Successfully pushed through unification of the Delaware River ports, ensuring the viability of the Port of Philadelphia and providing increased economic development and job opportunities.
- Established a nationally lauded heat emergency task force to protect older Pennsylvanians from heat extremes during an excessively hot summer.
- Opened the cabinet to public meetings with the governor for the first time since Governor Milton Shapp.

The statistics
- Approved over $270 million in capital construction projects.
- Signed 225 criminal extraditions.
- Signed 73 executive nominations.
- Signed 53 bills.
- Signed 64 executive board resolutions (dealing with collective bargaining issues, allocations of costs, and the reorganization of the Department of Public Welfare).
- Signed 16 executive orders, including orders establishing the Futures Council, setting state land use planning goals and objectives, amending a collective bargaining agreement, and reorganizing the state Department of Health.
- Signed eight pardons, one commutation (freeing Eddie Ryder), and one death warrant (Frederick J. Jermyn, who was convicted of killing his elderly mother).

During this process I had charted a path for my own political future, and it was time to get back to that undertaking on a full-time basis. I found myself ending the year much like it started: It was time to move on.

In the words of Art the Oracle: "What's next?"

I also had exceeded expectations in the fund-raising department. The press had already begun its previews of the 1994 gubernatorial campaign. The fact that I had about $2 million in the bank added campaign credibility to the generally good reviews that I received from the just-completed tenure as acting governor. At a holiday gathering with campaign and office staff I remarked that it was a good run and that I was ready to take whatever steps were necessary to be a good governor.

It was Jeff Hewitt who blurted out: "Hell, Mark, you're ready right now!"

It had a nice ring to it, and it would not be long before that became the campaign slogan: "Mark Singel: Ready Right Now."

However, there would be disappointments in the year ahead. In the last moments of an intensive effort for governor, a Board of Pardons issue would strike like a lightning bolt and derail an otherwise textbook campaign. Pundits forget that the Singel campaign led by no less than seven or eight points throughout that campaign cycle. Again, "Thou knowest his fall; thou knowest not his wrasslin'."

For now, at the end of 1993, I felt that I had emerged from a complex maze that had somehow started me back at a beginning.

It was as though I could see the shoreline and the mountains beyond—the promise of a great new adventure. But I still had some dangerous waters to cross.

Jeremiah tells the story of the Israelites in bondage in Babylon. The prophet brought word from the Lord that they were still expected to work and to live their lives in preparation for their return to the promised land. In this "meantime" between servitude and deliverance, the people kept their faith.

The route to my own political redemption was going to be an even steeper climb than 1993. The privilege of serving as lieutenant governor and acting governor was a glimpse of the expectations that I had for myself. While all of us are caught in the maelstrom, only a few are granted the intimation of what lies beyond Babylon.

I had confidence that I met the challenges and handled my stewardship well, but the fact is that it created in me a passion to emerge and return in my own right. I was headed toward a run for governor on my own and could not possibly have envisioned the exhilaration and ordeal of what was just ahead. But it was preferable to living in neutral.

The story of 1994 and the colliding worlds of politics, public service, and private realities is a long one that will have to be told elsewhere.

The record shows that Mark Singel lost his bid for governor in 1994 in a close race to Tom Ridge. An article from my hometown newspaper in late 1994 captured the intensity of that year in a Q & A session. I found the article to be fair and therapeutic at the time. I am including it in the appendix (following the postscript) as a way to summarize the year that followed the year of the quickening.

At commencements, I would often remind graduates of the exhortation of Horace Mann, the president of Antioch College and a great academician: "Be ashamed to die . . . before you have won some small victory for humanity." I like to think that I won a string of small victories in my public life; I believe that I rose to the occasion when my state needed me.

Still, I confess to a lingering sensation of restlessness. As I approach old age, I am left with a perception similar to the one that my father and brother share: "I could have accomplished more."

In moments when I begin to dwell on this, when the twists of fate and political realities begin to darken my spirit, I am comforted by a framed item that hangs on my office wall. A gift from my mother when I left public service, it is a simple verse from Micah 6:8, which reads: "This is what God asks of you: only to act justly, to love goodness, and to walk humbly with your God."

There you go.

POSTSCRIPT: LESSONS LEARNED

Lieutenant governors and those who serve as second-in-command in government, business, or academia, or any other junior executive looking at the next rung of his career ladder would do well to ponder the situation of every dog who has every chased a delivery truck: *What happens if you catch it?*

Those who have a responsibility to stand by and to support a partner, a boss, or any superior can learn something from Pennsylvania in 1993.

First: *Be prepared.*

It was no accident that I was able to assume the duties of acting governor when the moment arose. Not only had I taken my responsibilities as lieutenant governor seriously, I had assumed a number of other burdens assigned by the governor. This gave me additional insights into key policy areas like the environment, energy, emergency management, and ethnic relations. Beyond that, I made it a point to visit personally with cabinet secretaries and key decision-makers in both of my terms as the understudy.

At my first cabinet meeting as acting governor, I convened a group that I respected as professionals and admired as friends. Because I had reached out to them previously, they were invaluable to me when I needed their help.

Second: *Work hard.*

Before, during, and after my stint as acting governor, I made it a point to be the first one in the office and the last to leave. I kept a rigorous schedule of events throughout my political life in the belief that all experiences had an educational component. I was eager to master my craft and to take on as many assignments as I could to broaden my perspectives.

This hard work provided me with the experience to make the right calls—even under duress. It also had the side benefit of encouraging those around me to do their best as well.

Third: *Rely on smart staff.*

There is no possible way that a governor, lieutenant governor, or any elected official can possibly handle his or her responsibilities on their own. As the very least, an understanding spouse can be vital to handling the physical and emotional demands of the office.

Beyond that kind of "personal life coach," a trusted, tested, effective staff is vital. I was blessed with a team that could think clearly, write beautifully, and work tirelessly on my behalf and on behalf of the people of Pennsylvania. I cannot begin to explain how important their contributions were to whatever success we enjoyed.

Fourth: *Trust your instincts.*

As good as your staff and support team might be, there will be moments when YOU must make the call. When you are facing a thicket of microphones and cameras and you know that your next utterance will be taken as policy, when you know that you have just seconds to articulate something that will be analyzed by friend and foe, you do not have the luxury of calling "time."

If you have prepared and worked hard, you will rise to the occasion.

In these moments, it doesn't hurt to have some humility. Trusting your instincts can also mean trusting in something bigger than yourself. Subjugation to whatever higher power you believe in can provide the exhilaration of reaching heights that you did not think attainable. In those moments that I was able to use just the right phrase or defuse an explosive situation, I was not only trusting my own abilities but I was relying on help that came from that faith.

Fifth: *Don't sweat the small stuff.*

The slings and arrows of the maneuverings on the Senate floor never got under my skin. I knew that all of the players were performing their roles, and I didn't take any of their barbs personally. This allowed me to keep a clearer focus on the larger issues that really mattered.

It also assured that I would keep lifelong friendships with erstwhile adversaries. To this day, I treasure the memories and the collegiality that I enjoy with many of those who served in the arena with me—regardless of party affiliation or ideologies.

What *was* paramount was making progress for the people we represented. This was a responsibility that most of us understood and accepted willingly.

Sixth: *Be gracious.*

"Courage," it has been said, "is grace under pressure." Demonstrating that grace, even in the most stressful situations, commands the kind of respect that is necessary for doing your job. I was always impressed by the civility that truly great leaders demonstrated. Whether you agreed with their point of view or not, their ability to conduct business in a gracious way made them worthy advocates.

The consequence of "losing it" or of failing to be courteous is that you can expect bad treatment in return. One of the most finely-tuned political instincts is to detect weakness in an opponent. You insulate yourself if you simply maintain a steady demeanor. Don't let them see you sweat. Be gracious in victory and defeat.

Seventh: *Be grateful.*

As I was leaving the Senate floor for the final time as lieutenant governor, a dear friend and colleague who was also retiring put his arm around my shoulders and said: "We've had a good run." In that moment I realized that the disappointment of losing an election or two paled in comparison to the great experience of front-line public service. Being able to tell my children and grandchildren that "we got stuff done" has proven to be a real comfort to me as the years go by. I am grateful for all of the opportunities that I received through the goodness of my family, friends, colleagues, the voters, and my adversaries. It was a good run.

APPENDIX

By limiting this book to a year in my life, I sought to bring focus to an unusual period in Pennsylvania's history that could not otherwise be told. Since I was the keeper of the schedules and the repository of all of the administrative and legislative activities that occurred between June and December of 1993, I felt it necessary to put on the record exactly what transpired through my own perspective.

I admit to a certain self interest in that I remain painfully aware of the fate that, all too often, befalls folks who find themselves in the political crosshairs. Many are just cast aside as "also-rans" or bit actors in the play.

Throughout my service as acting governor, I was expected to shoulder the burden of Pennsylvania's daily concerns. I was also expected to walk the tightrope of a razor-thin majority in the Pennsylvania Senate with impartiality. The third requirement was to begin my own quest for the governorship without antagonizing a front office with decidedly divided loyalties and without taking on too much water from partisan opponents who wanted to sink my ship before it left the harbor.

There was a deafening silence from the Republicans when it came to legislative achievements. They were not about to give me any credit that could find its way into an eventual campaign ad. Quite the opposite; I was beset with every dart that they could fling, including a record number of law suits and an endless barrage of rhetoric.

Oddly, there were precious few accolades from my own party. This may have been because at least five other potential Democratic gubernatorial candidates were waiting in the wings and ready to pounce on any missteps.

What I hope this book shows is that there are circumstances in politics and in life that challenge us to rise to our own levels of competence regardless of the risk or rewards. When millions of people depend on you, it is important that you act with grace and style, hopefully, as John Kennedy said, "along the lines of excellence."

To lieutenant governors who may face a similar set of circumstances, or to any teacher, parent, or executive with a suddenly unexpected array of responsibilities, I wish you success and, just perhaps, a modicum of recognition.

There are two final addenda to this book.

At the beginning of 1994, I faced the daunting task of shifting into full campaign mode for governor. This included an "essay exam" that was prepared for me by the thorough and brilliant mind of Eric Schnurer. Eric's legal skills had kept me out of the courtroom for my entire tenure as acting governor. His perceptions about critical issues were vital to me gathering my own thoughts as I faced this new chapter. I thought it would be meaningful to show what kinds of things Pennsylvania and its potential leaders were facing in 1994 by including the contents of this quiz.

There are volumes that can be written about any "big league" campaign. My journeys throughout 1994 were exhilarating and exhausting. The events of 1993 put me in a position to contend for the governorship in my own right but, as it turns out, I came up short. There are plenty of stories about those who win; there are far fewer about those who spend themselves in the good fight.

What can be satisfying is a knowing nod from someone you truly respect or a "well done" from a loved one. Maybe even a forthright article that paints a final balanced picture when the fires of battle have subsided. The following Q & A from my hometown paper was fair and therapeutic for me. I share it with you as one public servant who did his best.

Finally, I am also including a final "farewell" article that appeared in the *Harrisburg Patriot*. Just because it makes me smile.

Attachment – Questions Before the Quest – 1994

Issue Questions for Lieutenant Governor Mark S. Singel

THE LIEUTENANT GOVERNOR'S VISION FOR PENNSYLVANIA

- Why do you want to be governor of Pennsylvania?
- What experiences or qualifications do you possess that would make you a better governor than other candidates for governor?
- What will be the priorities of a Singel Administration?
- What would be your first official state action if you were elected governor?
- Can you name one issue where you are in complete disagreement with Governor Casey and what is it?
- What would you like to be remembered for following your term(s) as governor?

THE ISSUES

ABORTION AND FAMILY PLANNING

- Do you support the Pennsylvania Abortion Control Act?
- Would you support any changes to the existing federal or state statutes regarding abortion?
- Should the state fund abortions?
- Should abortion be included within the state or federal health care options?
- Should the state provide funding for family planning centers? If the funding would support abortion counseling services?
- Do you support requiring parental consent for a minor to obtain an abortion?
- Do you support requiring spousal consent for a woman to obtain an abortion?
- Would you support a state abortion clinic access bill similar to the federal bill that provides fines and jail for violent and non-violent interference in women seeking abortions?

AGRICULTURE

- What further actions can the state undertake in promoting exports of Pennsylvania's agricultural products?

271

- What role should the state play in establishing land use policies for state and local governments?
- What actions can the state do to foster the use of PA agricultural products in addressing the hunger and malnutrition problems of poor children and families?
- What actions should the state take in farmland preservation efforts?

CHILDREN

- How can we combat the epidemic of teenage pregnancy?
- How can we address the problem of single parents and the need for both parental supervision and economic opportunity?
- How can we combat the epidemic of youth crime?
- How can we address the pressing problems of teenage hopelessness and teenage poverty?
- What are your plans for developing increased recreational and educational opportunities for children in Pennsylvania?
- Should condoms be distributed in the schools?
- Should the state require spousal and child medical support from a non-custodial parent if it's available to the parent?

CONSUMER CONCERNS

- Do you support capping credit card interest rates?
- Are there any further needed auto insurance reforms, particularly as it relates to the high Philadelphia auto insurance rates?
- Do you support plain language in contracts legislation?
- Do you support the continuation of the state liquor store system?

ECONOMIC DEVELOPMENT

- What role should the governor play in promoting economic development?
- Can you explain the reason for Pennsylvania's poor record when it comes to new business formation, job growth, and business retention? What would you do about it?
- What can be done to improve Pennsylvania's competitive position versus other states?
- Should the state economic development program be focused on attracting new business to Pennsylvania, retaining existing businesses, or developing new small businesses from within?

- What is your position regarding Pennsylvania's business tax rates?
- Do you support reimposing the Net Operating Loss (NOL) corporate income provisions for businesses?
- Do you support the establishment of a state investment bank to provide seed and venture capital to small and medium-sized businesses?
- Do you support the use of state and teacher pension funds for economic development purposes?
- What role should the state play in export promotion?
- What would you do to increase the amount of products Pennsylvania sells overseas?
- Which foreign markets would your administration target as areas of opportunities for Pennsylvania products?
- What should the state do to promote high technology and environmental firms?
- What can the state do to promote high efficiency manufacturing?
- What is the role of research and development in economic development? Should the state provide funding for research and development?
- Do you support relaxing environmental standards to promote the reuse of former industrial sites?
- What should the state do about converting former defense industry sites and retraining defense industry workers and how would it be paid for?
- Do you support riverboat or casino gambling in Pennsylvania?
- What can the state do to increase tourism? Do you support more funding for tourism promotion?

EDUCATION

- What is wrong with our educational system? What can be done to improve the situation?
- What is right with our educational system?
- What is your position regarding outcomes-based education?
- Should teachers be allowed to strike? How would you change the current process of negotiations to reduce the incidence of strikes in Pennsylvania?
- Are teachers overpaid or underpaid?
- Do you support a statewide teacher contract? If yes, how would you pay for it?

- Do you support providing incentives for recruiting teachers in curriculum shortage areas like science and math, including allowing alternative teacher certification for professionals seeking a second career in teaching?
- What role does inequity in funding have in poor educational performance? What can the state do to address the situation?
- Should the state increase its share of education funding? Should the state provide 50% of education funding?
- What can be done to improve the funding of schools from poor and distressed communities?
- Would you be willing to increase taxes to improve our educational system? Which taxes, and where should the money go?
- Do you support the recent change in special education funding, which switched from an excess cost funding system to a formula funding system? Are there any further reforms needed in special education funding?
- What is your position on school choice?
- Do you support the charter school concept that allows teachers and parents within the public school system to establish their own school?
- Should we increase the length of the school year? Of the school day?
- Do you support decreasing class size in the primary school grades, and how would you pay for it?
- Should the state provide incentives for school districts to consolidate?
- Do you support state funding for the Head Start preschool programs?
- What would you do to decrease the incidence of crime and violence in our schools?
- What can be done to reduce the number of high school dropouts? Are alternative schools such as those in malls the answer?
- Do you support a student losing their auto license if they drop out of high school?
- Do you support allowing prayer in school? Do you support the setting aside of a moment of silence in school?
- Do you support elimination of corporal punishment in school?
- Do you support requiring the Pledge of Allegiance in schools?
- Do you support the use of school buildings by church-based organizations to hold meetings in?
- Do you support continued funding for the Scotland private school?

- Is everyone entitled to a college education, if they are qualified? How would you pay for that?
- Do you support greater funding for higher education?
- Do you support requiring public disclosure of state-related university budgets like Penn State's?
- Should the state play a larger role in promoting apprenticeship programs for high school students not attending college, and how would you pay for it?
- How can the state help in providing a climate conducive to life-long learning and retraining? Do you support the use of tax credits to individuals and businesses that provide training and retraining?

ENERGY AND ENVIRONMENT

- Is the state taking full advantage of the natural resource base of the commonwealth?
- Should the state harvest parts of the state forest to raise revenue?
- Do you support market-based environmental policies?
- What would be some examples of how this differs from present environmental policies?
- Do you support breaking up the Department of Environmental Resources and giving some of their responsibilities to other departments? If yes, which responsibilities to which departments?
- Should the state move from an income-based tax system to one that is based upon pollution charges?
- What can the state do to promote the use of alternative fuels in both transportation and manufacturing?
- Do you support state funding for LIHEAP?
- Is the state doing enough to promote recycling and encouraging markets for recycled products?
- Do you support the establishment of recycling manufacturing enterprise zones, and how would you pay for it?
- Do you support a state bottling bill, placing a deposit on glass bottles to encourage recycling?
- Do you support the Duquesne Power Line project?
- Do you feel any more measures are needed to secure the safety of the Three Mile Island nuclear facility?
- What is your strategy for meeting the federal Clean Air Act requirements placed on Pennsylvania?

- What can the state do to ensure that people are protected from hazardous waste and that the wastes are cleaned up?

GOVERNMENT OPERATIONS

- Where would you cut costs in state government? Where would you increase expenditures?
- Are there agencies or programs that you would like to eliminate? Are there agencies or programs you would like to expand?
- What could be done to improve the efficiency of the state government?
- How should the state government interact with local governments in providing more efficient service?
- Should the state give incentives to local governments for mergers and increased cooperation, sharing of service, and mutual asset districts?
- Should the state establish a state revenue sharing program to allow local governments more discretion in the use of state funds?
- Do you support the continuation of the Independent Regulatory Review Commission? If so, are any reforms needed in the IRRC's mission or practices?
- Should the state establish an Independent Revenue Forecasting Board to provide expert insight on revenue forecasting independent of the general assembly and governor's office?
- Do you support reenactment of the Sunset Law?
- How would you, if at all, change the way legislative initiatives (WAMS) are handed out and funded?
- Is there anything wrong with legislative initiatives?

HEALTH CARE

- Pennsylvania already has a pretty good health care system. Why do we need to drastically change the program right now? Wouldn't it be better to just tinker around the edges?
- Why do we need to pass health care reform at the state level if the federal government is going to be passing a package also? Shouldn't Pennsylvania just wait?
- Do you support the president's health care package? What don't you like about it?
- Do you support Governor Casey's health care package? What don't you like about it?
- What else needs to be done about our health care system?

- Who should bear the bulk of the burden for paying for health care reform?
- Should drug and alcohol treatment be included as part of the governor's managed competition health plan or should it remain separate?
- Should the health care coverage provisions in auto insurance and workers' compensation be merged into the reform health care package?
- How do you propose to put more doctors in under served areas? How would you pay for it?
- Do you support greater use of non-physician health practitioners—physician assistants, nurse practitioners, nurse-midwives—in providing primary health care?
- Health care is a major employer in Pennsylvania. How will the various health care reform proposals you support affect employment?
- Do you support rationing of health care services as a means of controlling health care costs?
- Do you support medical malpractice reform, and in what form? Should a cap be placed on either pain and suffering damages or attorney compensation?
- Do you support the Pennsylvania Health Care Cost Containment Council, and if yes, increasing its funding?
- Do you support the present Certificate of Need program, and do you feel any reforms to the CON process are needed?
- Do you support efforts to establish statewide standards for tax exemption of hospitals and other non-profit organizations?
- Do you support a ban on physician self-referrals to labs or services a physician may have a financial interest in?
- Do you support funding of the non-preferred medical schools? If yes, do you support conditions to require a percentage of state funds to go to training primary care health practitioners?
- Do you support increased funding for AIDS education, counseling, and services?

HOUSING

- Do you support a dedicated funding source, such as a percentage of the realty transfer tax, for the building and rehabbing of affordable housing?
- Do you support funding for homeless shelters and services to the homeless?

- What state policies would you support to provide more affordable housing, and how would you fund these policies?
- Do you support selling of public housing to tenants for home ownership?

LABOR AND MANAGEMENT

- Does Pennsylvania have a labor problem? Can the state play a role in improving labor-management relations?
- Do you support repeal of the prevailing wage law?
- Should the governor take a more active role in solving labor and management disputes?
- Do you favor increasing the minimum wage?
- What if any further worker compensation reforms do you support?

MINORITIES

- How can we increase economic opportunities for minorities in Pennsylvania?
- What is your position regarding punishment and enforcement of hate crimes against minorities?
- Are minority set-aside programs good for Pennsylvania?
- Should minorities receive preference in purchasing, bidding, and in competition for jobs?
- What are the biggest problems facing our urban communities?
- What needs to be done to strengthen the role of families in our urban communities?
- Should the state promote bi-lingual education or declare English the official state language?

POLITICAL REFORMS

- Would you change the way legislators are compensated? How?
- Is the legislature too big?
- Should we have a part-time legislature?
- Which if any legislative perks would you like to see eliminated?
- Do you support legislative term limits?
- Do you support campaign finance reform? In what form?
- Do you support limits on PAC expenditures on statewide and legislative candidates?

- Do you support public financing of statewide and legislative campaigns? If yes, how would it be funded?
- Do you support merit selection of judges replacing election of judges?
- Do you support the establishment of voter initiative and referendum?

PUBLIC SAFETY

- What is the biggest threat to public safety?
- What is the role of the corrections system—rehabilitation or incarceration?
- How can the state help local governments to reduce the threat of crime on the streets?
- Do you support the use of state funds to promote local community policing initiatives?
- Do you support gun control measures? If so, how far would you go?
- How can the state help to combat the rising problem of gang violence and mayhem?
- What would you do about our juvenile justice system? Should violent juveniles be treated as adults, even in non-murder cases?
- Do you support the creation of boot camps for juvenile offenders?
- Do you feel the state is adequately funding our state court system? How would you reform funding of our state court system?
- How can we increase the speed and efficiency of our justice system?
- Do you believe in mandatory prison terms?
- Do you believe that our sentencing laws need to be overhauled? What would you do?
- Do you support a "three strikes" rule where a person convicted of three felonies receives a mandatory sentence without parole?
- Do you support alternative incarceration methods including home arrest with electronic surveillance?
- Do you support capital punishment?
- Do you favor the legalization or control of some currently illegal drugs as a strategy in reducing violent crime?
- Should the state be required to provide drug rehabilitation for persons convicted of crimes related to drug use?
- Do you support elimination of the PA Crime Commission or reforming the PA Crime Commission?

- How would you improve victims' rights and compensation?

SENIOR CITIZENS

- What are the implications for Pennsylvania of having one of the oldest states in the nation?
- Do senior citizens pay too much in the way of local property taxes?
- What role will the Department of Aging play in your administration?
- What is your position on reform of the long-term care system?
- How can we better utilize the talents, skills, and knowledge of older Pennsylvanians?
- Do you support repeal of the widow's tax?
- Will you protect and preserve the designation of lottery funds to senior citizen programs?
- If the Clinton health care plan is enacted with a prescription drug benefit thus eliminating the need for the PACE program, how would you use the money freed up in the PACE program?

TAXES

- How would you, if at all, change the tax system in Pennsylvania? Personal and corporate?
- What role do taxes play in attracting business to Pennsylvania?
- Do you favor changing the income tax to a more progressive, graduated income tax system?
- Did you support Governor Casey's 1991 tax increase? What role did you play in making those decisions?
- Would you support local tax reform? What type of system would you support?
- Should localities be given increased flexibility and more options for local taxation?
- Do you support statewide tax reassessment or requiring counties to perform tax reassessment? Do you support prohibiting spot reassessment?
- Do you support a tax on lobbying services?
- Should property taxes be eliminated?
- Do you support a tax amnesty program?
- Do you support a tax reform commission to look through the tax code to determine if specific state tax policies and credits should be changed?

TRANSPORTATION

- What are your priorities for improving our state's transportation system?
- Should the state's speed limit be increased to 65 miles per hour?
- How would you address the reverse and cross-commuting problems of the state's major urban regions?
- Do you support greater use of toll roads for financing road construction and maintenance?
- Do you support the PA Turnpike Commission purchasing I-80 from the federal government and making it a toll road to finance further turnpike expansion?
- Do you support the present motorcycle helmet law requiring motorcyclists to wear helmets?
- How do you feel about high speed rail? Where should it go? Who should pay for it?
- What can be done to strengthen business at the ports of Philadelphia?
- Should Pennsylvania increase its subsidization of AMTRAK rail service in the state? Should the state provide subsidization to add another "Pennsylvanian" rail line?

WELFARE REFORM

- How would you change the current welfare system?
- Is there a welfare cycle? How would you break it?
- What incentives would you offer to move people from the welfare rolls?
- Do you favor limits on the amount of time one can remain on the welfare rolls?
- Do you support elimination of the general assistance transitionally needy program that provides three months of cash assistance to able-bodied persons on welfare?
- Do you support workfare, requiring work or community service for persons on welfare? If yes, how would it be paid for?
- Do you support learnfare, penalizing welfare families whose children do not attend schools?
- Should the state create public sector jobs to move people off of welfare? If yes, how would it be paid for?
- Do you support the idea of creating a state-earned income tax credit for the working poor?

- How would you stimulate investment in distressed areas with chronic employment difficulties?
- Is the state doing enough to crack down on deadbeat parents? If not, what should it be doing?
- Should the state guarantee child support payments for women who have a child support order as a means to increase child support?

WOMEN

- What would you do to combat the problem of battered women in Pennsylvania?
- What is the role of the state in providing adequate day care facilities close to employment centers?
- What is your position regarding a woman's right to choose concerning the question of abortion?
- What is your position on requiring parental support in divorce cases?
- Should women be guaranteed prenatal care, no matter what their income level?
- Do you support legislation to guarantee equal pay for equal work?
- Do you support family leave programs that go beyond the federal law?
- What policies do you support to protect women against sexual harassment in the workplace?

Pardons issue cost me the governor's seat, Singel says

Q&A

Mark Singel

Position: Lieutenant governor of Pennsylvania; defeated Democratic candidate for governor.

Age: 41.

Career: Lieutenant governor since 1987; state senator, representing 35th District, 1980-86; 1974 graduate of Penn State University.

Quote: "One of the most reassuring things about this race is that I did about everything within my power to win."

(Mark Singel of Johnstown is completing his second term as lieutenant governor of Pennsylvania. He ran for the governor's office and was defeated in the November election by Tom Ridge of Erie. Singel spoke about the campaign, about his eight years in office and about his future plans in an interview at The Tribune-Democrat with Publisher Parade Mayer; Dave Hurst, editorial reporter; Bill Jones, chief editorial writer; and Burrce Wislinger, editor of the editorial page.)

You have had a little time now to recover from the rigors of the campaign and the results of the election. How do you feel today?

I'm pleased to discover that there's life after politics. I'm spending a lot more time with my family and enjoying the freedom. What I have discovered is that the importance of running for governor or running for United States senator. And I am grateful for that experience. I am very pleased with all of the positive memories that I take from it. Looking back, it was a grueling, rigorous ordeal, but it is something that I am pleased to have come through.

Looking back, is there anything that you would have done differently?

Not really. In fact, one of the most reassuring things about this race is that I did absolutely everything within my power to win. We put together a very effective, professional campaign team. We put together a broad base of support all over the state and really presented a full range on the positives. And if where should there be a campaign-funding limits imposed?

Absolutely.

Where would they be imposed?

I'll tell you precisely what I had planned to do had I been elected governor was to make campaign-financing reform and ethics changes in government the first order of business, because I think the people made a serious mistake about this campaign. It's very important that whoever is sitting in the seat of power at the state level, or at the national level recognize the need to restore the public confidence.

And a very integral part of that, I think, is to correct the imbalances in the campaign process. Frankly, it is outrageous that the two candidates for governor of Pennsylvania spent more than $20 million. And that places for too much emphasis on fund-raising.

It allows one candidate who has excessive access and family it puts people who don't have access to money out of the system. The solution, I think, is a system of public financing that allows for a voluntary participation in publicly funded campaigns like they have at the federal level.

And those who participate, there like they have a tax-checkoff system that would generate dollars and they have those who participate, would also have to abide by certain limitations.

Did then, Camp's standoff re-election cost you a race in which you've had what's your relationship with the governor today?

I'm going to back away from saying too much about that, be-

cause I really don't want people to think that I'm blaming anybody else. I think the inability for the campaign and has got to take the credit for the victory as well as the blame for its loss.

I'm willing to accept that perhaps the south can we blame Bob Casey or anybody else for the defeat. The only thing I will say is that we were rocked by an extraordinary circumstance that was the pardon campaign that played right into the opponent's hand relating to the crime issue. To me, that was the single-most important aspect of the campaign.

Were you too quick in admitting or saying what you had made a mistake?

No, and I'll tell you what I mean. It was more a blockbuster revelation in the middle of the campaign. And, you know, it was the worst nightmare for any lieutenant governor who presides over the Board of Pardons. I mean, understand that I make that decision thousands of time in my tenure and yet this was the only one available information you have. And in the entire history of the Board of Pardons has never happened. This was a lifer who was freed committed a similarly egregious crime.

Lieutenant governor who possibly over the Board of Pardons. I mean, there are people who have been caught shoplifting or doing a minor drug offence or committing like that, but this hardcore recidivist, the system is so meticulous and painstaking and what have you. So, every time that the lieutenant governor or the governor votes on a commutation of a life prisoner, they understand that there are political risks involved. But they also understand that it is

"In the entire history of the Board of Pardons it has never happened that a lifer (McFadden) who was freed committed a similarly egregious crime."

merited in some limited cases. What they hope for is that their trust is rewarded and we aren't what they're looking for. You put out and commute another crime.

Well, that's exactly what happened. That being the case, it became — you rely on your story. And in today's electronic media age, we had hundreds of prime calls pouring into the office and television ads that were completely without my comment and my version of the facts or to stand up, share of the responsibility and hope to minimize the damage.

I made a conscious decision to face the music and to do it as quickly and as directly as I could. And I think it was the right thing to do.

Can you give us some indication of what you're doing now and if you've met with any members of the Ridge team?

I have not yet. I recently had a very pleasant meeting with Mark Schweiker. And we were talking about the transition. There is precedent, where the incoming lieutenant governor has that Mark seems to be growing into. I told him — and I mean this sincerely — I intend to help him any way that I can.

What about your personal trans-ition? Why is going to happen to you and to your family?

I don't know yet. It's at the same time an exciting and an unnerving time. It's exciting because I have the opportunity to turn a new page in my life and take advantage of all of the connections and tage that I've learned and take advan-tion that into a brand new career.

Do you have a sense as to whether you might be stepping into academia, perhaps? There have been some connections with the Clinton administration in the past.

Money could be go to Washington, as I said, not associated with a government position. I may be about to go into private communi-ty or Washington area just on my own, but tacking functional with the Clinton administration has either been offered or so

campus about teaching and/or studying at the college. I have a personal interest that relates to personally history that I've been working on. It's kind of a personal research project.

The state Democratic Party obviously has to be reailing psychologically at this point. What does it have to do to pick up the pieces and go forward?

I wouldn't overestimate the damage. The truth is that the entire country was rocked by a tilt to the right. And I think most of that is due to a lack of focus at the national level.

For one reason or another, President Clinton just isn't com-municating well. He's just not get-ting across to the middle- or to the working-class families of Ameri-cans and so on. And that really had an effect all across the coun-try.

There was a great shaking of faith that went on. And I think that was precipitated by the uncer-tainty more than to an ideological perspective.

What I'm saying is that people are so disconcerted, they don't know why. And they're not quite sure what the solution is. So, I wouldn't abandon traditional Democratic or Republican values quite yet.

As you and Bob Casey step out of office, in mid-January, what condition are you leaving the common-wealth in?

It's solvent. It's stronger by far than when we first inherited those doors. We have initiated some nationally rec-ognized programs in the area of economic development, the environment, transportation.

I really have been proud to be part of an administration that has made more progress and has passed more landmark legislation than any administration in the last 30 years.

It has been a good experience for me. And as far as from 1st per-spective of this area, we brought home the bacon for this region. And I could have done quite a bit more as governor.

The National Debt

As of 5 p.m. Friday for the federal government, it was:
$4,771,329,929,826.52
- Since last update:
  Up $5,229,415,013.49
- Your share: $18,733.80

History lies in ground at lieutenant governor's mansion

Headstones tell tale about state officials, their families and pets

BY BETH WAGNER
THE ASSOCIATED PRESS

FORT INDIANTOWN GAP — Hidden in a cove of pine trees behind the lieutenant governor's mansion, a trail of headstones tells an historical tale about state officials, their families and their beloved pets.

The pet cemetery has been tended for the past eight years by Lt. Gov. Mark Singel and his family. When they leave their temporary home in January, they also will leave behind the remains of one rabbit, two hamsters, two cats, a bird and a chameleon.

When James Duff became governor in 1947, the stone mansion at the entrance to the military base of Fort Indiantown Gap was considered a "summer home" for the governor. But like his predecessor, Gov. Edward Martin, Duff and his wife spent more time at "the Gap" than in the executive mansion in Harrisburg.

It was at the Gap, in 1950, that Duff buried "Bomber" — one of his many dogs.

"You can just sense the kind of affection he must've had for this animal to build all this in his memory," Singel said as he brushed dirt from the stone.

In front of the mansion and a bit off to the side, shrubbery hides the gravestone where Bomber's date of birth and death are recorded.

The other graves sit behind the mansion.

Stones set flush with the ground mark the final resting places of animals of former governors, including William

Scranton and Raymond Shafer.

"Toby, Diane's dog, Died 1969," reads one gravestone, presumably that of a dog belonging to Shafer's daughter, Diane.

A more recent stone reads "Oliver Buella Confer. April 2, 1993 — Aug. 12, 1993. Rest in peace" — a neighbor's chameleon that Allyson Singel helped bury.

Jackie Singel laughs when she remembers her daughter and Carolyn Confer burying the reptile.

Carolyn played "Taps" on her trumpet at the end of the ceremony.

Plastic Lego building blocks marked the grave of 16-year-old Jonathan Singel's hamster, Sam, before the weather destroyed them.

Many animals are buried without headstones, Singel said.

Although their pets — and their final resting place — will be missed, the Singels said they will always have the memories of their burials and scary trips through the cemetery on Halloween night.

One memory involves Allyson's

rabbit, Cottontail, which gave Singel an opportunity to teach his children about death during a solemn ceremony attended by the whole family and a few neighbors.

"After I gave what I thought was an appropriate eulogy and discussion about life and death, Christopher, who was then 4 years old, stepped forward and said, 'I would like to make a few remarks,'" Singel said.

Chris, who is now 8, does not remember his speech, which the family says included something about "rabbit stew."

"I didn't think it was very funny," said Allyson, 12.

The Singels have not decided whether they will take Darryl, a stray cat, with them when they move out or leave him behind to take care of Lt. Gov.-elect Mark Schweiker and his family. Darryl's litter-mate Darryl is buried in the cemetery.

"Hey, Chris, how did you know that was your cat that got hit by the car?" Singel asked his youngest son.

"What did it look like?"

Chris fell to the ground and played dead.

"No, I mean before it was hit," Singel said.

With a shriek and a look of horror on his face, Chris held his arms out in front of his face as if about to be hit by a car.

Sweeping the dirt from another gravestone, Singel remarked at the meticulous care that was put into the marker.

"There's an inscription here, too," he said with a smile. "But it's written in Dog."

Pennsylvania Lt. Gov. Mark Singel (left) and his daughter, Allyson, 12, pause to read an inscription on a gravestone Wednesday in the pet cemetery behind the lieutenant governor's mansion in Fort Indiantown Gap. Many different types of animals, from many administrations, are buried alongside of each other in a cove of pine trees.

INDEX

ABOUT THE AUTHOR

Mark Singel served as Lieutenant Governor of Pennsylvania from 1987 through 1995 and, for a period of time, Acting Governor of the Commonwealth. The only person in Pennsylvania history to serve an extended time as Acting Governor, Singel received high marks for his stewardship. He led the state by enacting the first modern workers' compensation reform package, refinanced the state's park system through the "Key 93" program, and helped launch the high-tech era with landmark telecommunications legislation. He was also instrumental in reducing state and local taxes, the implementation of a statewide 911 emergency phone system, and the creation of thousands of new jobs in recycling and environmental technologies. He was the original author of the state's mortgage assistance bill that has saved 50,000 Pennsylvania homes.

Prior to his terms as Lieutenant Governor, Singel served six years in the Pennsylvania State Senate and was chief of staff to two members of the U.S. Congress.

Singel ran for U.S. Senate in 1992 and for Governor in 1994. He served as Chairman of the Pennsylvania Democratic Party from 1995-1998 and was the President of Pennsylvania's Electoral College in January, 1997. He was a delegate to the Democratic National Convention five times from 1992 through 2016.

Singel founded The Winter Group in February, 2005 and has developed it into one of the most effective and prestigious government relations firms in the state. He continues to provide consulting services to clients in retail, hospitality and gaming, manufacturing, technology, energy, nonprofits, and health care fields. Recent successes include a ban on public smoking, legislation to address child sexual abuse, and consumer protection in health care settings.

Singel served as Chair of Pennsylvanians for Judicial Reform which was instrumental in bringing talented, progressive jurists to the state's Supreme Court.

Singel has served in various capacities with Pennsylvania's governors and decision-makers and maintains strong personal and political ties with leaders at all levels today.

A magna cum laude graduate of Penn State, Singel continues to teach at the Harrisburg campus and other universities. He has served on the Boards of Penn State and St. Francis Universities and holds several honorary doctorate degrees. Singel is currently active with Harrisburg University and is a regular commentator on local and statewide political broadcast programs. He is a sought-after speaker at both political and academic events and is active in numerous community and philanthropic activities.

Singel has been married to Jacqueline for 40 years and has three children: Allyson, Jonathan, and Christopher. He has three grandchildren: Thomas, Felicity, and Henry Boots.

CPSIA information can be obtained at www.ICGtesting.com
Printed in the USA
BVOW08*0212110716

455101BV00004B/10/P